Gerhard Fischer was born in Germany, educated in the United States, and spent most of his professional life in Australia. He is an award-winning author, historian and literary essayist, with an extensive list of publications. He lives with his family in Sydney, Australia.

I0224525

The Dragon Mother's Dream

A Year in La Jolla
California Journal

Gerhard Fischer

ETT IMPRINT, SYDNEY

Exile Bay

Contents

PROLOGUE

This is the story of a journey to California in search of fame and fortune, to be achieved by playing golf. My wife Susan, Mandarin name Hui Qun, is a Chinese Tiger Mom, or more exactly a Dragon Mom because our son's Mandarin name is Xiaolong, meaning Little Dragon. (It's also the Chinese name of Bruce Lee, as in: Li Xiaolong.) Our son's European name is Maximilian (as in: *Max und Moritz*, Max Sebald, Emperor Maximilian of the Holy Roman Empire, and others). Maximilian Xiaolong was born in Sydney, where we lived and where Susan and I had first met back in 2001.

In Every Kid There Lurks a Tiger is the title of a book by Rudy Duran who was Tiger Woods' first professional coach (from age four to ten). Susan had recently become fascinated by the celebrity status of professional golfers and the huge amount of money they earned, and when she found out about this book, she immediately tried to get hold of it because she hoped to find something there that she had begun dreaming about, namely that her child one day could become a Second Tiger Woods, Number One Golf Player in the World. Susan found Rudy Duran's address on his website and she sent an email, asking him to send the book and an invoice; apparently, the book was not available in Australia. A few weeks later a hardback copy arrived by air, dedicated to our son: 'MAX, DREAM BIG AND WORK HARD TO MAKE THOSE DREAMS COME TRUE.' Signed: 'Rudy Duran, September 2012.' There was no invoice. The back cover of the book featured a photo of the author and his famous student, taken at an awards ceremony where Coach Duran received the PGA Tour's Card Walker Award for contributions to junior golf.

From that moment on, Susan was hooked. What if Rudy Duran could become Max's coach? A few emails followed, and it seemed that Rudy Duran was not averse to the idea. A decision was made: we'd go to America and hire Rudy to coach Max. A few issues remained vague: Could we afford it? What about visas? And: where exactly did Rudy live? He apparently divided his time between Norman, Oklahoma, Scottsdale, Arizona, and Southern California. His schedule for 2013, he wrote, was as yet undetermined. So where would we live? Arizona and Oklahoma were quickly ruled out: too far from anywhere. Susan wanted to go to Los Angeles where her sister lived, but I convinced her that was not a good idea: not for us the daily traffic jams, the air pollution, the nightmare urban environment of a metropolis spinning out of control. We considered San Luis Obispo, Rudy Duran's hometown on California's Central Coast halfway between Los Angeles and San Francisco, and nearby Monterey where I had lived from 1971 to 1972. A golf club in Seaside, in the Monterey Bay area, offered what seemed to be an excellent children's program. In the end, we opted for San Diego, or more exactly its northern beachside suburb of La Jolla: close to Los Angeles, in driving distance to Scottsdale. I'd been to La Jolla twice before, to attend a conference and give a lecture at the University of California at San Diego, which is located more precisely at La Jolla, and I remembered the natural beauty and pleasant climate of the area. San Diego also had an outstanding reputation for junior golf, probably second to none; this is where the tournament action was, notably the Callaway Junior World Championship at Torrey Pines. That's the one that Tiger Woods won when he was a kid, repeatedly.

When we told our friends most of them probably thought we were crazy, if not irresponsible. Some of them said so, others seemed a little envious. We had originally planned to spend the second half of 2013 in Berlin so Max could go to school there and learn German, now that became Plan B. We applied to the US consulate in Sydney for a visa (no problem: five years, multiple entries, but no permit to work), told Max's school he would not be back after the summer holiday, and we booked a flight to LAX on 8 February (note the lucky Chinese number), return flight 3 August. Susan quit her job, we rented out our house (to three guys from Barcelona, newly arrived in Australia), put my sailing boat (28-foot sloop) on the market (with a broker in Rose Bay who was not likely to go out of his way to make a sale), and we were ready. Or were we? There were endless discussions: 'This is insane! Where will Max go to school? Why are we doing this? What if Max is not interested? It is a just too much of a long shot. The chances of Max becoming a professional golfer are close to zero.' I remained the sceptic who always came up with another spanner to be thrown into the works. But there was one irrefutable argument I could not counter: If you don't try, you might regret. If it doesn't work out, we'll come back. As the Americans say: you can't get nowhere, lest you go. And anyway: I was retired, with nothing much to do. And I had lived in California nearly forty years ago. It took me a while to understand that I didn't mind going back. Curiosity and nostalgia won over reason. Thus, we left with two agendas in mind: to see whether Maximilian could become a top golfer, and to see what it was like living in the USA today – a time warp, California Dreaming, from Richard Nixon to Barack Obama.

My secret worry was about leaving my daughter Lina and her partner Richard behind. They had recently married in a fancy ceremony at the reception centre of Taronga Park Zoo overlooking Sydney Harbour; they were now looking to buy a house and planning to have a baby. In my speech as father of the bride I had encouraged them to explore the world together. I had asked Max, Lina's half-brother, to start the speech with a quotation from one of his favourite books by Dr Seuss: 'Congratulations! / Today is your day. / You're off to Great Places! / You're off and away!' And I had quoted Mark Twain: 'Twenty years from now you will be more disappointed by the things that you didn't do than by the ones you did do. So throw off the bowlines. Sail away from the safe harbor. Catch the trade winds in your sails. Explore. Dream. Discover.' Now Susan, Max and I were about to do just that, leaving the young couple behind. But Lina was as proudly independent and generous as ever; she agreed to look after our affairs (house, boat, car) and wished us good luck. She drove us to the airport in my Toyota that I left behind for her and Richie to use.

In September 2012, Max was five years and eleven months old. He had been playing golf for just under a year, and was quite skilled at it. He had made some good friends with kids his age (but mostly a few years older) whose parents had similar ambitions. Patrick had taken his daughter Sophie to an international tournament in North Carolina in 2012 where she had done quite well; she was now being invited to other tournaments overseas. Ken, father of Jeffrey (Max's golf buddy at Bexley Golf Club), was hoping to take his son to the Callaway tournament in Dan Diego, but was unsure whether he could afford the time off from work (and the money). All of them had the same dream: that their kids would make it to the top in golf. But none of them had a Dragon Mom like Maximilian.

It is well known, of course, that, in Chinese mythology, the dragon is a benevolent and all-powerful creature.

PART ONE
PACIFIC BEACH WINTER

FRIDAY, 8 February 2013

Email from San Diego:

'Hello from Up Over!'

'I'm writing from Pacific Beach, California, where we just arrived: working class neighbourhood, very friendly people. Just off the freeway there is a handmade sign in a tree: No Gun Control. The fancy San Diego suburb of La Jolla – the Village – is just north of us. We had rented a flat via AirBnB for two months: nothing permanent, see how we go. Our street address: Sapphire Street (many streets here are named after precious stones: Turquoise, Tourmaline, Felspar, Garnet, etc.) The apartment is part of a duplex, our landlord – 'your host' – Stan lives in the other flat at the back with his girlfriend, Hope. There are four parking spaces out front: one for Stan (Porsche 911), one for Hope (Honda SUV), two empty ones for us.'

I park the Mitsubishi, lean back, and close my eyes for a second or two.

We had left SYD Friday around noon, arrived LAX Friday 10am the same day to rain and cold, after a 14-hour flight.

We clear immigration and customs in under 30 minutes (pleasant surprise, if only registered in half a jetlag stupor), then straight into rental car office to pick up a pre-booked car. The Toyota Corolla turns out to be a Mitsubishi Galant (but we could have chosen from what's available, including several American models), then a three and a half-hour drive south down to San Diego, mostly San Diego Freeway (Interstate 5) with some excursions onto the Coast Highway when I feel I'm getting too tired behind the wheel.

We cross the San Diego County line and stop at Del Mar to open a bank account; the procedure takes about 45 minutes. The weather has cleared; we walk around the little town and notice the similarities with the Sydney scenery we just left behind: there are cliff walks and surf beaches, parks and malls, all bathed in the same brilliant sunlight. The flora, too, is virtually identical: palm trees, hibiscus, banana trees, bauhinias, bougainvilleas, jacarandas, oleander, strelitzias, frangipani.

Finally, we arrive: Sapphire Street, Pacific Beach, California. Mexico is only a few minutes away now.

Stan takes some freshly baked chocolate-chip cookies out of the oven to welcome us to the USA. He is tall and athletic, surfs and runs marathons. A magnetic sticker with his official finishing time for the New York Marathon is on the fridge of the kitchen: four hours, 36 minutes, eight seconds. (Or is this more likely Hope's time? Need to check with our friends in Berlin who are enthusiastic marathon runners.)

Stan shows us around and explains what's there. The flat is ok. The rooms are quite big, the furniture dated but comfortable. The shady backyard has some garden furniture and a barbecue. It's a good place to sit and write. There are a couple of beach chairs in the laundry that we are invited to borrow. The beach is two and a half blocks away. Sapphire Street is very quiet, but the main thoroughfare (La Jolla Boulevard) is just around the corner.

SATURDAY, 9 February

Today the weather is very friendly and sunny, it is Chinese New Year's Eve: Gong Xi Fa Cai!

Xiaofang (Susan's sister), husband Bill and daughter Brianna drive down from LA to have NYE dinner with us. They live in Torrance, near the coast a few miles south of LAX. First we go shopping together: there is a huge Chinese supermarket called Ranch 99, half an hour away on the other side of the SD Freeway. I follow Bill who has got satellite navigation in his car, worried that I might lose him in the maze of intersecting freeways, but he patiently waits for me on the side of the road whenever we get separated by the dense traffic. We buy stuff for hot pot, plus dumplings, a big flounder, a lobster, a case of Tsingtao beer. Twelve bottles for $9.99 plus tax, not too bad. Good variety of fish/seafood selection here, but mostly tired looking stuff. I am tempted to buy some oysters, they're good size Pacific oysters, but the staff don't know where they are from. When I look closer I find quite a few are open, don't smell too fresh. Forget it. But I buy an oyster knife for $1.49, just in case, for next time. Adding the sales tax (8%) when buying things takes some getting used to.

SUNDAY, 10 February

Golf at Torrey Pines Junior Clinic. Great golf course overlooking the Pacific Ocean, site of the 2008 US Open, won by Tiger Woods. It's a public course, owned and managed by the City of San Diego, actually two courses (18 holes each) next to each other, called North and South Torrey Pines. But we only get to see the driving range and putting green. Kids are split up into three groups and then rotate: warm-up exercises, driving range, putting green.

Junior Coach asks the kids in his group: 'Who thinks putting is boring?' Quite a few of his disciples raise their hands.

'What?' says the coach. 'What? If one putt is worth one million dollars?'

First American cliché confirmed – everything has a dollar sign attached to it, even the humble putt on the practice green.

Second cliché confirmed – the other coach is impressed with Max's swing and says: 'He's drawing a little, but we'll fix that and then he's gonna kill 'em!' The language of violence is the language of everyday life (and death).

We meet Samir and his daughter: they're originally from India, then lived in Melbourne, Victoria, then Toronto, Ontario, then New York City, now San Diego (more precisely: Rancho Bernardo, a posh neighbourhood in the mountains, some 20 miles inland). He's a keen golfer but does not want to push his daughter. Take it slowly, he says. He loves San Diego, the place he has been looking for. The expats of India: everywhere.

That evening on TV there is a portrait of Mr Nugent of the National Rifle Association, and we find another cliché confirmed: the American preoccupation with firearms. Mr Nugent has a farm in Texas where he keeps African antelopes, fast running animals, and he shoots them from his porch with a telescope-mounted assault rifle. Says Mr Nugent: 'Only I and no-one else determines how many bullets I need to defend my family. There is no gun violence. There is only criminal violence.'

Two big items on the TV news: President Obama's State of the Union Address / Hunt for Christopher Dorner. As the Dorner saga unfolds, the president's message is forgotten.

The Dorner story has been making headlines for a couple of days now. He is an Afro-American veteran and ex-cop turned rogue, fired by LAPD, and he has issued a 'manifesto' on the internet about his grievances, with a list of people/cops to be targeted, the apparent motive: revenge for racial discrimination. LA police publicly acknowledge that they will re-investigate his employment history, one of Dorner's demands spelled out in his manifesto. In the meantime, the hunt for the man goes on.

So far four people have been killed, including two cops, but Dorner evades being caught. Finally, he is tracked to some remote area in Northeast California where he hides out in a cabin; the matter ends, not unexpectedly, in a shootout straight out of Hollywood, *Die Hard*-style. It's all on TV: police moving in with armoured vehicles and incendiary tear gas, at the end there is a badly burned body lying in a burned-down cabin in the snowy woods of Big Bear Mountain. DNA is needed to identify the body. To no one's surprise, the LAPD declares that the fire was not started deliberately. (But why use 'incendiary' tear gas, I wonder?)

MONDAY, 11 February

We take Max to enroll him in school: Pacific Beach Elementary, around the corner from where we live. Public School: looks like a jail, high walls, hardly any windows, cemented interior schoolyard. I fill out the necessary papers. We need dental and doctor's examinations for Max. While I attend to the bureaucracy, Susan overhears dialogue in school office between secretary and boy who comes in with a bleeding hand and asks for a tissue. The health coordinator hardly looks at him and tells him to go to the toilet: 'Get it yourself.' We don't feel good about this school.

We drive straight to another, private, Catholic school: All Hallows Academy in La Jolla, up near Soledad Mountain, with sweeping views over the ocean. We arrive unannounced, but no problem, the principal has time for us, first she sends her secretary to show us around the school, then she asks us into her office: 'You're very welcome!' She is happy to take Max; the only question is: which grade? In Sydney, Max has just finished Kindergarten, but here we're in the middle of the school year. The principal suggests Kindergarten, but we prefer if Max goes ahead half a year. Ok, says the principal, in that case he will have to take an assessment test ($150) in the afternoon. There is no paperwork, except an earthquake emergency release form that we need to fill out in triplicate.

We come back in the afternoon. Max passes the assessment and can enroll in Year One. The school secretary takes us to the used uniform shed in the playground. We chose an outfit for Max for a couple of dollars: all set. The uniform is very basic: red or blue polo shirt and sweat shirt with school logo, long blue pants or shorts, mix or match, it's up to you. Shoes are supposed to be (mainly) white sneakers (called athletic shoes around here), again personal choice. You can hardly call it a uniform. Compared to the standard issue Australian school uniforms (stuffy and expensive, overly formal, different for summer and winter), it's a big relief, financially and fashion-wise.

We take Max to school the very next morning. A couple of his new classmates pick him up at reception and escort him to the classroom. He goes with them, a little hesitant, waving to us over his shoulder. But we're confident he'll be all right. He liked the school yesterday, especially the big soccer field next to the schoolyard.

We pay the first month's fee with credit card, hand in the Earthquake Emergency Kit (gallon-size zip bag with three non-perishable food items – fruit/nut bars – bottle of water, large rubbish bag and paper with contact names/numbers/addresses). This is supposedly in case we (the parents) are buried under some rubble in the earthquake to come, unable to pick up our son. We don't know anybody around here who could pick him up, so we put down the details of Xiaofang and Bill: doubtful that they would be able to come down from LA if there really should be an earthquake which, I read in the paper that day, is overdue, could happen any day. Be prepared.

After school we meet some parents, very nice people: come on over soon, kids can play together.

Third American cliché: confirmed or not? Do they really mean it? Superficial friendliness of the Americans? Or is it my own prejudice to doubt?

TUESDAY, 12 February

Next job: Buying a car; the budget is under $10,000. We find that cheap second-hand cars in the US are no more. 35 years ago, I bought a '62 MGA Convertible for $300 in New York, drove it down to Florida over Easter break, driving on the sand of Daytona Beach, top up, the proverbial wind in my hair. Two years later, a Plymouth V8 station wagon cost $680, and I drove it for nearly three years, across the country a couple of times and up and down the CA coast.

Susan would like to buy a BMW, and why not, so we look at a 250ci Convertible with a price tag of $8,900. It has 160,000 miles on the clock but looks brand new, sweet drive with top down, wind on my head (no more hair). During the test drive the dealer lectures us on Obama (he says the president's father was a communist, Obama himself a socialist – I don't ask about the difference), but he admits Obama is cool (that's why he got elected). Other car salesmen we meet afterwards all tell the same story. Selling a car in America seems to foster a sense of identification with the corporate outlook on the world. As we are foreigners, the salesmen are quick to give us some clues about how America is being run by the Washington bureaucrats – badly, they claim!

We check out a Mercedes-Benz dealer who presents a ten-year old S500 for $9,990; this dealer is all business, no interest in politics or anything else, no small talk; nice old car, only 90,000 miles, built 1999; no CD player, only cassette/radio; loaded with everything else, drives like a boat with driver feeling like sitting on a plush sofa. I'm tempted to buy it: silly idea! Costs of repairs would be astronomical! This dealer is the only one of half a dozen we talk to that day who later calls us back to check on our progress. I'm sorry: no deal.

Two days later, another dealer shows us a Lincoln Mercury Grand Marquis, saying this is the American equivalent of the Benz S500; it's loaded with everything digital and electric, just under $10,000, nice car, posh leather, velvety ride. I'm ready to buy, but customers before me (an old couple) snap it up: Rats! Fifteen minutes too late! This dealer is from Iran, his name is Shah, a nice fellow who tells us with quiet confidence that after driving the Mercury I would not like to drive anything else, ever. It turns out he came to the US on a scholarship to Harvard but that disappeared when, two years later, Shah Rezah Pahlevi made an untimely exit from power as Ayatollah Khomeini appeared on the scene. Now our guy here in SD – we dub him Shah of Iran – is a patriotic American car salesman, committed to give you the best service ever, as he says. Pleasant guy, but he does not call back.

We have become weary about spending so much money for an old car and decide to check out private offers. The choice on the internet is overwhelming, and it's very time-consuming to work out where the cars are located. We don't know the area well enough. The local paper, *San Diego Union-Tribune*, or *U-T* for short, carries very few ads; it covers a very big area (San Diego County, 4,500 square miles with 70 miles of coastline). I'm not really looking forward to drive to some out-of-the-way place all over the county to see some dubious proposition. Let's wait and see what comes up.

WEDNESDAY, 13 February

Max is happy at his new school. All Hallows Academy is years K to Eight, very small, only one class per year, 24 kids in Max's class, mostly girls, with two permanent teachers (one a qualified teacher's aide), friendly and enthusiastic staff. Max has found new friends: James, Pablo, Quentin, Ricky. The drop-off and pick-up car line procedure before and after school is very similar compared to that of Max's primary school in Sydney. It's perhaps even more stressful because All Hallows is situated right next to a major intersection, and there's limited parking in front of the school. But there's one difference: in Sydney, the school and the parents also have to battle council officers who constantly threaten to enforce the 'No Stopping' regulation, and sometimes do. Here, we find no authoritarian 'nanny state' attitude, and things generally work quite smoothly.

In the afternoon, we walk along the beach to the pier at the end of Garnet Avenue. It's a beautiful old timber structure with little cabins built on either side of the first 100 metres or so of the pier. The cabins turn out to be motel rooms. The reception of the 'Crystal Pier Hotel – Sleep over the Ocean' ('No Vacancy') is just outside the pier in a little hut; you check in, a gate opens to let you drive your car onto the pier, you park next to your cabin and enjoy the view from your balcony. If you wish, you could throw a line over the railings and catch a fish for dinner.

Of course, you could also just stroll along to the end of the pier, as we do. Fishing is encouraged, and there is a sink with a little stone table attached where you can scale and clean your catch. But it is cold this late afternoon, and as the sun sets over the water to another picturesque spectacle (lots of people watching and taking photos), we find only one intrepid old fisherman out there at the end of the pier – except he's not fishing, he's crabbing. He's got two crab pots over the side, the line firmly attached to the timberwork. It's an impressive effort: we're at least eight metres above the water at this end, and there's probably another six metres or more to the bottom. We watch as he pulls one pot up, it's a substantial wire construction. He usually leaves it in the water for about half an hour, the old-timer tells us, but now it comes up empty. He says, upon enquiry, that it would cost probably around $70 to set me up for crabbing, including the annual licence fee. Hmmm: a tempting prospect. Crabs are fairly expensive here, almost like in Sydney. At Ranch 99, they sell the local dungeness crab, alive and out of a tank, for under $10/lb, that's over $20 a kilo. But they're not Australian mud crabs, of course.

THURSDAY, 14 February

We have rented the Mitsubishi for two weeks, so we decide to make the most of it and drive to Arizona. It's a long weekend, no school on Friday and Monday. The plan is to meet Rudy Duran who will be in Scottsdale for a few days, play some golf, then drive up to the Grand Canyon and on to Las Vegas, return via LA. We've set up a date with Rudy Duran to meet in Scottsdale on Friday morning to present Max for a practice round of golf.

We ask Max's school for permission to take him out of school early on Thursday: no problem. We leave around 1pm and head straight east. For much of the way, the road (Interstate 8, or I-8 for short, also known as the Kumeyaay Highway after the local Indian tribe) runs parallel along the US-Mexican border; there is hardly any traffic. We admire a stretch of spectacular mountain scenery coming into Arizona, but mostly it's flat desert.

Déjà vu: I remember driving here in 1970 coming from the opposite direction, at the end of a long trip from Minnesota down to Texas and then west to Monterey, California. It was mid-August, temperatures in the high 90s, and my over-loaded old Plymouth station wagon huffing and puffing trying to make it up the hills, in a late afternoon with a blinding sun in our eyes. We needed to stop every half hour or so when the engine was overheating, waiting by the side of the road to let it cool down and fill up the radiator again (from plastic gallon-size water containers that we carried along in the back). Regular oil refills were also needed. Even though, the car left behind a billowing black cloud of exhaust fumes as we were coming down the *sierra* into California, and soon enough we were stopped by a cop who gave us a ticket for polluting the air.

Today, the drive to Phoenix is uneventful and tiring. When we reach Yuma just past the California-Arizona state line, it has become dark. At Gila Bend, we turn off I-8 and head north. It is only some 350 miles from San Diego to Phoenix, and we were told it would take us about five hours. But 'by the time I get to Phoenix' it's after 9pm, I've been behind the wheel for almost eight hours, with one little break, and I'm exhausted. We find a motel on the outskirts of town and go to sleep, too tired to eat.

FRIDAY, 15 February

Today is the great day: we are to meet Golf Guru Rudy Duran, Tiger Wood's first coach, at Quintero Golf Course. It is a private, gated golf and country club, almost an hour north of Phoenix, in the foothills of the mountains. When you enter, the attendants at the gate take your name, and after you parked your car a golf cart is waiting for you, with your name on it. Nobody walks here. The course is in the middle of the desert and must have cost a fortune to build, not to mention maintenance. Everything is spotless, there are juicy-green tees and fairways, water hazards, sand bunkers and greens surrounded by a rocky wasteland. While we're waiting for Rudy, I read the notices at the pro shop board: a limited number of club memberships are available at $20,000 application fee, plus $450 a month.

We meet in front of the pro shop at 10.30am, introduce ourselves and shake hands, then get into two golf carts (Rudy/Max; Susan/Gerhard) and drive out to the practice area. Rudy is very nice, he likes Max, who conducts himself like an old pro ('I know what I'm doing!'). Our son is a little bit too cocky, and I have the distinct impression he realises that this day and his meeting with Rudy are supposed to be important, so he's hiding his nervousness behind an attitude. But Susan and I agree: it's better to be over-confident than under-confident. On the driving range, Max hits some good shots and some crappy ones, overall: good swing, good technique. Max knows how to correct his shots and manages to hit a good one from the same position after one or two so-so ones. But Rudy does not seem overly impressed or excited.

Rudy is also not impressed by Dragon Mom telling Max what to do. Max must learn to 'own' the game, he must make his own decisions. Rudy says: 'Don't worry about bad shots, focus on the good ones and forget the others, confidence is the most important thing, mental issues destroy your game.' His coaching is very hands-off, he does not say much, lets Max do his thing, repeatedly asks: 'Did you like that shot?' Golf, according to coach Rudy Duran, is art not science; it's about creativity, fun, wellbeing. The spirit of the game must come first. Technique is not so important, maybe one tenth of the overall experience, but rules and etiquette are because they're part of the culture of the game and of what Rudy calls the 'intangibles' (which I take to be the creative side of things). For children, golf practice is about teaching life skills – the 'virtues' according to Rudy: honesty, respect, discipline, commitment, sportsmanship. Max has to learn the P-T-M-E-S-S of Golf: Physical, Technical, Mental, Emotional, Social, and Spirit of the Game. Rudy is thinking about setting up a Golf Academy with his wife, somewhere in Southern California. But it's only an idea at this stage, there are no concrete plans.

While Max practises, Rudy and I talk (technique, aims, philosophy, emotions, art vs. technique, the holistic approach). We talk some more during a break for lunch at 12.30pm (clam chowder for Susan; hot dog for Rudy; Hamburger for Max and I, sharing), total bill comes to $40 (including tip). Rudy asks me where I'm from in Germany and then tells me that he was stationed at Ramstein for two years while he was in the air force. This is where he learned how to play golf. I cannot hide my surprise: apparently, there was not much to do over there in the military during the Cold War. After two years on the base and playing golf every day Rudy was ready to turn pro. He regrets not having made more of the opportunities offered to him at the time, like travelling in Germany or Europe: too young. But so what – he learned to play golf over there!

More out of Rudy's Gospel of Golf: you must look at it as a recreational activity, chances of becoming a touring pro are practically zero. He himself tried on the Canadian tour but quit early on, deciding to become a teaching pro instead. He speaks a lot about research, that's what his wife (PhD in Sports Education) does in golf education; she teaches at the University of Oklahoma but works for universities and high schools across the country. She writes curricula for golf courses taught at secondary and tertiary institutions. In essence, says Rudy, research shows that you'll need a minimum of 10,000 hours of practice to become a top player, that is approximately three hours a day over nine years, in other words something like one hour on the driving range followed by two hours or nine holes of golf, day in and day out, from six years of age onward until the candidate is 16 and can turn pro. Basically it's the same with any other kind of top performance, I suggest: if you want to become a world-class professional ballerina or tennis or piano player, you'll need to start early in life and put in a few hours of practice every day. Yeah, says Rudy, you need long-term commitment and discipline.

Later I think it's interesting that Rudy's book *In Every Child there Lurks a Tiger* is mostly about technique. Has he changed his approach after meeting his wife? The educational-philosophical theories of teaching junior golf might be a result of her input. But Rudy and his wife don't play golf together, as I find out after asking. I regret not having asked more questions about her. I would have liked to know more about the theoretical aspects of golf pedagogy. But there's too much to absorb over half a hamburger, in an hour or so.

After lunch, we're back on the course to play six holes. We join up with a twosome of lady players. They are visitors, not members, and they hack around the course in a pitiful display of skill (or lack thereof) that at times is painful to watch. It does not look as if they are having fun either, and I wonder how much they had to pay for the green fees. Max easily outplays them by a couple of shots every hole. Later, Quintero's director of golf drives up in his cart to say hello. I find out he has waived the cart rental and green fees for us; he used to be a student of Rudy's. Max gets tired after playing five holes, and Rudy suggests we call it a day. It's 3.30pm, and very hot. Back to the pro shop for some iced coffee/water/lemonade, and more talking, different options regarding coaching.

Reality Check No. 1: We never talked money before, now we ask Rudy what we owe him for the day, and he says: 'Make it $300.' It's a bargain: he usually charges $200 per hour (adults) or $125 (kids), plus expenses (whatever they may be: airfares from/to Norman, Oklahoma, taxis, green fees, accommodation, food, etc.). He is being very generous with us, no expenses for us to pay on the day, he has organised the course, carts, everything; and he drove an hour out of Scottsdale to meet us and spent most of the day on the course with Max. I'm very impressed by the man, his manners, his friendliness, his stories/anecdotes, his easy-going chattiness. We pay him the $300 for the day, but we can't afford him. We'll stay in touch, we say.

Reality Check No. 2: At the end of the day there is no beating around the bush – Max plays well, but he is not as good as Dragon Mom would like to believe. Max 'Little Dragon' Fischer is good, but Tiger Woods was better. TW usually scored 36 or less over nine par-three holes at age five, Rudy says. Max's best score to date was 47; the better kids today at US tournaments also score in the mid-30s. The chances of Max becoming a PGA tour player are 0.001 percent, says Rudy (which of course we knew all along, even Dragon Mom realises it, though she prefers not to think about it). There are a hundred million golf players around the world, and only some 200 PGA tour players, Rudy says. I say, to myself: *Du hast keine Chance, also nutze sie.*

Rudy drives off in his old gold-coloured Mercedes SL Convertible, and we wave goodbye.

We decide to go to Sedona instead of the Grand Canyon ('Leave that for another day!'), as it is quite late already. On the highway, we chew over the consequences of meeting with Rudy. Dragon Mom is not impressed with Rudy's coaching, nor with his assessment of Max. Why can't Max be as good as TW? Maybe not today, but in a few years' time. Anyway, it's a long shot. We'll need to plan for the next ten years or so. There's no rush, she tells me, no point in pushing Max to peak too early. No burnout.

A new alternative is appearing on the horizon. Maybe we should take Max to Hollywood, Susan observes, casually. He is smart and good looking, he likes singing and dancing. That's true enough. Especially now, on these long drives when there is not much to do, Max does not get bored, he entertains himself with his song repertoire, top of his current list is *Gangnam Style*, the original and half a dozen covers. He gets quite excited about *Mitt Romney Style* that he watches time after time on his iPad. Yeah, Hollywood – somebody might discover him there.

As far as Dragon Mom is concerned, Rudy is history.

SATURDAY, 16 February

Sedona, Arizona: Cowboy town in Red Rock mountain area, spectacular location, some 100 Westerns made here. But the place is very spread out, we get lost a couple of times, dirt roads like in Australia. The next day Max is happy when we let him climb a big rock, taking the direct route up to the top, the *diretissima*. While I slowly meander up following a hardly recognizable track, Susan waits for us at the bottom.

More talk of Hollywood during the long drive to Las Vegas. We arrive as it is getting dark in the early evening. Spectacular view coming down the mountains into the valley: lights everywhere, as far as your eyes can see. Max: 'Wow! That is amazing.' It is. We stay at the 'Circus, Circus' Casino and Hotel, a special family resort with an indoor amusement park, and Max has a ball.

SUNDAY, 17 February

Las Vegas is mostly *déjà vu*, just as I remember it from my first visit here, except the neon lights of old have given way to giant digital video displays. The cult of celebrity has joined the art of impersonation in the service of selling gambling and prostitution. Impersonators rule, 'Tributes to...' shows seem to be the order of the day. For your instant wedding you can hire actors dressed up as celebs as official witnesses and guests. The current star attractions appear to be Gordon Ramsay and Cirque du Soleil; they are seemingly everywhere. Las Vegas, then and now, is the self-appointed 'Entertainment Capital of The World' (same old all-American hype as in Garlic Capital of the World or Artichoke Capital of the World: rural places near Salinas that I remember from years back).

What I don't remember: that the Casinos are so huge, they occupy whole super-sized city blocks, there is free parking everywhere, and people are walking along the Strip (Las Vegas Boulevard) in huge numbers. A week later I read about a drive-by shooting on the Strip: somebody in a Range Rover fires into a Maserati at three o'clock in the morning near Bellagio and Caesar's Palace Drive, the driver of the Maserati ('aspiring rapper') is killed while his car ploughs into a taxi, there is a pile-up with a few other cars, Range Rover driver escapes.

There are 40 million cars on the road in California, one of the car dealers in SD had told us. After lunch, I begin the drive back from LV to SD, long straight stretches of freeway through the desert. I chose the inland route via Riverside which has much less traffic. Susan wants to visit her sister on the way and stay overnight at her and Bill's place in Torrance. Next day, Monday, is President's Day, a public holiday, but I'm tired of driving and want to go home. Besides, I have no intention of making a detour to drive around Hollywood looking for potential agents who might be lurking behind a corner to discover a new child superstar.

We drive on Route 66 for a while (ghost road today, potholed two-lane highway, with rusty and gimmicky remnants of the old glory days). We stop for a hamburger and coke at Peggy Sue's 50s diner a little further just off the freeway, a cute little original three-booth eatery with a 50s menu (Richard-Nixon-Burger) and an add-on five-and-dime shop (full of kitschy 50s souvenirs: Elvis cups and Marilyn Monroe tea towels, commemorative plates, lighters and what-have-you – quite an impressive collection). On the wall, there are lots of photos featuring owner Peggy Sue posing with various celebrities. Peggy Sue is the owner's real name, apparently. She wouldn't be the inspiration behind the Buddy Holly song, would she now?

MONDAY, 18 February

We sleep in, taking a rest. In the afternoon, we drive around to look at more cars. Endless dealerships, everybody offering special sales.

TUESDAY, 19 February

Bought a car today from a private seller (newspaper ad), a retired air force officer in La Mesa. It's a 1997 Mercury Grand Marquis that has been meticulously maintained and documented for the last eight years since the owner bought it for his wife: 4.5 litre V8, 113,000 miles on the odometer, new Michelin tires, loaded with everything power/electric/digital, mahagony timber on the dashboard, a radio/cassette player but also a six-disc CD stacker installed in the trunk. Nice car, with a murky green colour, but except for that miraculously the same car we almost bought from the Shah of Iran at the dealership the other day. We saved almost $7,000. The car drives like a boat, but the big leather seats are hugely comfortable.

The seller Riley L. ('Lou') Watson has been everywhere, including Australia (remembers wide streets of Adelaide).

He confides that he dreams of winning the lottery to buy a plane; he says his eyes are not that good anymore, but he keeps up his licence just in case. I suggest a Piper Cherokee might be the plane to go for, but he laughs: 'Something better than that if I win the lottery.' My other suggestion, a GulfstreamV, is off the mark as well, in the other direction: too fancy. I try to think of something in-between but cannot come up with anything. Later I regret that I did not ask him about his rank, and whether he's seen any action.

I spend the whole evening trying to get the car insured, via phone and internet, invariably earning a refusal because I don't have a CA licence. (Ironically, I used to have one, in the 70s. It would be out of date, of course, but I wonder now what happened to it. Did I just throw it away?) Finally, I get through to somebody from the AAA who calls back regarding my internet application for a quote, and after the usual 'don't-know-wait-have-to-ask-my-manager' rigmarole, she puts me through to somebody in head office who manages to find somebody else who is the exact specialist; he calls back straight away, quotes a ridiculously high premium (but what am I to do?), then prepares the documents online, I initial and sign online, and we're done: c/c payment is accepted, car is insured. Whew!

The next morning, we buy a GPS at the local Radio Shack store. The sales assistant shows us how to operate it, and we're all set. California: here we come!

WEDNESDAY, 20 February

Email from Rudy: he enjoyed meeting us, is impressed with Max's personality and golfing ability. He suggests we'd come to Scottsdale for coaching once every three months or so (he usually spends ten days there each Fall, Winter and Spring), so he can keep an eye on Max's development in addition to the work of a main coach. But Susan is no longer interested. Rudy is history.

I write a polite email back: congratulating Rudy on his birthday (he is 64 today), expressing our hope that we might meet him again when he comes to Southern California, and that we will enroll Max in his Golf Academy as the first student, if and when that institution will open its doors.

We need to find a coach, urgently.

WEDNESDAY afternoon

After school, we drive to Colina Park Golf Course in San Diego, via two freeways. The Mercury handles ok, except for a bit of swinging two and fro when you change lanes too quickly. I'll have to get used to it. The big car does not like dips (plenty of them around here): too heavy, too much overhang, soft shocks.

Colina Park is on 52nd street off El Cajon Boulevard in a section of town called Colina del Sol, the Sunny Hill. It's only about 30 minutes away from Max's school (like driving from Woollahra to Bexley Golf Club in Sydney), in an area nick-named Little Saigon: Vietnamese restaurants, supermarkets and shops everywhere. It's a little bit like Cabramatta.

New golf strategy: to enroll Max in First Tee/Pro Kids junior golf program at Colina Park. Rudy Duran, one of the original founders, had told us about it. We plan to play here as often as we can. They have afternoon golf coaching, other sports, excursions, supervised homework. It's an interesting program directed at the 'underserviced' children of the area: teaching life skills through the gentleman's game of golf. The kids come in all multicultural shapes and colours: black, Hispanic, Asian, African, girls in burqas and boys in low-hanging board shorts with underpants exposed.

We pay 100 dollars (membership fee) and five dollars for a round of golf: 18 holes, all par three. It's a public course like Torrey Pines, designed especially for children, although a lot of adults play here to practise their short game. The course is in good shape, a new driving range is under construction, it's on a hilly site with alternating uphill and downhill fairways, on some holes you can putt downhill from the tee box onto the green. Some of these greens are very tricky, fast and undulating with multiple breaks; there is also a little lake (well, pond is more like it) that has even got a cascading waterfall. Colina Park is no ordinary golf course, of course: it is the home of the Callaway Junior World Championship, age group six-and-under, played every July. This is why we're here. This is the event Max will be practising for.

It's dark by the time we get back to Pacific Beach.

THURSDAY, 21 February

In the morning, I drive the Mitsubishi rental car to the airport and hand it back, one day early. No refund: weekly rate. I go back by bus via Old Town, a traffic hub just north of downtown San Diego where buses, trolleys (light rail) and the coastal train meet. When I get home, I discover that I left the house key for our flat in Sapphire Street attached to the car key ring. Damn! I call the rental car company, but too late: the car is already gone with new renters, they can't be bothered to track them down, and nobody noticed that there was an extra key.

Fortunately, Susan has her key on her. Otherwise we wouldn't be able to get into the house: landlord is away on business in NY, his girlfriend is away as well, the back of the house is rented out to six guys from Belgium who stay for a week. I get a duplicate key cut for $2.50 at a little locksmith shop off Garnet Avenue. Little things: in Surry Hills shopping centre back in Sydney, they charge $5.00 for cutting a key. Later I discover the local post office people in Pacific Beach cut keys, too. They charge only $2.25.

THURSDAY afternoon

After an early lunch, Susan and I explore the public transport system. Bus No. 30 stops conveniently at the corner of Turquoise Street and La Jolla Boulevard, a few steps from our house; it goes to the University of California campus one way and to downtown San Diego the other. At Old Town we change to the Green Line trolley to Santa Fe Plaza where we change to the Orange Line downtown, and then the Blue Line takes us to the Mexican border. From here you can walk across into Tijuana. There is a huge Californian flag on one side of the border and an equally huge Mexican one on the other. We walk to a gigantic outlet mall that is about half a mile away and a whole mile long: one shop/boutique next to the other, all the major and minor brands are assembled here, but business is slow. There are hardly any customers. We find the first shoe shop and Susan buys a pair of *Aerosoles* for herself. They cost $29: ok, but not exactly a major saving. We get back by trolleys and bus, just in time to pick up Max from school.

Surprisingly, the SD Urban Transit system is not bad at all: one prejudice about America corrected. Of course, you still need a car to survive around here unless you limit yourself to your neighbourhood. But there are plenty of buses, the trolleys and the coastal train connect to the northern suburbs of SD county (Oceanside), and all seem pretty well integrated. A day pass is only five bucks and valid on all transport. There is a smart card, of course, called Compass. (Hello, Sydney?)

After school, we drive again to Colina Park and find out that Max is ineligible for the First Tee program for a number of reasons, and anyway: minimum age is seven. Manager refuses to budge, says employee the day before made a mistake to enroll Max. He'll get us a refund. Max can play golf, of course, this is a public course, owned by the city of SD, but he is ineligible for the teaching program.

We talk to the man in charge, Todd Smith, PGA, the Director of Golf who also confirms: sorry, nothing we can do, insurance issue, etc. He explains the aims of the program: principal aim is education, not to train top golfers. Golf is to help underprivileged children to acquire life skills, to give them a better chance through learning discipline, self-confidence, making friends through teamwork, keeping the kids off the streets, all through playing golf (and other associated after-school activities on offer). The kids get points for doing things: finishing homework, presenting report cards, doing voluntary work, and they can exchange the points for goods and services: free play, excursions, golf equipment, etc. The program also arranges scholarships. The ultimate goal is character development and building leadership potential. Very admirable!

But this is golf, and this is America, and America is business: the three go hand in hand. Todd Smith is proud of Colina Park's association with the Callaway Championship. Players from overseas and all over the United States usually come here for a few days of training before the tournament: not unlike us, really. Except we're here already now, mid-February, so we'll have a head start. Todd tells us that he personally coached two out of the last three six-and-under champions, the last one from Japan. Dragon Mom's eyes light up. She has found a new Guru. Todd will be Max's coach.

Todd is the director of the local not-for-profit First Tee organisation, but he is also a PGA teaching pro, on the internet list of the fifty best coaches in California. He charges $100 per session, which could last anywhere from 20 minutes to one hour, depending on the child's attention span. He also has a flat rate of $1,000 per year, with one session per week. We are going to be here for something like five months, at least, so we're better off with the annual rate. We pay $1,000 on our credit card and are in business. Weekly coaching lesson is booked: Friday afternoon, 3pm. The timing works out perfectly: Friday is early release day at 1.45pm at All Hallows, the other days school is not out until 3pm.

FRIDAY, 22 February

Over breakfast, I read that 'Turner's Outdoorsman' has a display ad for a gun sale in the *U-T.* You can get a good deal on a Ruger LC9mm with a built-in laser ($489.98) or a Remington 700 SPS 308 Tactical (rifle), the latter for only $799.98. My favourite is a Heritage MFG Rough Rider 22LR single-action six-shot Colt, the cowboy's friend of old, the weapon that opened up the West. Today it comes with wood grip and alloy frame, 100% made in the USA, and costs $139.98. Wouldn't mind having one of those to defend the family against the baddies, as Max would say. But would they sell me one? I'll probably have to wait until I have my CA driver's licence. There's a gun show on at Del Mar next weekend.

In the same issue of the *U-T* is a page-long article about fish substitution practices in US supermarkets and restaurants. A nation-wide study (covering 22 states, including NY and CA) has found incredible practices among fishmongers, grocers and restaurateurs: about a third of grocery stores label fish incorrectly, substituting cheaper species for more expensive ones, and a staggering 95% of sushi restaurants do the same. There are no uniform labelling laws across the US. Consumers are being ripped off.

I remember the fish substitution racket in Australia way back in the early 80s: a species of fish – ling, of the cod family – was being sold as barramundi, then the scam was discovered and for a while ling appeared as 'equal to barramundi' in Australia's fish shops. Today, ling has taken its rightful place among the other Australian species and is just as expensive as barramundi. Which in turn is mostly fish-farmed these days, conveniently plate-sized, whereas 'pink ling' is still caught in the wild, though stocks are declining.

Another little thing that makes a difference: artificial sweeteners (essential for my coffee habit) are sold in units with the equivalent of two teaspoons of sugar. In Australia (and everywhere else, I think), tablets are equivalent to one teaspoon, but these are not available here (neither at Vons nor Albertson supermarkets where we usually shop, nor anywhere else where I try later). Isn't this the country of consumer choice par excellence? I'm beginning to have my doubts. I have no choice but to buy the doubly-sweet sweeteners. But I choose a brand that comes in little sachets, each one worth two teaspoons of sugar. I will use only half a sachet for my cup of coffee, I promise myself. Later, when I open the box, I find it is only half full: another great achievement in packaging!

FRIDAY afternoon

First lesson with new golf guru Todd Smith. He seems quite the opposite to Rudy Duran: more science, less art, although he does stress the philosophy of the game as well. We begin by checking out Max's swing on a computer simulator in a little darkened room fitted out with a tee mat, video camera, computer monitor and a wall-size digital display of a fairway with a flag in the distance and a net in front of it. Sensors are hooked up to Max's lower back, his shoulder and his hands. Then Max takes a swing towards the virtual hole, and the computer measures: speed and trajectory of ball, height and

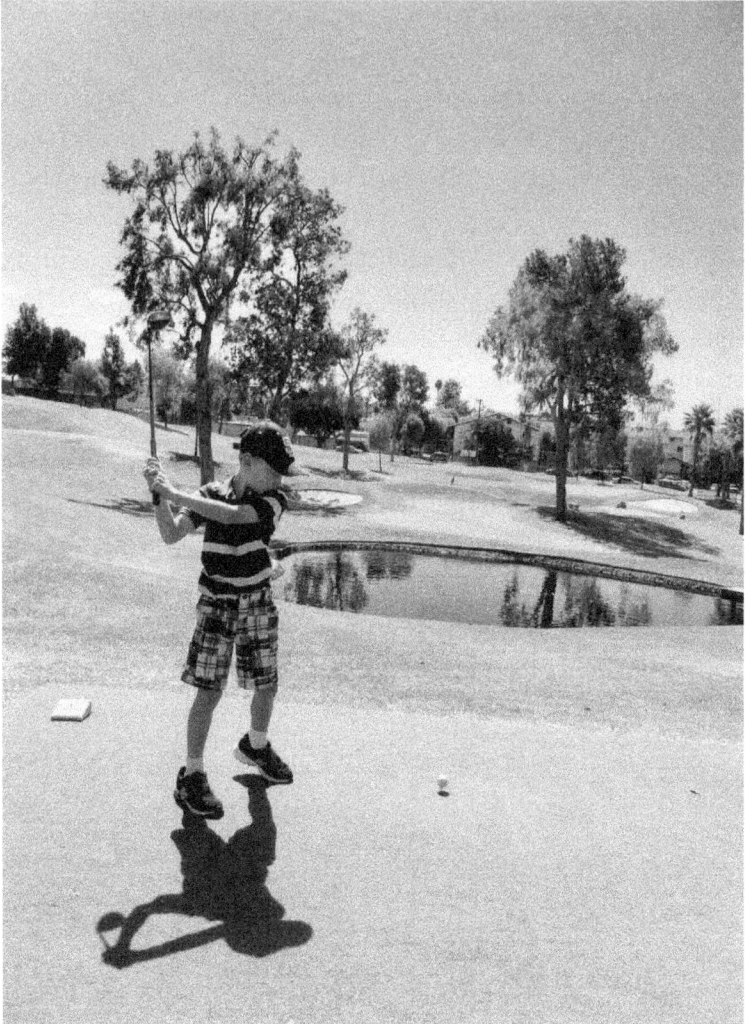

Water Hazard: Max Teeing off at Hole 17, Colina Park

distance achieved. Most importantly, three curves measure the movement of hips, upper torso (shoulders) and arms/hands.

Todd explains by showing a diagram of a touring pro: the three curves are separate until they join at impact with the ball to achieve maximum power. It's the same principle like a boxer hitting a punch or a baseball player throwing a ball. The all-important rotation begins with the hips, then the shoulders turn and lastly the arms. In Max's diagram (saved on the computer for future reference and comparison), the curves partially overlap, his body moves more as one piece (as I would have expected). This, explains Todd, prevents him from reaching maximum impact and speed (which equals distance on the fairway), but it may also cause injury down the track. We have our work cut out: over the next ten years or so, Max will have to work on his swing to separate the elements, as it were.

Susan and I are quite impressed by the demonstration. It's easy to see how the theory works, but how to separate the different movements of hips, shoulder and arms consciously within the one movement of hitting the ball is another story. Todd shows an exercise Max is supposed to do every day: he lies down on his back, vertically raises his legs angled 90 degrees at the knees, then turns over to the left to (almost) touch the floor, back up to the middle, then over to the other side, back to centre again. The shoulder is not supposed to move, only hips and legs. 'Repeat five times!' Max is eager to lie down on the mat and follow suit, but he finds it's not easy to keep control of the legs.

Todd is happy with Max's swing and impressed with the power he can generate. For the Callaway though, he says, the important thing is mastering the greens. It's all about putting: getting the speed/distance right, 'reading' the green, the lie of the ball, the curvature and breaks. Which way will the ball roll? 'That's what we'll be concentrating on over the coming weeks.'

Dragon Mom is over the moon. Her son's golfing career is on track.

Max likes Todd who is a quiet, cool guy. He's a tall, handsome Afro-American, with a winning smile; he speaks slowly and enunciates very clearly, deliberately. We talk about food (Max's favourite: fish tacos), and I ask Todd about a fish market in San Diego. There isn't any, but he knows and recommends a restaurant called 'Fishmarket'. He seems to be a fish-and-seafood fan like myself and mentions a couple of other good places in our area: the 'World Famous' (that's the name!) on the beachfront walkway at Pacific Beach (lobster tacos during happy hour for $1.50), or the 'Fish Shop' on Garnet Avenue.

SATURDAY, 23 February

We decide to further explore San Diego by public transport. At the bus stop, we come across a disabled bus with a flat battery. The driver tells us that on weekends kids under 12 ride free: just as well, as we were about to buy a compass card for Max. Five dollars saved! We only need to wait a few minutes, then a replacement bus arrives.

Our destination today is the *USS Midway*, a decommissioned aircraft carrier that is now a floating museum near the downtown pier of SD harbour. Apparently, the 'Fishmarket' restaurant is just across the pier. A possibility for lunch.

But we never get there: on the bus we meet Cindy and David, Chinese mom and son (18 years old), who are on an outing to Balboa park. They are from Shenzhen. We decide to join them, and they are happy to have us strolling along. We change from bus to trolley at Old Town and then to bus again. Balboa Park is the site of the famous SD zoo, a couple of museums, a theatre (apparently used for children's shows). There is a kind of fake Spanish-Mexican village with lots of artsy shops, people showing off their juggling or yoga skills, or just happily browsing like us. We visit the natural history museum, a nice little Greek-style palace with the usual dinosaurs, fossils, etc. In the lobby a Foucault pendulum is merrily swinging to and fro, and I explain to Max and David what it is all about: visual proof of the earth's rotation, a famous experiment named after the 18th century French scientist. David thinks I'm a physicist and is surprised when I tell him I teach (or used to teach) history and literature. Max is more interested in the dinosaurs. He chats with David in Mandarin.

We invite Cindy and David back to our place for dinner: steamed dumplings from the freezer. David is a freshman at the University of California at San Diego, UCSD for short. He is a polite and clever young man, well mannered. He applied to six US universities but received only one offer. Luckily it was the best one, I suggest. He agrees, he quite likes UCSD. His major is structural engineering, as architecture (his first choice) is not taught here. He is living on campus which is a requirement for freshmen, and I can hardly believe that they have not changed the rules since my student days in the 1970s. Sharing an apartment in a dorm with four other students costs him some $10,000 a year for room and board; in addition, he has to pay $40,000 tuition. Not cheap, but probably cheaper than Australia.

David's mother is visiting with a six-months visa; she is divorced, hardly speaks any English. Cindy tells us that she has paid a lawyer $5,000 to apply for refugee status, on the ground that she has been forced to have an abortion. I can't quite work out whether this actually happened or not, and I cannot imagine that China's one-child policy is sufficient reason to be given political asylum. Seems too easy. But then, this is 'America – One Nation under God'. Religion is politics, and the Chinese communists are godless people: here's one way, maybe, to show it to them. Her lawyer should know about her chances, I suppose. But does he or she work on a no-win no-fee basis? What happens if Cindy is refused? She gives me a sly smile and says she will appeal. She naively believes she can appeal year after year after year. I'm sceptical, but she is seemingly not worried about the prospect. I wish her good luck (and, in silence, that she has an honest lawyer).

Cindy is optimistic. Someone she knows went through the procedure and is now in possession of a green card. Cindy is determined not to go back to China, and if she is successful her son can stay as well. If not, he'll have to go back on condition of his student visa.

Immigration reform is one of the key issues in Obama's reform agenda. Later we hear in the news that in California the Department of Immigration has released numerous 'unauthorised immigrants' from detention because there is not enough money to pay for their stay at government's expense. I learn a new word: SEQUESTRATION. Government shutdown due to lack of funds. The spectre of sequestration is casting a menacing shadow ahead.

SUNDAY, 24 February

On Sunday morning we drive to La Colina. Max plays golf with Kenny, eight years old, who we have met earlier in the week with Maggie, his Chinese mom. It was a lucky coincidence: Kenny does not normally play here during the week. But the San Diego Unified School District is short of funds and has closed all schools for the week, so the kids have an unexpected holiday. Apparently, teachers must come to school but students must stay at home. Maggie works in real estate, and that could be helpful as we have asked our landlord about extending our stay, and he is not very forthcoming.

After golf we stop at our house for lunch: Max and Kenny and his little sister eat some dumplings and then play on the giant corner sofa, there's plenty of pillows and cardboards for building hide-outs and cubby houses, while the adults have a proper meal: tomatoes and basil and mozzarella, salmon and asparagus (all bought from a Vietnamese supermarket). Maggie's husband David has joined us on the way home, and with four adults and three kids the place is full. I get annoyed when everyone keeps speaking Mandarin, so an effort is made. David's English is very good, he's been here for 17 years. They live in Rancho Bernardo in the mountains, quite a way away. David has taken up golf after his son discovered the game: usually it's the other way around. But he does not have much time to play: he works as an engineer, defence software applications, his company does a lot of business with China, he travels often. Maggie also has a degree in electronic engineering but works part-time selling real estate. She mainly works from home. She has two kids to look after; her daughter is only four.

MONDAY, 25 February

We pick up Max from school half an hour early and drive to the Department of Motor Vehicles. You take a number and wait; the girl next to us has been there for over two hours already, she says. But we have an appointment, and things move smoothly. Car transfer and registration are done quickly, after one thorny issue is finally resolved: on the application, you must provide a Social Security Number or tick a box that says you never had one. I used to have one, way back, but have no idea what the number was, or what happened to it. The friendly guy behind the counter consults with the manager who goes away to make a phone call, then comes back and says it's ok, too long ago. I can sign, and I tick the box 'Never had one'. Fortunately, the computer link to the Department of Social Security does not come up with an objection.

Now the driver's licence test. I have my picture taken, thumb fingerprinted, and then move on to a little cubicle to take the written test. I get a sheet with thirty-six questions, the usual multiple choice stuff, and start brooding. I realise right away that I am silly doing this, I'm certain I won't pass, I have no idea about current traffic rules in California. Why I do try anyway? I tell myself: relax, you can pass with six wrong answers. Maybe I can get away with it? What's the speed limit in a residential area? 25, 30 or 35mph? I have no clue, so I tick the most conservative option. Correct! How many months in jail for being over the limit? Six months or 12 months? I tick the latter, preferring to err conservatively on the side of a strict, punitive regime. But the law is more lenient than I thought: the right answer is six months.

I fail the test: eight questions wrong. I should have had a look at the Driver's Handbook, I say to the officer who checks my test sheet. Highly recommended, he observes.

In the evening, I study the handbook. Not a very attractive publication: bad print, no index, the set-up does not seem overly thought through, text meanders haphazardly from one issue to the next. I search for a free practice test online, but there isn't any. You can do one for $19.99 plus tax. I think in Australia you can practise online for free as often as you wish.

TUESDAY, 26 February

At Colina Park, we meet Louise, a very competent golfer, who is eight years of age and plays all by herself, following her lesson with Todd Smith. She is very shy and speaks very softly. We ask her whether she'd like to play with Max, and the two play a few holes together. After golf, she will go to her weekly art class. Louise knows German, her mother is from Flensburg. Her father who picks her up is a lawyer, Hispanic background. He proclaims proudly in German: '*Ich bin Rechtsanwalt!*' The family spent a year together in Berlin. When Louise lines up for a putt, he tells her: 'You better get this, otherwise you won't get any dinner.' It's a joke, of course.

Later that evening, we go online and book a holiday to Mexico City for the Easter Holiday.

COLINA PARK WORDS OF WISDOM, FOR THE BENEFIT OF AMERICA'S YOUNG

On the Colina Park course, white sandstone benches are placed next to the tee boxes to give players a chance to sit down for a break while their partners/opponents tee off. These solid pieces of park furniture were donated by individual sponsors who have their names inscribed on a brass plaque along with what seems an inscription of their choice. Here's a list of featured quotations, from an eclectic list of gurus:

Hole No. 1: 'I'm not a saint, unless you think of a saint as a sinner who keeps on trying.' Nelson Mandela

Hole No. 2: 'No one can make you feel inferior without your consent.' Eleanor Roosevelt

Hole No. 3 and Hole No. 6 (one bench for adjacent tees): 'Courage is resistance to fear, mastery of fear, not absence of fear.' Mark Twain

Hole No. 5: 'Often, the most moral choice is the hardest, endure with perseverance.' Unknown

Hole No. 7: 'Winners never quit and quitters never win.' Unknown

Hole No. 8: 'The best way to predict your future is to create it.' Peter Drucker

Hole No. 9: 'Success is not measured by the position someone has reached in life, but by the obstacles he has overcome while trying to succeed.' Booker T. Washington

Hole No.10: 'As you climb the ladder of success, check occasionally to make sure it is leaning against the right wall.' Unknown

Hole No. 11: 'The object of golf is not just to win, it is to play like a gentleman, and win.' Phil Mickelson

Hole No. 13: 'Nothing can stop the man with the right mental attitude from achieving his goal; nothing on earth can help the man with the wrong mental attitude.' Thomas Jefferson

Hole No. 14: 'Make a game out of practice. You're still a child at heart.' Harvey Penick

Hole No. 15 and Hole No. 18 (one bench for adjacent tees): 'Faith is the substance of things hoped for on the evidence of things not seen.' Hebrews 11:1

Hole No. 17: 'Never give up. No matter how dark it may look, always stay the course.' Lee Elder

Holes No. 4 and No. 16: no plaques yet. Sponsors wanted.

WEDNESDAY, 27 February

We've got to find a new flat. We had asked Stan whether we could extend our stay, but he did not give a clear answer. He's presently in New York doing his job: finding accommodation for overseas students who enroll in a Manhattan dance school run by a friend. Usually he does this from his place here in

California, via internet. But after the recent winter storm that flooded parts of the city, accommodation in Manhattan is in short supply. His presence is required on site. Now he tells us, by email, that there is an issue with Max: our son jumps around too much (he does!), and the floor tiles are 'like bass drums'. The owners, says Stan, are not able to promise that we can stay beyond March. He goes on to complain about the weather in NY: it is freezing, one blizzard after another.

We're not quite sure what to make of it. We thought Stan was the owner. I think he's playing games with us. We turn to the internet again, searching for accommodation. There's quite a few flats on offer, but most are unfurnished and mostly for longer term rentals. We finally find one a little further up the coast, right in the middle of the La Jolla village, corner Draper Avenue and Pearl Street: two bedrooms, two bathrooms, balcony, fully furnished. It's perfect, just down the hill from Max's school. This is exactly where we wanted to be. Amazingly, it's five hundred dollars cheaper than what we're paying now in plebeian Pacific Beach, and just as close to the beach.

We're lucky that we found Maggie who knows about real estate. She promises to get in touch with the owner.

FRIDAY, 1 March

We drive up to LA after school to stay at Xiaofang's and Bill's place for the weekend. Max will play his first tournament on Sunday morning. I have a terrible time driving on the I-5 with stop-and-go traffic. I leave the freeway to get to the coastal highway but the traffic there is even worse. The weather is too good: everybody wants to go to the beach. I drive back to take the San Diego Freeway, but then the GPS tells me to go on the Long Beach Tollway. However, it does not tell me how much it costs. Can I pay cash or do I need a tag? We don't have any change on us. I refuse the tollway option and stay on the freeway. It takes forever, although everybody is driving above the speed limit whenever there is a clear space ahead. Finally: Torrance, exit right. It took us over three hours to cover the 110 miles. I'm exhausted. Before dinner, Bill and I drive to a nearby liquor superstore that just opened at the local mall. It's gigantic, twice the size of your suburban Dan Murphy's in Sydney. I could easily fall back to my old wine-drinking days here. We pick up two bottles of Kim Crawford Marlborough SauvBlanc: nice drop. We (well, mostly I) finish them off over prawns, steak and some Chinese vegetables. I think I could get used to drinking white wine again.

SATURDAY, 2 March

We drive north along the coastal highway to do some LA sightseeing. We visit the usual places. In Hollywood, we try whether we can match the footprints and handprints of the stars in front of the Chinese Theatre; we check out the boutiques on Rodeo Drive, get lost while driving the winding roads up and down Beverly Hills, and finally end up strolling along Santa Monica Pier.

On the way back, we stop at Venice Beach and admire the body-builders who are religiously devoting themselves to their six-pack workout. A large sign outside a shopfront on the beachside walkway says: 'The Doctor's in! No Appointment Needed.' In front of the door, a man in a white lab coat is handing out brochures to the passers-by who are leisurely strolling, skating, jogging or pan-handling along the promenade. There seems to be a general air of merriment around the building, and a whiff of pot is hanging in the air.

When we get closer, I realise it is a doctor's surgery specializing in cannabis therapy. Apparently, you can get a prescription here, no waiting required, and you can get your script for medicinal marijuana filled at a dispensary a few doors away. Cannabis is not quite a panacea, but according to the good doctor's brochure it is good for all sorts of indications: chronic pain, nausea, glaucoma, to name a few. There is also evidence that marijuana can kill cancer cells: in tests with rodents suffering from breast, liver, pancreatic and brain cancers, tetrahydrocannabinol (THC, one of the active ingredients in cannabis) was found to have a powerful tumor-shrinking effect. Studies involving clinical trials are on the way.

In California, the medical use of cannabis was first allowed in 1996, but in San Diego the City Council has not yet been able to make up its mind about how to regulate marijuana dispensaries. As a result, marijuana shops have opened in all sorts of places, in downtown San Diego as well as in Pacific Beach, Point Loma, La Jolla and University Heights. These establishments are illegal, but Mayor Bob Filner, a staunch pro-cannabis advocate, has directed council officers not to prosecute, and city police will look the other way. However, customers still need to be on the look-out: federal law classifies marijuana as a 'first class drug', in the same category as heroin and ecstasy, and an FBI agent may be lurking behind a corner to catch you in possession.

On the car radio, we listen to Canadian pot heroes Cheech and Chong. The hilarious hippie comedy and pop-singing duo from the 70s (famous for *Up in smoke*, the movie featuring the mother-of-all-joints) have made a comeback with the 'Medical Marijuana Blues'.

AMERICAN REVOLUTIONS

It occurs to me that there are at least three revolutions going on in America right now: the Pot Revolution, the Energy Revolution, the New Warfare Revolution.

Here's a preview, captured in three quotes of the week.

Quote of the Week No. 1: 'I've gotten a lot of good ideas from pot. Including smoke more pot.' (Bill Maher, *Rolling Stone Magazine*.)

Quote of the Week No. 2: 'This water is most likely safe. If you have any concerns about contamination due to hydraulic fracturing, expose water to flame.' (Poster with picture of dripping tap and lighted match found in bathroom of NYC gym, and elsewhere. Hoax.)

Quote of the Week No. 3: 'Don't nuke 'em, drone 'em!' (Sticker on back of pick-up truck.)

BILL'S DREAM

It's Saturday, late afternoon, and Bill is not home yet when we get back to Torrance after our sightseeing drive. He usually arrives home from work only after 7pm. He's a postman, and he's been delivering the mail the whole day. Bill tells me he works eight to ten hours a day, six days a week. The normal working week is 40 hours, the rest is overtime. Staff sizes have been declining over the last few years, now he's always asked to work longer hours. Not asked, he corrects himself: told to. I ask him about the government proposal to suspend Saturday deliveries to cut costs and reduce the huge deficit the postal service is running up year after year. Bill says he wouldn't mind not working a day less. But he hasn't got a choice, he adds.

Bill has a dream. He would like to retire, not quite yet, but in a few years' time when he has reached his maximum pension allowance. He would like to become a personal trainer. He is in good shape, thanks to his job, walking eight hours a day, but he also exercises at home, doing pull-ups with a bar he has installed in a doorway in his house. It's a do-it-yourself kit you buy in a sports store and put together yourself. Max likes it a lot and tries to imitate Bill, but he can't quite get his chin across the bar yet. Bill also has a bench press and other gadgets that he keeps in an open shed in the garden.

Bill is tall, slim and very fit. I can easily see that he would make a good personal trainer. But how would he find his clients? Bill says he knows a guy, a Hollywood celebrity, who was with him in elementary school in Torrance. This guy was the martial arts trainer of David Carradine (who starred in the *Kung Fu* TV series). He has got all sorts of martial arts belts, black and otherwise. He is on TV all the time, Bill says, on all the talk shows; he's got his own website, but these days he is getting to be a little bit..., well, obese. Bill would like to work out with him, he says, and then the guy would introduce his friends to him, and they would become Bill's clients. The two would just hang out together, they'd do some exercises and fitness drills, and his friend would see Bill's potential as a personal trainer and would refer all his overweight acquaintances to him. He must know a ton of people, Bill says.

I'm sceptical, of course. If this guy is a martial arts expert, he could get in shape by himself, couldn't he? And he probably wouldn't want to be seen in public with a personal trainer, would he? But Bill has got all this covered. It's not about training his friend, he says. They'd just work out together because they're old friends; it's the celebrity contacts that Bill is after. He could become the personal trainer of some Hollywood celebrities. And besides, his friend does not care about his image in public. He doesn't give a damn, doesn't need to. He jokes about his fatty appearance on his website, Bill says.

I don't ask Bill when was the last time he had seen his friend from Torrance Elementary School. A dream is a dream is a dream. Everybody's got a dream of some sort. The hobo's dream of the Big Rock Candy Mountain. The actor's dream: Hollywood, California – The Dream Factory. The golfer's dream – Rudy Duran said, 'Dream Big and Work Hard, Max.' The Dragon Mother's Dream: You can be what your mother wants you to be. The Chinese Dream: Gong Xi Fa Cai! The All-American Everly Brothers had a dream, too: if ever they wanted a girl, or boy for that matter, all they had to do was dream. And then, of course, there is Bob Dylan who famously invited you to be in his dream as long as he could be in yours.

Bill and his wife Xiaofang are doing reasonably well. Bill is not dreaming his life away. He has got a secure job with the US government: he delivers the mail, an essential service (even though email seems to be taking over at breakneck speed). His wife has a degree in accounting, but right now she is looking after their daughter, full time. They have a comfortable house with a renovated kitchen, next to a park and playground, not far to local shopping and schools. The house is big enough to accommodate us as regular weekend visitors. Bill drives a small pick-up truck that takes him to work, Xiaofang has got a new Honda SUV. They have a beautiful daughter who speaks mostly Mandarin, but she'll pick up English in no time next fall when she'll start attending pre-school. Life is good. Still, you need a dream in your life, as a back-up. Or faith, the 'substance of things hoped for on the evidence of things not seen'.

SUNDAY, 3 March

We drive north on I-405 and then west on CA-118, aka as the Ronald Reagan Freeway. Rich agricultural land as we descend into the lovely Simi Valley: there's orchards and vines with table grapes. We pass a turnoff sign to the 'Ronald Reagan Presidential Library and Air Force One'. We wonder whether Reagan was born in this area, and whether he parked his presidential plane here after he left office. Later we pass a turnoff that says: American Jewish University. One of the 4,500 degree granting colleges in the country.

Our destination is Moorepark, a tidy and learned town. There's a Moorepark College for the local kids, and the streets are named after famous universities: Cambridge, Amherst, Loyola, Berkeley, Duke, Purdue. Everything is very clean and orderly, and on a Sunday morning very quiet and peaceful. We drive down Princeton Avenue.

There's nobody around.

The Rustic Canyon Golf Club is on the other side of town, located in a wide valley enclosed by mountains on all sides. It's Western country, very beautiful. The land must have been a ranch previously; there's broken down, rusty fencing and what seems like old bullock cart tracks across the fairways. Now the desert has partially reclaimed the land. There are ravines, cacti and brush. The local rules warn of poisonous rattlesnakes that are apparently at home here: 'Be extra careful when looking for a lost ball.'

This is Max's first US tournament, part of the LA Junior Regional Tour. The tour is sponsored by U.S. Kids Golf, the major manufacturer of golf equipment and accessories for young people. It's big business. The routine is pretty much the same as in Sydney, but there's a bit more formality: at the first tee, the players are introduced to the gallery (which consists of half a dozen family members): 'Our next player, from Sydney, Australia: Maximilian Fischer.' Polite applause, and the game is underway. The tees for the six-year olds are halfway down the fairways, quite a long walk on most holes. Some parents have rented a cart, it's only $10 a piece, but the kids are not allowed to ride with them. Max plays in a group of three with Jack who is Afro-American, and Joseph who is Hispanic. He is the youngest, but only by a few months. Jack's dad is obviously trying to emulate Earl Woods, Tiger

Woods' father. He has already taken his son to tournaments all over the country, he tells us, but that's finished now: no more money after this summer, only local tournaments.

There's a lot of parental coaching going on although it is officially frowned upon. Jack's dad is standing right behind his son telling him how to approach the ball and where and how to position himself. He says: 'Left foot forward, again, a bit back. Good. Look at the pin. Look at the ball. Ok. Go ahead.' At least Jack and Joseph listen to their fathers whereas Max can hardly be bothered. He just steps up to the ball and hits it. The play is slow. We must wait for the group of girls ahead of us, along with the group behind us. There is a rule of 'fifteen minutes per hole' but it does not seem to be enforced, even though there are quite a few stewards on the course, watching and taking notes. This part of the game is new to us: the whole group gets a 'red card' (one penalty stroke) if it falls behind. Time is money, as poet Georg Herwegh already observed: in Germany, in 1863.

The kids play nine holes: three par-threes, three par-fours and three par-fives. Max begins nervously and wastes a couple of shots early on and towards the end, when he loses patience and concentration. But he plays well and scores 45, nine over par. He finishes second in his age group, after Jack. He gets a silver plate and a medal that he parades around in school the next day, showing off like a peacock to the girls.

The return drive to San Diego at night is much easier: less traffic. This time we take the Long Beach Tollway. We stop at a booth manned by a lady cashier and pay cash: $5.25. The toll road is nearly empty. It's a fast detour on the way to and from LA, skirting Irvine then joining the I-5 again. When we get home, Max is sound asleep and we take him straight to bed. We watch David Lettermann who's hosting Bruce Willis who appears with a bishop's mitre and declares that he is 'pope material'. The other guest is much nicer

Runner-up: Max with Medal and Trophy

to look at than Mr Willis: the winner of the 2013 *Sports Illustrated* swimsuit competition, couldn't catch her name, Ms Kate Something-or-Other. She has won twice in a row now, the lucky girl; this time the shoot for the cover photo spread was done in Antarctica where she had to change her skimpy bikinis to some other next-to-nothing outfits, on and off all day long, all camera work outside in the open, on the snow with icebergs in the background and penguins looking on, freezing her shapely butt off, the lovely poor thing. Letterman has a special surprise for her. In an eye-catching stunt, a huge poster showing off the curvaceous Miss Swimsuit USA is unfurled across several floors on the building opposite the Manhattan theatre where the *Late Show* is being taped.

MONDAY, 4 March

Mitt Romney has come out of hiding, I read in the *U-T*.

It 'kills' him not being president, he says in his first interview since he lost the election, but not because of unfulfilled personal ambition, of course not, far from it: it pains him to see the country go to ruin due to the lack of leadership by President Obama. It turns out that Romney and his wife have been living in their 'secluded home' in La Jolla since last November. I am surprised because I thought his home was in Boston, but then La Jolla is perhaps a logical choice for a man with such past achievements.

La Jolla is today and has always been a most exclusive place. It had the most expensive houses in the US in 2008 and 2009; the average price of a four-bedroom home was $1.842 million in 2008 and $2.125 million in 2009. There are Rolls-Royce, Bentley, Ferrari, Maserati and Lamborghini dealerships in a town of just over 30,000 residents. Plenty of Porsches, Mercs and the occasional Cadillac can be seen cruising along La Jolla Boulevard, but if you want to buy one of these lesser luxury marques you'll need to go elsewhere in San Diego county.

And what about Mitt Romney? What vehicle might he be driving today? Remember Ry Cooder's *Mutt Romney Blues*? The car chauffeured by Romney some years ago from Boston to Toronto with the family dog tied up on the roof was a good old-fashioned American station wagon, type 'country estate' (with fake wooden panels), and not one of them fancy imports. And where in La Jolla do the Romneys live, I wonder. Down by the beach, or up in the hills among the palatial mansions on Muirland Drive that I pass every morning on the way to Max's school?

THE CROSS ON SOLEDAD MOUNTAIN

The peak of Soledad Mountain is just a few minutes away from All Hallows, so after school we drive up there to have a look: the view is panoramic. You look far out over the ocean to the west, there's a long pier (part of the famous Scripps Institute of Oceanography) jutting out into the surf a few miles to the north, still further north a hazy LA beckons, then you look east towards a clear sky above the desert and mountains on the way to Arizona, and finally south to the SD skyline, with a faint brown smog line over the horizon cutting across the landmark Coronado Bridge. A Latin cross, nine metres high, built out of white recessed concrete stands at the very pinnacle of Soledad Mountain, on top of a circular pedestal that you can ascend like the stairway to heaven.

The school secretary had told me the cross is a war memorial, but that's not the right term: it's a veterans' memorial, dedicated to American soldiers whether they have seen action or not. Below the cross are concentric circles of chest-high walls covered with black granite plaques, commemorating individual servicemen. Some have photos, most have the soldiers' service record and pictures of medals earned, capped off by salutations like 'For God and Country' or 'In Loving Memory'. Plaques donated by corporations attest to the patriotic spirit of local businessmen: 'HBO Salutes and Supports our Veterans and Active Duty Personnel!' or 'The Del Mar Thoroughbred Club

Stairway to Heaven: School Excursion to the Easter Cross, Soledad Mountain

remembers its War Veterans.' There are also engraved brick pavers available to people without family members who have served in the military. One paver simply states: 'God Bless America. Dave and Jill Payne.'

It's the usual display of all-inclusive American patriotism, but I'm intrigued by the Cross. I think of the Australian war memorials: the typical pose of the Anzac digger with slouch hat and bowed head, rifle at hand. I ask a volunteer who is glad to answer such questions: 'It is customary at American war memorials to have a cross?' I don't get a clear answer; the volunteer man seems a little uneasy when he evasively explains that the site is administered by a private organisation.

Later I google and find that there's a quite a history behind that cross. A wooden cross was first erected by local citizens in 1923; known as the Easter Cross, it was stolen a few years later. A replacement cross was burned down by the Ku Klux Klan in 1932 after a black family had moved into the area. It was the Klan's customary show of terror to warn unwanted people and frighten them away. In 1934, a new cross was erected that was blown away in a storm; the present one dates from 1954. To my surprise, there is a chapter of the Klan operating in San Diego County today: their website seems to be mostly about selling T-shirts with rather inoffensive slogans in praise of love of Family, God and Country.

Since 1989, the Soledad Cross has been the object of ongoing litigation. Civil libertarians, including war veterans, want the cross removed while patriotic American Christians want to keep it. Various courts have repeatedly ruled that the city of San Diego is in violation of both the California Constitution ('No Preference Clause') and the First Amendment of the US Constitution, concerning the principle of the separation of church and state. The cross, as a symbol of the Christian religion, ignores the neutrality obligation of state agencies as it clearly favours one religion over others by allowing the public display of a religious symbol on publicly-owned land. To deflect the issue, the San Diego City Council offered the management of the site to the not-for-profit Mount Soledad Memorial Association which then constructed the

Veterans' Memorial around the cross. In defiance of the court, the Memorial was officially dedicated on Easter Sunday. However, this did not stop litigation, and finally, in 2006, President George W. Bush intervened, signing into law a bill to transfer 'City of San Diego property from Mt. Soledad Natural Park along with a Latin Cross to the federal government by applying the powers of eminent domain.' The property thus transferred measured 225 square feet: the exact footprint of the cross. This move was again promptly challenged. A lawsuit was filed by the American Civil Liberties Union on behalf of the Jewish War Veterans of the United States of America against the US government and Defence Secretary Donald Rumsfeld, charging 'that the continued display of the Mt. Soledad Latin cross on federally owned land unlawfully entangles government with religion.'

As of today, the matter is not settled. It is likely to be decided by the Supreme Court.

IS YOGA A RELIGION?

There is yet another dispute about the question of state neutrality in religious matters that is currently dividing opinions in Southern California. At issue is the teaching of yoga in state schools: is it promoting religion or just physical education? At Encinitas, in North San Diego County, a yoga program has recently been introduced into the school district's physical education curriculum. It is called *Ashtanga*, a supposedly dynamic version of yoga based on the teachings of a late local guru, Sri Krishna Patabhi Jois. According to the curriculum, the program 'provides a good physical workout' that 'also brings calmness and clarity to the mind,' along with other benefits such as helping students to 'connect more deeply with their inner selves.' Supposedly, 'yoga brings the inner spirit of each child to the surface.'

Dean Broyles, a lawyer based at Encinitas who represents a non-profit organisation devoted to religious freedom, has described the program as unconstitutional and has issued a legal challenge to the school board. According to Broyles, there are a lot of critics who ask him: 'What do you have against a little sweating and stretching?' His answer: 'Absolutely nothing. I'm not even against people doing yoga. I'm against the government teaching Ashtanga Yoga.' The language of the curriculum statement, he argues, clearly shows that Ashtanga Yoga is not just about physical fitness: 'Why in P.E. class are they concerned with connecting with inner selves?'

Encinitas lies at the geographical heart of Southern California, and it is no surprise that there are quite a few old-time baby boomers living in the area who strongly believe in yoga and other 'new age' practices that date back to the hippie days of the late 1960s. They reject the argument that the curriculum developed for the Encinitas School District violates the neutrality clause of the constitution. The supporters of *Ashtanga* claim that the yoga program taught in the schools has been conscientiously secularised; there is 'no chanting and no use of the traditional Sanskrit names of the postures, no attempt to indoctrinate the children.' But there are also many old-time religious conservatives in Encinitas who see yoga as part of an Eastern spirituality that is fundamentally opposed to Christian values and teachings, if not the work of the devil as the fundamentalist pastor and best-selling author Mark Driscoll has claimed. In *Real Marriage*, a hard-hitting Christian-values sex manual for his followers, Driscoll describes yoga as 'demonic' and claims that 'by definition' it is 'a worship act to spirits other than the God of the Bible.'

Does the truth lie somewhere in-between? Would hybridity or syncretism work? Christian groups elsewhere in the country have tried to combine yoga exercises for children with aspects of Christian spirituality, by replacing Sanskrit chanting with scripture readings. There is a program out of Oklahoma known as Praise Moves, a 'Christian alternative to yoga'. Of course, Dean Broyles would not be happy with that either and would probably challenge. But wait – there is more: a third alternative for public schools called Power Moves involves kids doing yoga exercises with some 'sweating and stretching' while 'character-building quotes' appear on a video screen. I imagine they would be like the ones that I read on the golf course benches at Colina Park.

RETURN TO THE OLD WILD WEST

What about another American cliché: the rising crime rate? Actually the crime statistics in California are generally on a downward trend, except one crime is up: cattle rustling. According to the Bureau of Livestock identification, 1,317 head of cattle were stolen last year, a whopping 22% increase from pre-recession numbers. In other parts of the Old Wild West, the problem is worse. The Texas and Southwestern Cattle Raisers Association reported 10,400 head of cattle stolen in 2012, a 36% increase since 2010. The trend coincides with record high cattle prices in 2011 and 2012 reported by the US Department of Agriculture.

In the Old West, when a cattle rustler was caught, he more likely than not ended up swinging from the next tree, or so the movies tell us. These days, they'll probably plea-bargain to get probation and a fine. In California, there are no set penalties for stealing cattle, but a new law coming into effect in January 2014 will treat cattle rustling as a felony or misdemeanor, with a $5,000 fine. With a steer costing around $1,000 a head, that does seem quite a deterrent.

So, who does the cattle rustling in 2013? Is it the home butcher on the suburban half-acre block, trying to cope with the rising price of minced beef for their hamburgers? Or the interstate trafficker, loading up a dozen steers at a time to be shipped across the state line to the next slaughterhouse to make a few quick bucks? Who knows?

What we do know is that there are an estimated three million head in California. There's a lot of bull around.

LITTLE SAIGON AND THE ART OF BRANDING

The area around Colina Park is known for its high crime rate. Now San Diego City Council has unanimously voted to 'brand' a six-block section of El Cajon Boulevard in City Heights, between Highland and Euclid Avenues, as the 'Little Saigon Cultural and Commercial District'. It's an area with a concentration of Vietnamese grocery stores and restaurants, and it is home to some 40,000 Vietnamese-Americans, the second largest Asian-American community in San Diego (after the Philipino-Americans). 70% of the businesses in the area are owned by Vietnamese-Americans. It is hoped that the 'branding' will help establish this neglected part of town as a centre of Vietnamese art, music, culture and food.

We have come to know the area quite well from our regular visits to Colina Park. Driving back to La Jolla, we usually stop and shop in one of the huge Vietnamese supermarkets, stocking up on fruit and veggies, Asian beer and other staples. Along El Cajon Boulevard, we pass plenty of dilapidated buildings and storefronts, pawn shops, fast-food joints and all sorts of small businesses trying to eke out a living. Our friends tell us to be careful when we take Max to golf there, but we have not seen anything unusual, certainly no evidence of any crime. But then we're there usually during the day, it's perhaps a different story after dark.

The area certainly needs a facelift. The name change is to make it more marketable. It's quite a challenge.

TUESDAY, 5 March

We have decided we'd like to extend our stay in Southern California until the end of the year, and Maggie has managed to persuade the owner of the flat at Draper Avenue to rent it to us. The usual rental term is a minimum of six months: we will rent for three months, until the end of June, and then for five months from September to January. During July and August the place is always let to regular customers, and we'll need to go somewhere else during that time. But that's ok: it's the school holidays. We can rent a place for a couple of weeks somewhere closer to Colina Park for the Callaway tournament and then go on vacation.

It turns out that the owner of the La Jolla apartment is a Chinese woman with the same surname as Susan; she lives in Washington State. The contract is sent and signed via internet. We pay the whole amount in advance. Our contract with Stan runs out on 8 April. We'll be coming back from Easter holiday in Mexico on 6 April, stay a couple of nights at Sapphire Street, and then move on to La Jolla.

THURSDAY, 7 March

Today, we've been here for 4 weeks. A daily routine has set in. Taking Max to school at just before eight o'clock, breakfast while reading the local paper, walking along the beach, writing, lunch, picking Max up from school, driving to Colina Park (15.5 miles one way), taking Max to play golf, homework, dinner. The weather is sunny, if a little cooler than usual.

FRIDAY, 8 March

Ricky, one of the boys in Max's class is seven years old today, and he has invited Max to his birthday party. I drive him there after school. The house is in a cul-de-sac, closed off by yellow witches' hats and a sign saying: Drive Slowly, Kids at Play. The birthday party has taken over the street, kids everywhere, playing ball, riding their bicycles and skateboards or jumping around on pogo sticks. Susan is already there, helping Ricky's mother Marianna with the set-up. It's the usual affair, very much like a kids' birthday party in Australia: a buffet set up in the garage, finger food, marshmallow cupcakes, do-it-yourself tacos, lolly bags, beer and wine for the adults. Max tries skateboarding for the first time. Later the kids play video games and dance in front of a huge flat-screen TV. The usual favourites: One Direction, Gangnam Style, etc.

The adults gather in the backyard around an open fire in a circular brick pit (gas, lava stones). They are a group of friends who have known each other for 20-odd years, having lived in the same neighbourhood after moving here from New Jersey. The wives complete the usual American melting pot: Marianna is originally from Brazil, another mother from Mexico.

The men all share one vital interest: surfing. We get a glimpse of what the famous Pacific Beach surf culture is all about. Pete, birthday boy's dad, has an impressive collection of surfboards stacked up in his double garage, and a couple of boards ready to go in his pick-up truck. He says he's going to the beach every day for an hour or two after work, longer on weekends, always the same spot on the beach down the road. Kevin, another parent, is a teacher at a local high school who surfs a couple of hours every day after school. Four or five of them usually spend their holidays together; they have been to a few exotic places like Costa Rica or some Indonesian island I've never heard of, where the surf is supposedly the best in the world. I mention Australia, and they laugh. Of course, they've heard about surfing down under, and they would like to go one day: but it's a bit far and too expensive. They will spend the Easter holiday week at Cabo San Lucas, at the tip of Baja California. Great place for surfing! We tell them we are planning to be in Mexico City and are happy to hear that's a good choice: don't worry, it's safe unless you do something stupid, it's a great city, you'll like it there.

We spend a pleasant afternoon that turns into evening, chatting and drinking, with lots of laughter and well-established camaraderie. Everybody is very curious about where we are from and why we came here. They are quite amused by Dragon Mom's dream story, as I tell it, and respond with a great deal of admiration: Wow! Awesome! Good luck! But golf is not really their thing. The other main topic of conversation is schools and education. Kevin has a son in second grade at Pacific Beach Elementary. He says he is very impressed by the school. His son is in the math and chess clubs, plays baseball and soccer; he is learning well and likes the school. The other parents voice their scepticism; the consensus seems to be that PB Elementary is not really up to scratch. They think very highly of All Hallows and tell us we've done the right thing.

We don't mention our short and abortive visit to PB Elementary. I'm pretty sure Kevin is right, and the others are too. It's a matter of perception, and there's always a good teacher in a bad school and a bad teacher in a good school, you can be lucky one year and it's a disaster the next. Later we learn from Marianna that Ricky went to PB Elementary the previous year; he is quite small for his age, and his parents soon found out that he was being bullied in class. When they reported this to the school, nothing was done, so they took him out and enrolled him in All Hallows.

On the way home, Max informs us that he'd like a pogo stick.

SATURDAY, 9 March

It's sunny again today, after it had rained all night: very unusual. But rain is very welcome here, and badly needed. We take a late morning stroll down to the pier.

On the beach nearby, the One-Way Church of God has set up an open tent with a makeshift altar table and some thirty folding chairs. The chairs are empty, awaiting the faithful. At 11am there is nobody around yet except two church ladies who are arranging literature on a table on the adjacent walkway. A large banner proclaims: There is only ONE WAY! It seems the church is operating out of a van parked nearby. The van doubles as advertising billboard: it features a cross next to the name 'One Way Church' and a logo that replicates the one-way street sign with the arrow going straight up to heaven. It's a mobile church. I wonder whether there are drive-in churches in America, too.

On TV, later that day, we watch a new pope being elected in Rome. A curious ritual: the Catholic Church allows itself the luxury of a democratic vote (highly selective, to be sure) to choose a plenipotentiary who will rule over his flock with near-absolute power until he dies like a monarch, or – new precedent by the previous office-holder – chooses to resign like any other mere mortal CEO.

In the afternoon, we drive to Lake San Marcos for another kids' golf tournament. The course is part of a country club community in the mountains between Carlsbad and Escondido. There is a man-made lake with meandering canals and bridges, waterfront homes with jetties, a desolate, deserted *piazza*. Fake Italian architecture. We drive to the clubhouse and unpack Max's golf bag, only to be told by the pro that this is not the right place. The kids' tournament is at another course, half a mile down the road. It is rather less impressive, slightly run-down, the pro shop is a shed, there is no practice area. We meet up with Louise and her brother and sister and their parents; I chat with mother Dorothée in German. They spend most of their weekends taking their kids to golf, just like us. Max is in the same group with Kenny who has come up with his father; Maggie is staying home today to look after the baby girl. Max plays without great enthusiasm. This is the first time he is in the eight-and-under group; he's the youngest of the bunch but taller than most of the eight-year-olds. After four weeks of intensive practice and coaching, I don't see much improvement in his game. Susan, as usual, cannot resist telling him what to do and how to do every shot, and he gets angry at her. It does not help his game, of course. He finishes with a score of 12 over par. But he lands in fifth place, gets a medal to wear around his neck, and he is happy.

SUNDAY, 10 March

More sightseeing in SD. We take Bus 30 to Old Town and change to the Green Line Trolley to Seaport Village. It's a pleasant walk along the waterfront to the *USS Midway*, the decommissioned giant aircraft carrier that has been turned into a museum. It's a huge ship, to be sure, but the biggest surprise is that it is steam-powered. It has four turbines fed by huge boilers that run on diesel fuel, and the steam generated runs all the ship's propulsion (four props), the powerful catapult system that launches the planes into the air, as well as providing electricity to power the ship's communication and service functions. It's a very entertaining and informative museum, with volunteer guides (seemingly all veterans) at hand everywhere to explain things. The animatronic captain speaks to us at his desk in his cabin, and an interactive video lets you control the ship's power output, in virtual reality. The flight deck and the hangar below are huge open spaces, but the rest of the ship features the same infrastructure as any traditional vessel: narrow companionways, steep ladders, hatches, galleys, bunks and heads to accommodate some 3,000 sailors. The bridge is a pretty cramped affair, too, and the steering wheel not bigger than that of my 28-foot sailing boat. There is also a jail, the *brig*, equipped with two individual cells and a holding cell for eight. Inside, there is a huge circular mirror that allows the guard to see from outside the brig into every corner of it.

I talk to a volunteer who served in Vietnam. He remembers an R&R visit to Sydney, especially the beach at Bondi and the beautiful girls who were so impressed with the courtesy and good manners of the American sailors. By comparison, he says, the Aussie men were somewhat – he hesitates one second – 'rough'.

THE PYRAMID MAN

Along the seawall walk, there are the usual buskers plying their trade: a magician, a blues singer with acoustic guitar, a psychic offering card or palm readings, portrait painters, the guy who plays a statue (not quite clear of what). Next to the tarot card lady, who is dozing away in her beach chair under a sun umbrella, there is one truly amazing act: the pyramid builder. A small man, perhaps just over five feet tall, who looks part Mexican part Indian, has built half a dozen stone pyramids as tall as himself. He uses rocks lying around on the seawall behind him. He starts with big rocks, places smaller ones on top and then finds a larger, triangular, roughly cone-shaped stone that he places on the top stone with the pointy bit down. Miraculously, it stays in place, in perfect balance. We watch him putting the final touch to one pyramid. He chooses a heavy stone with a sharp, pointy end, lifts it up with both hands and places it carefully on the top stone. He rests it there, supporting it with both hands, and holds it in place for what seems a few minutes at least. Then, ever so slowly, he opens his hands and moves them away from the stone that remains standing up, precariously balanced on a tip that is no larger than a dime. Later we watch him seizing the top stone of another pyramid, equally balanced upside down, slowly lifting it up in the air and slowly putting it back again on its pivot. A handwritten sign on a piece of cardboard confirms his act: there is no glue or anything that keeps the stones in place, and a donation is requested for taking photographs.

CALIFORNIA DREAMING

At night, I can't sleep. I worry and keep thinking of Bill's dream and his overweight friend from elementary school who coached David Carradine in martial arts. I would like to get fit myself. One of the reasons to go to California was a vague idea to change my lifestyle. I've more or less given up drinking wine (in Sydney it was usually a bottle of white with dinner, sometimes more), now I drink some beer, but irregularly. I go walking, but not enough. I wonder whether I have lost some weight. I think I did, my belt is feeling a bit loose around my waist. But I have no scale here, it's hard to say for sure. I have not checked my blood pressure since we got here. I'll do that tomorrow, maybe.

I remember David Carradine was found dead in a hotel room in Bangkok. Cause of death: accidental asphyxiation. A case of sexual experimentation gone wrong? Or suicide? Michael Hutchence died a similar death in a hotel in Double Bay, Sydney. Inconclusive evidence in both cases. Carradine was 72.

The Carradines are a famous Hollywood family of actors/performers/singers. I remember David's brother Keith playing the laid-back hippie folk singer who performs 'I'm easy' in *Nashville*, one of my all-time favourite movies. He also wrote another song for that film, 'It don't worry me', sung at the very end after the shooting on a concert stage of two of the main characters in this story with its truly panoramic cast, country singers Haven Hamilton and Barbara Jean (the 'King' and 'Sweetheart of Nashville', respectively).

Why can't I fall asleep? Why do these pictures from old movies keep drifting around my head? Why do I worry so much? I should take the advice of Keith Carradine, I say to myself, and take a leaf out of his book on the *Wisdom of American Country Folk Music*.

Does Keith Carradine worry about the price of gas? – It don't worry him.

Does he worry about the promised tax reform that never comes? – No, it don't worry him.

But what if life turns out to be a one-way street? – It still don't worry him.

And if someone says that he ain't free? – Well, it really does not bother him.

WEDNESDAY, 13 March

Blood pressure, at 10am, measured at the CVS Pharmacy and Drugstore on Pearl: 148/80, mild hypertension. Ok result. No reason to worry.

The *U-T* reports that an earthquake occurred on Monday over the San Jacinto Fault, 4.7 on the Richter scale. The epicenter was some 70 miles northeast of San Diego, no damage was done. We certainly did not feel a thing. Yesterday, a smaller quake (3.5 Richter scale) followed. These are classified as moderate quakes, according to a seismologist from San Diego State University. There have been three such quakes since 2001. A Big Quake, according to the seismologist, occurs on average every 220 years. The last one was on 22 November 1800.

HOLE IN ONE

Today is a historic day in golf. Max shot his first hole in one: hole 7 at Colina Park, 76 yards, eight iron. We celebrate by eating at Sammy's Pizza, supposedly the best in La Jolla, at the corner of Pearl and Draper, in the building we will be moving into after returning from Mexico. The pizzas are not bad at all: a thick crust prosciutto with artichokes and *rucola* costs $12.50 (compared to $24 [Australian dollars] without artichokes at *Pizza y Birra* at the corner of Crown and Arthur, Surry Hills, a block up from our house). I try a couple of glasses of Estancia Sauvignon Blanc from Monterey County. Not bad either. I don't remember they were growing wine in Monterey in the 70s, a new development in California viticulture?

In the evening news on TV: a pope has been elected. A reporter from CNN comments that the new Bishop of Rome is supposed to be 'a butt-kicker (pardon my French), and that's what's needed around here.' Oh, dear! Where is Dave Allen now that we need him and his pope jokes that he used to tell on late-night TV in Australia?

THURSDAY, 14 March

Driving test, 12.05pm. I pass. I get four questions wrong, two of them I suspected being dodgy from the start. Speed limit in a school zone where children are present? I err on the side of caution and tick the box that says 15mph. Wrong, it's 25mph. And another thing: I find out that it is legal to use a mobile phone without a hands-free device to make an emergency call while driving. Interesting: wouldn't you be likely to cause another accident by dialing 911 on your phone to report an accident, all the while driving at 65mph on a ten-lane freeway?

Later that afternoon, we stroll along Garnet Avenue. There is an advertisement sign for sale in one of the street's hippie souvenir-cum-curio shops. It shows a picture of an automatic handgun with the company's logo 'Colt' beneath it, and the slogan: 'We don't call 911.'

FRIDAY, 15 March

I spend almost an hour on the phone to make an appointment for the road test. I can't book online or use the automated, voice-activated phone service because I don't fit the usual pattern: no learner's or prelim licence. Finally, I speak to a 'technician' (no operators here). I get an appointment for next Monday, 10.45am. 'Good luck,' I say to myself.

SATURDAY, 16 March

Another weekend at LA. More sightseeing with Xiaofang, Bill and Brianna, this time Universal Studios. We pay $80 admission, no concessions, kids under three are free, but what's there for them anyway? The whole park has written 'rip-off' all over it. You've got to wait in line for everything. We stand in a queue for almost an hour to get on the studio back lot tour, which is pretty much the same as I remember it, including the *Psycho* house on the hill and some actor playing Norman Bates running after the bus wielding the famous kitchen knife. The rubber shark (*Jaws*) is still jumping out of the water as if to swallow the bus, and the earthquake in the Manhattan subway station (what movie was that?) still features crashing trains, trucks falling through huge cracks in the ceiling, fireballs and a mini-tsunami rushing down the stairways. It's all pretty lame. A new addition is a 3-D battle between King Kong and a bunch of dinosaurs that's not too bad (scary, and very loud), the digital technology at work here makes a difference.

I remember there used to be a shootout performed live by actors in front of a Texas saloon in the Wild West section of the lot, but that's gone. Actors are obviously too expensive, computer animation in 3-D is the order of the day. The newest attraction that's No. 1 on Max's list is 'Transformers: The Ride', but the waiting time is 85 minutes, so we give it a miss and tell him: next time. Instead we head for the low-tech attractions with shorter waiting times: Animal Actors (very lame show; the zoo in Sydney has more exciting stuff), Special Effects (pathetic), and the Blues Brothers Show done by four impersonators who do a reasonably good job at singing. It's on an open-air stage, and it's cold by the time we get there; but the kids get a chance to warm up on stage to the tune of 'Twist it', and the parents are excited to see the budding talent and star quality of their offspring. Before that, I stood in line for a quarter of an hour to get us some overpriced deep-fried chicken, with mashed potato and grey-brown gravy and a piece of baked floury something. The food is awful.

At the end of the day, we are exhausted, all of us. We agree we won't be coming back, despite our ticket that's valid for the whole year. This is America at its worst, I tell Susan. The whole hyped-up 'Entertainment Center of LA' should self-destruct. She doesn't agree. She thinks it's ok, so-so.

SUNDAY, 17 March

Another golf tournament of the LA Regional Tour, this time at Los Robles, not far from Rustic Canyon. Again, very beautiful mountain scenery. Max ends up equal third (with Jack) and gets another medal. Susan says she is happy with his progress, but – as she is convinced that her son will win the Callaway – I venture to question whether it isn't time for him to top something.

The winner is a newcomer we have not met before, and the runner-up (one stroke ahead of Max) is Korean boy Nathan who has been playing golf since he was two-and-a-half years old, as his father tells us. Nathan is a cute, lively boy who looks exactly like a miniature Mr Oddjobs, the Korean tough guy in *Goldfinger* who crushes a golf ball in his hand and shows off his astonishing skill of throwing a steel-rimmed bowler hat like a frisbee, in the process decapitating a fake Italian marble statue of Venus. That part of the movie could have been shot on any of the fancier golf clubs around Southern California, but it was probably done on some studio back lot.

MONDAY, 18 March

I take my driving test and pass. The instructor/tester tells me I need to pay more attention to my speed. I'm surprised because I did not go particularly fast, but he says I was too slow. On one stretch of the test route the limit was 40mph, and I accelerated gently up to 36mph. Again, I erred on the side of caution: my strategy (if you can call it that) was to drive carefully, look left and right and back over my shoulder when doing turns, and remain under the speed limit. The main idea after all is to demonstrate safe driving, isn't it? But I learn an interesting detail: the maximum speed posted is also the speed that one is supposed to drive. I could have failed if I had driven ten miles below the posted limit, the instructor tells me. Obviously, driving safely is an important thing in California, but keeping the traffic flowing seems no less important. After all, there are 40 million cars on the road here. You don't want them to crawl along the roads (though this is what happens all too often). I tell the instructor I got the message: 'Yes, sir, officer!' I promise to do a better job from now on! Put the pedal on the metal!

The DMV Officer is a height-challenged Philipino man with a thick accent, hard to understand. I ask him about his languages, and he says he speaks Tagalog, Spanish, (a kind of) English, plus three or four local dialects that he learned while he was stationed with the Philippine army in different parts of the country. He was in Sydney ten years ago. I ask him whether he liked it there, and the answer is yes. Then, after a minute he adds, on his own account, that he likes it better here. What is it he likes better here, I ask. There's more opportunities here, he confides in me. Ok, I say.

It's astonishing that so many people seem to have internalised the idea of America as the 'Land of Unlimited Opportunity'. *Das Land der Unbegrenzten Möglichkeiten* – that was the slogan about the USA when I went to school in Germany. Here and now, it's what you hear, read and see every day: dream big, work hard, make that dream come true. You can be what you want to be. The sky's the limit.

There's no time to carry on the conversation. The test drive is over, business completed. The officer congratulates me and signs the paper that I take back to the window in the DMV office where dozens of people are waiting. I'm told the licence will be mailed to me within one month. By that time, I will have another address.

LOCAL NEWS

La Jolla resident Mitt Romney and wife Ann, of Dunemere Drive, have won an appeal against their development proposal to rebuild their oceanfront home. The plan is to demolish the existing 3,009-square-foot villa and to build a new 11,062-square-foot, two-storey MacMansion, including excavation work to construct a 3,668-square-foot basement and underground parking structure, including a car elevator for four cars. The proposal had been passed unanimously by the San Diego Planning Commission in June, but was held up pending an appeal by a local architect, Tony Ciani, who had previously lived on Dunemere Drive and is a well-known advocate for public beach access. According to Ciani, the Romney proposal is out character with the local community because of its size and bulk. Also, it does not conform to local planning regulations and land development codes because it is based on a calculation that artificially inflates the size of the property by including the beach in front of the home in order to increase the allowable floor-area ratio. The Romneys, supported by their land surveyor and city planning staff, contend they own the beach down to the mean high tide line. But Ciani says it is the city that owns the beach, and at the hearing of the California Coastal Commission he produced a map of the La Jolla Community Plan to prove it. Furthermore, he asked, can an area that is clearly not suitable for building purposes, i.e. the beach, be included in a calculation to establish the allowable floor-space ratio? This is a moot point, conceded Commissioner Jana Zimmer, who voted against allowing the development. The guidelines of the Local Coastal Program do not expressly forbid counting unbuildable areas on a sandy beach for the purpose of calculating floor-area ratios, but they do so with regard to other kinds of unbuildable areas, such as canyons and gullies.

The commission noted another area of concern, namely possible beach erosion due to rising seawater levels. Further north in San Diego county, residents occupying cliff-front homes are in danger of losing their valuable properties while the beaches below are being washed away during storms and king tides. They are trying to protect their houses by building seawalls at the bottom of the cliffs, but the coastal commission maintains that this will only make matters worse in the long run. It seems the Romneys are not worried about possible long-term damage to their holiday home. Perhaps they don't believe in global warming. Their lawyer reports that the couple are happy with the outcome of the appeal: reason and common sense have allegedly prevailed.

The Romneys had paid $12 million for their home back in 2008, but this is by no means an unusual price for a piece of real estate along this stretch of California coastline.

WEDNESDAY, 20 March

SEALS ON THE BEACH AT CHILDREN'S POOL

San Diego Mayor Bob Filner has ordered the La Jolla Children's Pool beach closed from sunrise to sunset until mid-May. This is in response to night-time video footage showing unidentified people harassing the seals that live on the beach during the pupping season. The beach is under 24-hour surveillance by a 'seal cam' that has been donated by the Western Alliance for Nature.

At around 5pm we drive down to the Children's Pool to get an idea what this is all about. A bunch of activists have assembled on the beach adjacent to a rope barrier that warns people off close contact with the seals that are lolling about a few metres away. Three swimmers in wetsuits are snorkeling in the water. The demonstrators are holding up signs protesting against 'King Filner's' allegedly unlawful decision to close the beach. A TV crew is interviewing a spokesman of the group, while a couple of park rangers and an imposingly tall policeman are on duty: they keep a watchful eye on the seals, the protesters and a few dozen onlookers who have gathered to witness an act of civil disobedience in the making. But nothing much happens. As the sun goes down, the people on the beach and in the water are in breach of the mayor's ordinance, but nobody is arrested. The onlookers slowly disperse, the activists have made their point. It's getting dark and cold; a chilly wind is blowing onshore.

We are puzzled, and I ask the police officer (his name badge identifies him as Mr Freymueller, with Germanic roots no doubt) what is going on. He explains that the beach is closed for a limited period and only at night, to protect the seals from harassment by local 'teenage hoodlums'. Officer Freymueller of 'San Diego's Finests' confirms that it is not illegal to swim during the day although it is not advisable. There are signs warning that the water presents a public health hazard due to high levels of 'fecal coliform' caused by seal excrement. We explain to Max what that means. Wow, he says and giggles. Poo in the water? Why would anyone want to swim here?

Casa Beach, as the children's pool used to be known, is a small crescent-shaped beach, perhaps 80 metres across, protected by a semi-circular seawall and promenade that dates back to 1930. The construction of the seawall was paid for by Ellen Browning Scripps, one of the many public projects donated by the local philanthropist, as a gift to the city of San Diego. An act of the California state legislature subsequently confirmed the gift, stating that the beach 'shall be devoted exclusively to public park, bathing pool for children...and recreational purposes,' including fishing. At that time, there were hardly any seals around, but since the 1970s they have been making a comeback under protective state legislation. Now, here is an interesting conflict: the *historic rights* of the good citizens of La Jolla who want their children to be able to swim at a beach that has been theirs for eighty years, and the *natural right* of the seals who nurture their pups on a man-made beach that is ideally suited for that purpose.

The protesters say they are not anti-seal, rather: they want to share the beach with the seals. They point out that the seals have become used to people and can often be seen playing with the humans swimming in the waters. But they also say that the seal population is growing, that the seals are taking over the beach.

What to make of these arguments? The seals may be cute (if hardly cuddly), and they certainly accept the presence of humans, but these are wild animals after all. They are

Seals on the Sand at Children's Pool, October 2005

smelly, they pollute the water and will bite if harassed. On the beach, they appear sluggish and somnolent, but in the water a child (or adult for that matter) could be in dire straits if an angry seal might feel the need to assert its claim to territorial sovereignty. I suspect what the protesters really want is to have the seals removed from the beach altogether.

But the good citizens of La Jolla who have formed the Friends of the Seals Association have other ideas. They want the beach turned into a marine mammal reserve, advocating the rights of animals over the rights of humans.

The good citizens of the La Jolla Chamber of Commerce have also expressed an opinion on the matter. They have come out strongly on the side of the seals. The beach has become a tourist attraction, and tourists bring money into the area.

Not surprisingly, there has been ongoing litigation, even to the point of questioning the legality of the rope-barrier. The police have been called on several occasions to settle

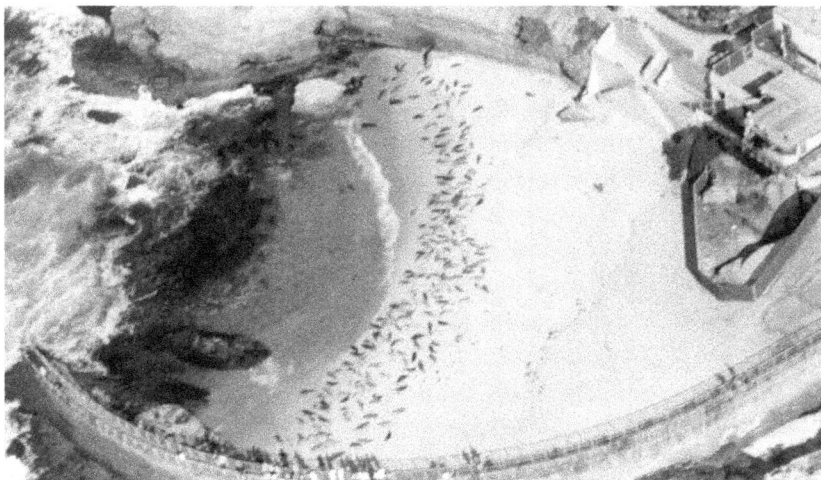

Aerial View of Children's Pool, May 2011: The Seals Have Taken Over

confrontations between seal advocates and beach lovers; citations have been issued and people taken into custody. A man has been indicted for sending death threats via email to members of the Animal Protection and Rescue League.

I like the seals. They are lazy, fin-footed bums, just lying around and sunning themselves on the warm sand, happy to occasionally scratch themselves with their flippers. Every once in a while they go for a swim and a bit of fishing. The mommy seals crawl down to the water, pups right behind them, using their bellies with that inimitable rocking motion, until the first wave gives them a shove forward, and they merrily dive away into their element. I also like it that they are quiet, not like the sea lions I remember from Monterey who had made their home at the bottom of Fisherman's Wharf. Those seals were a different species of pinniped; they made an awful racket, roaring day and night. The seals at La Jolla Children's Pool are harbour seals; they are much smaller and very civilised by comparison, they keep quiet and to themselves.

We are tourists, of course, so we also walk down to the beach, stop two or three feet away from the seals, take some group photos with ourselves on centre stage and the animals in the background. They cast a weary eye towards us, but don't bother to move. On the other side of the little headland there is a small beach that the seals have also taken over, but there is no rope barrier here to separate humans and animals. The tourists wander around and between the seals, almost stepping on them. Max takes some photos with his iPad; we can hardly drag him away. But he will not swim in the children's pool, he says: too much seal poo in the water.

THURSDAY, 21 March

I finally decide to pay a visit to UCSD. It is on a huge, sprawling campus north of La Jolla, between Torrey Pines Road and the I-5 freeway. I take the bus because I'm not sure about parking on campus (it turns out there is plenty, you pay four quarters for 45 minutes), and because the bus route runs along La Jolla Shores with some good views, especially down the escarpment overlooking a long stretch of beach with the huge pier of Scripps Institute of Oceanography a prominent landmark. There are plenty of eucalyptus trees on campus. They give the place an unexpected Australian appearance.

I'm pleased to find that Theodore 'Dr Seuss' Geisel is prominently represented here. The Geisel Library, funded by the writer, is named after the man himself. It's the university's main library, built atop a hill in the centre of the campus, with a little forest below that features a meandering path through the trees reminiscent of some of the fanciful illustrations of Dr Seuss' stories (*Oh, the places you'll go!*). The library is a modernist, futuristic looking concrete building, partly underground; it looks like a space ship that just landed on top of the hill. The university bookstore is also well-stocked with the products of Theodore Geisel's pen, and I'm quite surprised, and again pleased, to discover this, given the fact that children's literature does not usually finds its way into establishments that cater to serious tertiary or scientific interests. But we have a special case here, of course: the famous writer of juvenile picture-and-poetry books is also a famous local identity and philanthropist. Most of the Seuss books on offer here are expensive hardcover editions; I find none of the cheap paperbacks that I bought for Max in Sydney.

I meet with John Rouse of UCSD's theatre department who I know from a conference some years ago. He picks me up at the bus stop on campus, and we drive to a small mall a minute away to have a coffee. Peet's Coffee shop is apparently the place for coffee around here. It's a mini chain, three outlets in San Diego with one in downtown La Jolla, but clearly no competition for Starbucks that seems to be around every other corner. I tell John the story of our coming here, Max's golfing and my writing. Wow, he says. I ask him about his background, and he tells a story that by now has become quite familiar. His father was in the air force, and he grew up on various bases around the country, moving from school to school. I ask where his home is, and he thinks about this for a while. I suggest it might now be San Diego where he has been working for 16 years, and he finally nods. Berlin is the other place he feels strongly about, he says: Berlin in May at the time of the annual theatre festival.

John used to spend a lot of time in Berlin, but he has not been there in the last few years. He confirms that UCSD is very strong in science and technology, especially electronic engineering and bio-medical sciences, but the scientists and technocrats have a faible for the arts, says John, so the visual arts, music and theatre departments are well endowed. John's theatre department has received a great deal of money from one of the local benefactors of the university, the founder of Qualcomm. His department is now ranked third in the country, behind Yale and NYU. It has great facilities. There is a veritable 'theatre precinct' on campus, built around three different performance spaces, with the highly-regarded, semi-professional La Jolla Playhouse as its centrepiece.

We sit on bar stools around a small round table. John dunks chunks of a croissant into his latte, I sip on my cappuccino. The coffee is ok. Another customer from an adjoining table comes over and introduces himself. He has overheard our conversation about things German and is keen to share his expertise. His name is Bernd Kienen, he's got a PhD in chemistry and works for a local bio-pharmaceutical company. He came from Germany 20 years ago. I ask him whether he knows someone who's got a boat. There is this Italian guy, he says, but he has not seen him for a while. Bernd is a member of a German Club, and he invites me to come over some time to one of their meetings. I answer evasively, mindful of the German clubs I've experienced in Australia: the German penchant for *Vereinskultur* ('club culture'), the mindset of immigrants who have somewhat distorted views about the contemporary realities of the homeland they left behind often decades earlier. Bernd tells me that his club is called *Schlaraffia am Stillen Meer*. Now, this is intriguing: not the usual 'Concordia' or 'Germania' that I would have expected.

Later I check out the website of *Schlaraffia*. It is the weirdest thing: a mixture of *carnival* (fancy dress costumes with dunces' caps), medieval knights' banquet and freemasonry rituals. I send an email to Bernd, saying I'm curious and would not mind attending a meeting of the club. He writes back saying that *Schlaraffia* is perhaps in need of a bit of reform. He also writes that he is into wine; he is a wine consultant for riesling and burgundy. Wow, I say to myself.

I wouldn't mind being a wine consultant myself, preferably Marlborough SauvBlanc. What would be the benefits? Free grog? How do you become a wine consultant? Need to check further details with Bernd.

SATURDAY, 23 March

Max plays a tournament at Lawrence Welk Resort, some 40 miles north on I-15. It's a very pretty but difficult course, 1,700 yards for the nine holes the kids play. We tee off at noon, the last group. There are only two players in the six-and-under age group, Max and Tim. Max finishes first, Tim second. Both receive a trophy. Max is ten months older and one head taller than Tim, and the two get along famously. We have a pizza at Pizza Hut for lunch, Tim's favourite is pepperoni, Max would prefer a cheese only pizza but Dragon Mom insists on a Hawaiian because she wants to feed her son meat, with extra cheese. The pizza is not too bad. The weather is good. There's palm trees and flowering shrubs with humming birds hovering around. Life is ok.

We sit outside on a little plaza of this resort community, in front of the Lawrence Welk Centre for the Performing Arts, a theatre that is currently showing *Chicago, The Musical*. The plaza is all but deserted, except for the life-size bronze statue of Mr Welk as a conductor, smiling and swinging a baton. He is described on a plaque as 'America's Mr Music Man'. I confide to Chuck, Tim's father, that I have never heard of Mr Welk, but he hasn't either.

SUNDAY, 24 March

Sightseeing, SeaWorld, San Diego. We have arranged to meet Tim and his parents and little sister to spend the day together. They are an interesting family: here we have a Caucasian

Tiger Dad rather than a Chinese Tiger Mom. Chuck is from Northern California. He met his wife, Claire, in New York while studying at Columbia. She is from Queens, of Chinese background but born in the Philippines. She does not speak Mandarin, but Chuck does, quite fluently according to Susan. Chuck now teaches his son to speak Mandarin. In the afternoon, Tim attends a Chinese school in Carmel Valley (the local public school he attends in the morning only lasts four hours). He is also a scholar at the 'Great China Whole Brain Academy' in Sorrento Valley where he plays chess and learns Mandarin in addition to doing speed calculations with an abacus. Tim has an impressive command of mathematical knowledge for a five-year old, unlike Max who is struggling at the moment. Max does not do well in the speed tests in his class. He never finishes them. He takes his time, finds it hard to focus. At home doing his homework, he prefers to clown around.

Interestingly, Tim looks very much like a Chinese boy, while his sister, who is nearly three years old, has no Asian features at all. The family have only recently moved to San Diego from San Francisco.

I ask Chuck what he does, and he says he invests in technology companies. A lot of his business is with Chinese companies. He has been going there for nearly 20 years. But business is coming to an end, he explains. The Chinese have enough money of their own now, they don't need foreign capital anymore. He has witnessed the recent transformation of the Chinese economy first-hand, for instance the development of the Beijing airport from a one-hall barrack to the gigantic superstructure it is today.

We have a great day at Sea World. There are many attractions for the kids, notably a variety of roller coaster rides, and of course the marine life shows with killer whales, sea lions, dolphins and otters. They have a pet show as well, much better than the one at Universal Studios. There are no long lines either, because there's so much more to do and see. Some things are predictably similar, like the patriotic display at the start of the orcas show that begins with a salute and a 'Thank you' to our brave boys in the armed forces. Chuck tells me that this would have provoked some 'boos' in San Francisco.

The food is awful. I buy a barbecued turkey leg at a BBQ hut that features a rotisserie spit big enough to do a small whale. The turkey leg costs $8.99. It looks more like a baby dinosaur drumstick, and it tastes like that as well: tough and chewy and nasty and so salty it is really inedible. I should have taken it back, but I didn't. If this was a normal restaurant I would have.

We have now visited two amusement parks, world-famous icons of the California tourism industry: Universal Studios (Personal Rating: two out of ten); SeaWorld (PR: eight out of ten). There are two parks to go: Disneyland, Legoland.

MONDAY, 25 March

I take the bus to the airport to check out how long it will take us to get there for our flight to Mexico City on Friday. Parking at Lindbergh Field is quite expensive; we want to save some money. The first Bus is No. 30 to Downtown San Diego, corner Broadway and Fifth Avenue, where I change to Bus 992 to the airport. The trip takes some 90 minutes, including 15 minutes waiting for the connecting bus.

Downtown San Diego looks pretty desolate, despite the promise of the street names that suggest a mirage of Manhattan on the Pacific. It is lunchtime, and this is the heart of the CBD, but very few people are about. There is a huge construction site next door to a new Westin hotel that is adjacent to a Westfield Mall ('We are open during construction'). A substantial building is being demolished, a pre-historic looking crane is picking up debris and piling it on a truck. A new park is being built that is supposed to re-vitalise the area.

From the bus, I notice a small group of demonstrators in front of the Federal Court building, holding up placards and walking around in a circle. I suppose they are demonstrating to influence the Supreme Court in Washington that is currently hearing arguments to decide on same-sex legislation. Similar demonstrations are happening all over the United States. I cannot make out whether the demonstrators here are pro or contra, or whether both groups are represented, trying to out-demonstrate each other. The country seems deeply divided over the matter. There is endless speculation in all media about how the Supreme Court is likely to decide. One enthusiastic newspaper correspondent has an ingenious suggestion that links the issue of gay rights with the ongoing debate on how to get domestic consumption back on track in order to fix the American economy: 'Gay marriage bridal registries'!

SUMMARY OF PROGRESS: MAX AT SCHOOL

Easter marks the end of term three of the California school year, and Max gets a report card from Miss Higgins at All Hallows Academy. He has done ok, not great but acceptable, considering he jumped ahead half a year and had to get accustomed not only to the first (serious) school year, after the fun and games of Kindergarten in Sydney (*Kindy*, as the Aussies have it), but also to the American way of doing things, notably the frequent tests in class for which he was utterly unprepared. On their report card, the kids are marked out of Four, with One being the lowest score. Max has two Fours in reading (decoding skills, comprehension), otherwise a lot of

Threes. Mathematics is his weak point: one score of One in 'knowledge of basic facts', and one of Two in 'mathematical skills'. We have been working with him on speed calculations, and lately it seems to be paying off. On the last day before the end of term he proudly tells us that he passed the final math test: progress is in sight.

Miss Higgins also notes that she 'would like him to participate more in class.' It's not that Max is a quiet or shy kid, on the contrary. But in school he seems to be keeping mum. We can't get a proper answer from him as to why, and make an appointment to see Miss Higgins to discuss the report card and other business.

BIG BUSINESS IN PACIFIC BEACH

If you walk along the streets of Pacific Beach, you will notice that pest control is big in Southern California, just like in New South Wales. There are cockroaches, rodents, ants, bedbugs, and termites that eat you out of house and home. TV ads inspired by horror movies show gigantic insects at work, chomping away at the foundations of multi-million dollar MacMansions. Just like in Australia, there are plenty of pick-up trucks – 'utes' as the Australian vernacular has it – loaded with hoses and barrels of insecticide parked in front of suburban homes, and pest control tradies in safety masks going about their toxic business. But the Americans also do it in a big way that has not made it to Australia yet. This is tent fumigation: whole houses are being covered, tent-like, by giant strips of plastic sheeting that are zipped together, with sandbags placed around the bottom perimeter to form an airtight cover. I imagine that inside the tent all the doors and windows are wide open, as are all drawers and cupboards; foodstuffs and other delicate items have been removed, the residents and their pets have gone on vacation for a few days.

Tented House on Cass Street

And then the pest controllers move in and pump the tent full of gas until the very last critter bites the dust.

There are quite a few of these tented houses around our Pacific Beach neighbourhood. The multicoloured sheeting makes them look like little circus tents. There is even a whole church on Cass Street that is being fumigated under a tent. One could think that Christo and Jeanne-Claude the Package Artists are at work here, but as far as I know the only work they have done in California was building the *Running Fence*, from the little inland town of Sonoma to the coast north of San Francisco. That must have been in the early 70s, at the beginning of the Christos' career as wrappers, probably just after they had done the *Wrapped Coast* at Sydney's Little Bay, the first of their big projects. The *Wrapped Reichstag* in Berlin was still a pipe dream then.

Postscript to Pest Control: Termite Stimulus?

A San Diego company, Mariners Pest Control, offers a special '2013 Termite Stimulus Package', hopefully meant to exterminate, not to excite the little critters. It offers eco-friendly orange oil as the preferred poison.

NEIGHBOURHOOD WALK: CASS STREET TO GARNET AVENUE

On Cass Street, the American preoccupation with religion becomes strikingly apparent. There are churches all along the street, and they are spacious. There is the pretty, mission-style St Brigid's Catholic Church with adjacent rectory on Cass and Diamond that occupies a whole block. Next door, the more austere Christ Lutheran Church Pacific covers a similar-sized block. On the opposite side of Cass are the flats of the Lutheran Retirement Home, and the block adjacent to the church serves as a parking lot. There is a row of garages that has 'God's Garage' in large lettering written on it, somewhat impiously I find.

There are about half a dozen other churches on Cass and adjoining streets down to Garnet Avenue, but on that thorough-fare we enter un-Christian territory. Garnet is an amusement strip, the favourite hangout of local college students who frequent the bars and pubs, the smoke shops, the new age hippie and surf shops, the taco and hamburger joints. The Hare Krishna Temple is on Grant Avenue, a further block down. Towards the beach, the street scene becomes a little more upmarket, with some fancier restaurants and boutiques. If you walk the other way, inland to the East, you'll notice the opposite trend: tattoo and body building establishments, car accessories, adult and dollar stores.

BIRD ROCK WALK

Sometimes my daily walk takes me towards Bird Rock, north of the long stretch of sand along Pacific and Mission Beach.

The beach here gives way to a coastline of jagged cliffs. An uninterrupted line of expensive homes facing the ocean afford the privileged residents sweeping views over the Pacific while shutting out mere passers-by like myself. Only a few openings allow a view of the sea or an access to the rocky coast below the cliffs. A substantial home on Sea Ridge Crescent features the inscription 'Jesus is Lord' over the entrance door. In the front yard, the pious owners have erected a nativity scene: baby Jesus in the crib, the proud parents, shepherds, animals and angels, all in vivid polychromatic fibreglass, half-life size. I don't get it: is this a permanent installation? Or have the owners simply forgotten to remove the thing after Xmas? It is a week before Easter. Isn't it time for a spring clean-up and getting the crucifixion scene out of the garage?

A block further on, the owner of a cliff-front home next to a pathway to the coast has installed a shower (with taps and a showerhead) at the corner of his front yard. There is a neat little tiled enclave, open to the street, surrounded on three sides by a picket fence. A sign attached confirms that this is a public shower, albeit made available by a private individual on his or her private property. 'Dear Surfer,' the sign says, 'this hose is provided for your convenience. Feel free to use it to rinse yourself. Please conserve water as much as possible. Thank you, the Owner.'

Here we have one Christian American family presenting itself to the world, I say to myself, and over here we have another one.

EASTER COMING UP: THREE LOCAL ENTERTAINMENT TAGLINES

1. The San Diego Opera company's production of *Murder in the Cathedral*, an apparently rarely produced work by composer Ildebrando Pizzetti, opens this Saturday. The advertising tagline: 'Would you die for your faith?'

2. The House of Blues San Diego advertises a gospel brunch with a Southern theme for Easter Sunday. An all-you-can-eat buffet is on offer (made-to-order omelets, buttermilk biscuits with country gravy, chicken jambalaya, peel-and-eat shrimp, and more), and there will be a live performance by Elwert Waltower & Friends. Tagline: 'Praise the Lord and Pass the Biscuits.'

3. The Old Town Temecula Community Theatre presents 'Passion of the Christ', an original two-act dance show performed by the Inland Valley Classical Ballet Theatre. The performance tells the story of Jesus in his adulthood. Tagline: 'His ministries and miracles, changing water to wine [have they consulted a wine consultant about this?], healings, the Last Supper, his discussions with God, the betrayal of Judas, the judgment and crucifixion, and the resurrection and the spreading of the Holy Spirit.'

It is a family show, so I assume they will have left out most of the violent bits (rather than being inspired by Mel Gibson's script of *The Passion*). But otherwise it's the whole epic story, all told in dance. Ticket prices are modest: $16–$22. This could become big: Oberammergau in Southern California.

EASTER BREAK, MEXICO CITY

We're off to Mexico City for Easter Break. We have been admonished to be careful: it's very dangerous, people are being mugged, kidnapped, killed and what not. Undoubtedly, there is an alarming amount of gun-related violence south of the border.

Ironically, Mexico has one of the strictest firearm laws anywhere in the world. In other words: the guns that kill people in Mexico are illegal, unregistered. And where do they come from? Why, the United States of course. A recent study in my trusted *U-T* reports an estimated revenue of $172.2 million for the US firearms industry is due to cross-border trade. There is a 'superabundance' of gun shops along the U.S.-Mexico border, and efforts by the customs authorities to stop the southbound gun trafficking seem largely ineffectual. Drug dealers apparently use their cash profits to buy weapons in the US that are smuggled back into Mexico and then used to put away business competitors or other unwanted humans.

We conclude we are probably relatively safe if we can stay away from muggers and pickpockets in dubious areas of Mexico City at night, and if we don't get involved in any drug business activities (which we don't intend to). It's unlikely that we get caught in a crossfire between feuding gangs of drug barons. Nevertheless, I suggest to Susan, maybe we should get some bulletproof body armour? We recently saw an ad on TV for bulletproof vests, now also offered in children's sizes. Discounted school orders are available.

Postcard from Teotihuacan, Mexico: Los Piramides

PART TWO
SPRING AND SUMMER IN LA JOLLA

APRIL: National Poetry Month

April is National Poetry Month in the United States, and the *U-T* asks its readers: 'Is there a poem hiding in your soul?'

I am tempted to add: 'If yes, it should perhaps stay there.'

SUNDAY, 7 April

The *Concours d'Élégance* is an annual auto show and social event at Eleanor Scripps Park adjacent to La Jolla Cove, with all proceeds to benefit the La Jolla Historical Society. There are automotive artwork shows, musical entertainment, VIP receptions and cocktail soirées, and, of course, the cars lined up on the green grass: the *concours* is a highlight, no doubt, of the social calendar of La Jolla High Society.

After our late-night flight back from Mexico City, the rest of the family is either tired or watching teenie soaps on TV, so I decide to check out the show by myself. Up the hill on Prospect Street, the newer and lesser classic cars are displayed, mostly American muscle cars and European sports cars from the 1960s onward. This is for the riff-raff among the car enthusiasts; the owner-exhibitors of the truly fancy *Concours* cars obviously prefer to be among themselves on the grass in the park below.

When I finally get down there, the party is almost over. It's just as well: entry is a whopping $35, $100 gets you into the VIP section. I'm not prepared to part with that sort of money to look at a few old cars, so I just watch across the low picket fence to see some Rolls and Packhards being towed away onto their trucks while workers are dismantling the barricades. I would have loved to see the 1930s Bugattis, but they're already gone. Eventually, the last car left on the grassy lot is a VW beetle, built 1957, an original model, nothing restored. It's in mint condition, absolutely sparkling in deep black colour. I chat with the owner and tell him that I had a car like this, some forty years ago, and he smiles and says: 'Didn't we all?' Thinking I'm one of the exhibitors, he asks, 'What's your car?' I laugh and say: 'A 1997 Mercury Grand Marquis, in murky green, that I bought a few weeks ago for under $3,000.' 'Oh,' he says, 'you're only visiting.' And he adds: 'Great car, good buy.' I thank him, and he says 'Auf Wiedersehen!'

I drive back to Stan's flat at Pacific Beach. Better start packing, I tell Susan and Max, we'll get out of here early in the morning.

MONDAY, 8 April

We move from suburban Pacific Beach to downtown La Jolla. The name of our building on the corner of Draper Avenue and Pearl Street is *Bella Capri* – yet another dream of the European imagination: the tourist's fantasy love of Italy, the fishermen of Capri (Rudi Schuricke and Max Raabe singing about the red sun sinking into the Mediterranean), Gina Lollobrigida and Sophia Loren, pizza, pasta and wine, and so on. But here, on the shores of the Pacific? We don't care about the name; we're glad to be here.

There are shops at ground level (Sammy's Woodfired Pizza, Family Dentist, Antique Designer Boutique, Bridal Shop, and, last – but not least: The Salt Room, for breathing therapy, which instantly reminds me of my Himalayan salt blocks that I had to leave behind in Sydney, to my great regret: each block was as heavy as a brick). There's underground security parking and two floors of apartments. You enter through a sort of Italianate archway, past a kind of forum (empty except for a few undistinguished potted plants), access to the lift is via security code, once inside the lift you need to punch in a second code to get moving. We're on the second level, in a flat with two bedrooms and two bathrooms and a big balcony facing west. We can just see the ocean across the roofs of the houses opposite.

Our new apartment is a pleasant improvement over the one at Sapphire Street. It is modern and reasonably tasteful. Tumbled marble tiles in the bathrooms, small kitchen with stone benchtops and all the standard appliances (except for a mixer for smoothies or cocktails). There is a dining table with six chairs, comfortable furniture and a nice thick carpet in the living room, outdoor table and lounge chairs on the balcony. I can sit and write here in the sun, keeping an eye open on what's going on in the street below. We have everything we need, and the rent is very reasonable, $2,400 a month, TV and internet by Time/Warner cable included: unbelievably cheap, according to everybody who knows something about this. There is nothing below $3,000 advertised around here, we are told, often flats in less than impressive buildings. We are very lucky. Only Max complains: there's no Disney Channel that he started watching in Pacific Beach, notably the awful teenage sitcoms. That's a good thing, of course! But Max is not happy: he will have to make do with Sesame Street, the 'baby channel' in his considered opinion.

The location is great. Two houses down on Draper is the La Jolla Library, further down across the street The Bishop's School (expensive, private, Presbyterian), next to it the La Jolla Tennis Club and then the La Jolla Recreation Centre with basketball courts, tennis practice wall, playground outside and playrooms inside, tables and benches for picnics. You can hire raquets, balls to play, and it's all free – thanks to Ellen Browning Scripps who put up the money for this in the first place. There is even a soccer-sized stretch of lawn where the kids can kick a ball and run around freely. Regrettably, this is also an area favoured by dog owners and their pets who should be leashed according to a posted city ordinance – well, at least the pets should be, but they rarely are.

La Jolla Recreation Centre is a hub of community activities. There's classes of all kinds for people of all ages. For seniors, iPhone tutorials have become very popular. Some of the tutors are high school students, volunteers from the neighbouring Bishop's School and from La Jolla High. The aim is to bridge the technology gap between the generations. Not a bad idea, I think. I wouldn't mind learning how to use a smart phone myself. Use it properly, I mean.

At the end of Draper is Prospect Street, the main shopping district and the seriously expensive strip of La Jolla (fancy boutiques, restaurants and hotels overlooking the ocean). You can also walk down Pearl to the coast: three blocks to the San Diego Museum of Contemporary Art, and behind that – just down the hill – the endless expanse of blue water, the children's beach, seals lolling about on the sand, a small contingent of protesters with placards *en permanence*, and further on La Jolla Cove and La Jolla Caves. It's all very pretty and neat, with spectacular coastal scenery.

And then there's the neighbourhood restaurants: apart from Sammy's downstairs, there are plenty of eating places within the next block up and down Pearl Street. On the corner

opposite is Wahoo Fish Taco, right next to Mitch's Surf Shop
(with a giant 'Occupy Everything' poster in the window).
Next door is El Pescador Fish Market, a fish restaurant
despite the name (soon to be relocated opposite Sammy's on
the other side of Draper), and next to that China Chef ('Voted
best by *La Jolla Light* readers in 2012') followed by Ortega's
Place (a Mexican hole-in-the-wall taco joint) and Pizza on
Pearls. The Tandoori Chef is the last one on the block, but
around the corner on Cuvier Street (next door to the OhLaLa
Dance Academy) is the Sahel Bazaar: International Market &
Deli. Despite its name, the Sahel is mostly about the Middle
East and Iran, but they do sell fresh *neglet dour* dates from
North Africa. The owner proudly makes her own Persian
hummus with a secret ingredient she is not willing to divulge.
I buy some to try but decide that I prefer the classical Syrian/
Lebanese hummus, particularly the one made by my favourite
Turkish baker in Sydney, *Erciyes* on Cleveland, that has by far
the best bread and hummus anywhere, except for the old city
of Damascus, now sadly in ruins.

On the other side of Pearl, we have the Copy Cove Print
shop on the corner, next to it the Café Milano Italian
Restaurant (advertising lobster ravioli, 2012 *U-T* Readers'
Choice Award). Next to it is Libby's Crepes Café and Bistro
(which seems permanently closed, however); then comes
Chedi Thai Bistro (big restaurant with lots of happy hour
specials: looks promisingly yummy), and finally, to round
things up perfectly, Nick's Liquor on the corner with a good
selection of cold white wines in a couple of fridges. The
supermarkets here don't usually bother to sell their wines
cold, which is a shame.

So, all in all, we are well provided here. We won't have to
go hungry or thirsty. And if you feel like American fast/junk
food, there is a Jack-in-the-Box (euphemistically known as a
family restaurant) two blocks down on the corner of Pearl

and Cuvier. The stop for bus No. 30 to UCSD or downtown San Diego is right in front of our house.

Regarding Max's TV choices: we rejoiced too early, of course. Two days after we moved in, he had worked out the remote control, and the Disney Channel with teenie soaps was back on.

GOLF: PREPARING FOR THE CALLAWAY

At Colina Park, Todd Smith's coaching always involves competitive play. First stage is putting: we spend a lot of time on the practice green, working out the 'breaks', learning how to 'read' the slopes of the green, how the ball will roll. The greens at Colina Park are notoriously difficult to play. The whole course is built on a hill, there is a kind of in-built force of gravity that makes the ball want to go downhill. If your ball lands short, it invariably will roll back. In addition, some of the greens are layered up or down the steep hillsides with breaks in all sorts of directions. Todd tells us this is the main job of the caddy: to advise the player on how to play the ball on the greens. To prepare for the Callaway Junior World Championship, he says, we should draw a map of all the 18 greens and indicate the various breaks. That sounds easy enough, except when you consider that the ball might lie anywhere on the green, and there is not just one hole on each green but three. On each day of the tournament, the hole with the flag pin in it will be moved to a different site: front, middle or back of the green. The possibilities of hitting the right shot (or missing it) are endless.

Max will be allowed one caddy during the Callaway Championship; there will be no spectators on the course. Max does not like Susan to caddy, because she never stops talking to him, in an odd mixture of Mandarin and English, and sometimes I wonder whether he really understands what she is saying. But, of course, Dragon Mom believes she is the ideal caddy because, naturally, she knows her son best, and apart from that she thinks she knows everything there is to know about golf. To be fair, she has soaked up a few things over the last twelve months or so. Before that she did not have a clue, she would not have known the difference between a bunker and a birdie, and even today she is woefully ignorant about many things (not to mention the myriads of rules). Not that I know the rules that much better. Reading the book (*Rules of Golf*) gives me a headache.

We leave the question of the eventual caddy open; there will be three rounds, so perhaps we take turns (and claim credit if Max does better on one's respective day). Another option is to hire one of the guys who work at Colina Park. Todd Smith tells us that a lot of parents do it this way, and that the older kids in his First Tee program are keen to act as caddies and earn a few extra dollars. We agree it's probably the best solution, not only because the competing parents are kept out of the ballgame, but it stands to reason that the local caddy knows the course much more intimately and can advise Max better. On the tricky greens here, this could be decisive. Whether Max will listen to any advice, though, is another story altogether. He usually prefers to 'know' already and do his own thing. Then again, this is Rudy Duran's philosophy. The player needs to 'own' his game. This is what he taught Tiger Woods, and who can argue with that.

Putting Practice No. 1: Distance control

On the practice green, Todd stakes out a half circle, marked with tees, in a radius of 17 inches behind the hole. This is the distance, he explains, from where a player should be able to hole the ball 'comfortably'. Quite often that does not happen, of course. Then he places six tees in a straight line away from the hole, each one two feet apart from the next. Thus, there are six putts ranging from a two feet-putt to a

12-feet putt. This is a fun game: you start with the shortest putt and go on to the next one, to be repeated twice, for a total of 18 putts, i.e. one round of golf, played on the putting green only. The scoring is simple: plus, minus, or even. If you hit the ball into the circle, it's counted as even or zero (for a par; assuming you would hole the ball with the next putt); if you hit the ball behind the circle, it's a plus one (for a bogey); if the ball lands in front of the hole, it's counted as plus two (double bogey); and if it lands in the hole, it's a minus one (birdie). So, after 18 putts, you end up with a score of either zero (even par), or plus some number (over par), or minus some number (below par). And then you go again and repeat the 18 putts, with the aim of improving your score: if you don't, you'll be penalised (three push-ups) before you go again. And again. And again. And one more time.

Initially, I don't quite understand why it counts as a double bogey when the ball lands in front but still close to the hole, i.e. within under 17 inches. I suppose the idea is to learn to avoid short putts: if your putt lands short, it won't make it into the hole, ever. If, on the other hand, you hit the ball a bit harder (even if it will roll further than the prescribed 17 inches), there is still a chance that it might roll into the hole for a birdie if the aim is spot-on.

Max likes this game, and he takes it very seriously. He concentrates as hard as he can. He doesn't mind the penalties (there are quite a few, at first), but we find out that he is not strong enough to do repeated push-ups, so Todd changes the rule: the penalty now is running three laps around the green, which Max does quite enthusiastically. And again.

He improves quickly, and after a couple of weeks his putting score is usually close to where it should be: even par, or better.

Putting Practice No. 2: Reading the greens

After the mission 'Distance Control' is accomplished, we go on the next phase, putting on a real green. Todd places four tees on opposite ends of the greens, close to the edge and roughly at a 90-degree angle to each other. The distance to the hole is usually at least 12 feet, but quite often substantially longer. The idea is to putt from different positions on the green to correctly identify the breaks.

Max plays a ball from a tee of his choosing, and then moves on to the next one until all four are played. The goal is to hole each ball in two putts, i.e. score a par; if you miss (i.e. three-putt the ball and score a bogey), you will have to go back to the beginning and start again. If you manage to hole the ball with either birdie or with a two-putt four times in a row, you can move on to the next green. And so on.

Again, Max makes quick progress.

Long Game Practice: Reaching the greens

Next, Max is ready to play holes. All holes on Colina Park are par three: it's a short course especially designed for juniors. The aim in practice is quite ambitious from the start, as Todd explains: Always try to reach the hole in three strokes. If you don't, you'll have to play the hole again. And again. And so forth.

It sounds easy enough: you hit the tee shot straight onto the green, or very close to it, and then hole the ball for par with a two-putt (or a chip plus one-putt), or with a one-putt for birdie. You need to choose the right club and do the proper pre-shot routine to prepare and line up your shot. You hit a near-perfect tee-shot, and then comes the putting: with the correct aim (mind the breaks!) and distance control, the first putt must go close to the flag and the second putt into the hole: par three. Even better: one putt for a birdie. No worries, says Max, he understands.

That's the theory: quite easy, really.

In real life, it is quite tough, especially on the holes that go uphill. During practice, if Max misses par, Todd orders him to walk back downhill and start again. But Max remains enthusiastic, and he doesn't complain, except for an occasional 'Oh, man!' – his expression of frustration mumbled under his breath.

Initially, Max's tee-shots are somewhat erratic. We have not really focused much on his 'long game'. When he played long shots in tournaments, i.e. on par-four or par-five holes, he used his driver and usually did all right. Even if a shot ended up in the rough, the balls could mostly be quite playable. Here at Colina Park, the holes are rather short (between 54 and 109 yards), and if you miss the green on the first attempt, it is very hard to make par. Max uses his driver only on the two longest holes. Unlike his peers who need their drivers, Max can reach most greens with his 5-iron or 7-iron. He is quite tall for his age, and that's a good thing, according to Susan. She is convinced that, in the future, her son will hit the ball further than anybody.

Todd realises that Max needs some more practice with his tee-shots, and he lets him hit some extra balls. It's trial and error: Max needs to find the proper club for each hole. Equally important, Todd makes him correct his stance. Max usually pays no attention to how his feet are placed, he often does not look at the flag before he shoots. His pre-shot routine is woefully undeveloped. He simply can't be bothered. He has a pretty good swing though, and he manages the distances easily enough. Thus, his tee shots are usually not too bad, but there is no consistency, not enough control.

Todd is optimistic. We'll get there, he says.

WEDNESDAY, 10 April

THE CHAUVINIST

I gradually explore the new neighbourhood. Fay Street, which runs parallel to Draper two blocks to the East, is a favourite stroll; it's full of little bistros with small outdoor eating areas, furniture and art shops, and plenty of fitness studios. There is even a butcher advertising 'home grown beef' (must have a cow in his backyard, I presume).

The Chauvinist, also on Faye, is a 'Consignment Store for Men'. It has a mural of the Lincoln Monument next to its display window, with three boys depicted from behind curiously looking up to the dead president, a prominent victim of American gun violence, who is sternly looking back down on them. The Chauvinist is where the gentlemen of La Jolla depose of their used clothes: slacks, shirts, socks, shoes, cowboy boots, belts, cufflinks, suspenders, jackets, hats, coats, you name it. Apparently, they don't give it to charity, they sell it second-hand, on consignment, and The Chauvinist is where you can buy the stuff.

The store also has a range of new things, designer items like silk ties and handkerchiefs, plus some panama hats, so I go inside to have a browse and try on some hats for size. The owner is Señor Salvador J. Viesca who runs the place with his son, Salvador Jr. Mr Viesca sen. tells me the story of a customer who came in and looked around, finally finding a pair of pants that he liked and that fit perfectly, only to discover that he was the original owner who had consigned the piece to the Chauvinist in the first place. True story? Hard to say. It probably has been told a few times over the years, perhaps with different items of pre-loved clothing substituted.

I ask Mr Viesca, who is impeccably outfitted with white suit and yellow bow-tie, about the name of his shop and the curious mural. No deeper meaning or story behind it, he says; he just likes the word: *Chauvinist*. And the picture, too. I suspect Señor Viesca is a bit of a self-conscious Macho-Man. And why not?

THURSDAY, 11 April

In the evening, Bernd picks me up and we drive to an evening at the *Schlaraffia* Club: a promise of *in arte voluptas*. The *Schlaraffenland* of the Grimm's Brothers tales is the fabled land of *Cockaigne*, the medieval land of idleness and plenty, where wine flows in the rivers and roast ducks are flying straight into your mouth while barbecued pigs are strolling around with knives and forks stuck in their backs, ready to have a juicy cut taken out of them. It's a promising name, but from what Bernd has told me and what I have seen on the website, I have some reservations about what to expect. We drive from La Jolla towards downtown San Diego, and to my great surprise, we end up next to Colina Park Golf Course – that's so weird, of all the possible meeting places in the greater San Diego area, why here?

The Faith Lutheran Church has a basement that doubles as a church hall, down a few spooky steps from a darkly-lit parking place. It's a rather austere, uninviting room. There's about twenty people sitting on opposite tables, facing each other, and an elevated table at the front with what seems to be the officer in charge, the President. Another member, who introduces himself as Axel Best, the Chancellor, has his own little table to the right. They are all wearing robes reminiscent of academic gowns except for their bright and shiny multicoloured patchwork, and the funny hats resembling the traditional headgear of officials of a *Karnevalsverein* in Mainz or Cologne, except these hats are entirely individualistic with a fantasy name embroidered across the sides. I am warmly greeted and asked to sit down and don a straw hat because I am a *Pilger* (pilgrim, or visitor) for the evening. The others are *Ritter* (knights) or *Knappen* (squires), with names that are puns on their original profession: Bernd is Ritter Laborius because he works in a lab, there is Ritter Banquero who used to be a banker, and so forth. The most interesting man is 90-year old Lord Henry who seems like a kind of *eminence grise*; he takes over the role of chair during the performance part of the evening. He tells me later that he used to be based in Melbourne during the 1960s where he managed the Crown Hotel, and that the owners at the time wanted to keep him so they offered him Dunk Island if he stayed. He could have owned his own island, he says, but he declined. Bad mistake, I say, and he laughingly agrees. I am not quite sure what to make of his story. He is a very witty man, and apparently well connected.

The *Schlaraffen,* as they call themselves, date their origin back to the 1850s, an original bohemian anti-authoritarian social club founded by actors and artists in Prague who mimicked and satirised the respectable society of their time, adopting the popular mythology and iconography of the medieval knights with their travelling journeymen, minstrels and pages, to poke fun at the decadent aristocrats who were the social role model of the time.

All the proceedings are in German, but it is a curious lingo of invented, anachronistic-sounding phrases. The individual chapters of the club are called *Reych*, so when the members are asked to stand, the Chief Knight announces *das Reych erhebt sich* (the empire rises), and when they are to sit down again, *das Reych wird sesshaft* (the empire settles down). Instead of saying *Prost* they say *ehe*, and when they want to indicate approval, they shout *lulu* and slap on the table with one hand. It's all supposed to be good fun, of course, but really, it gets rather boring rather quickly. There are no women.

Bernd introduces me, and I say a few words about what I'm doing here. The *Schlaraffians* listen very eagerly, seeing a potential recruit in me to prop up the dwindling and ageing membership. They shout a few hearty *lulus*, but I remain noncommittal. Bernd points out I'm here conducting research.

After a break for a frugal snack (bread, sausages, cheeses: all German, all very basic), the official business of the evening begins. The theme is music, and everybody who feels like it is invited to perform something. Axel Best offers a piece on his classical Spanish guitar, then plays keyboard to accompany his son (a squire) who plays guitar along with another newcomer (pilgrim with straw hat like myself, a lawyer originally from Erfurt in East Germany) on saxophone. I volunteer a little musical number, a Berlin cabaret song dating back to the naughty 1920s, to express my appreciation of the warm welcome: *Ich lass mir meinen Körper schwarz bepinseln* ('I'll have my body painted black'). The improvised performance creates a little stir because of its risqué content (going native on Fiji Islands, Fiji Doll, bamboo shack, nudist culture), and Lord Henry points out that the *Uhu* (statue of an owl) who watches over the proceedings should have had his head covered prior to my song. Oh well, I'm not sure to what extent they are serious. Later I find out that three topics are taboo in *Schlaraffia*: they don't talk about politics, religion, and sex. They play it safe.

THURSDAY–SUNDAY, 11–14 April

MASTER'S WEEK

It's tournament time at Augusta, Georgia. One of the players who makes a lot of headlines is Guan Tianlang, at 14 years of age an amateur and the youngest player ever to be invited to the most prestigious professional golf tournament in the world. He plays with Bill Crenshaw in the first round and shoots an impressive one over par, including a spectacular 12-foot birdie putt from just off the green on the 18th hole. If he plays like this again on Friday, he will make the cut.

We had met Tianlang last November at the Australian Open at the Lakes Golf Course in Sydney. The conditions were very rough and play had to be interrupted because of strong winds. Tianlang did not make the cut then, so he had a day free and we invited him and his parents to come sailing with us on Sydney Harbour. They thoroughly enjoyed their day off, even though the winds were still fresh and the water quite choppy. As a souvenir, we took a photo of Tianlang at the helm of 'Stardust Dancer', the standard shot for visitors: Tianlang at the helm, sailing north towards Rose Bay, with Opera House and Harbour Bridge in the background. We asked him about what the papers said about him: that he hits 500 golf balls every day, both on the driving range and on the course, and that he uses every club in his bag doing so. Not true, he said. He does not play every day, and when he does he hits perhaps 300 balls. His mother is very strict about school; she makes sure he does his homework regularly. He goes to a normal school in Guangdong. Apparently, he does not travel as much as we thought. He plays tournaments mostly in Asia and in the US during the summer or other vacation. Even though, he has been around a lot. I ask him what place he likes best, but he cannot say. He has travelled everywhere but has not seen anything. The routine is always the same: airport – hotel – golf course – hotel – airport.

The Masters is one of the great sporting events in the world, just like the tennis grand slams. I've made it to Wimbledon, and Susan and I have been to the French and the Australian Open; the US Open is on our list to complete the spectator slam: we're planning to take Max there this August. It would be fun to go to the Masters as well. Back in Sydney, I had asked Tianlang's parents whether they could get us tickets to the Masters in 2013, since we would be in San Diego at the time. Maybe, was the answer: they would try. Now Susan sends an email to wish Tianlang good luck, and to remind them of the tickets. But we receive no answer. Very slack of them, I say. They are probably too busy and can't get tickets anyway, Susan says. That's likely to be true; even Rudy Duran was surprised when I told him we might be going to the Masters ('very hard to get tickets'). Still, it would be nice if we could go.

Tianlang has made the cut: he scored 75 on Friday, ten shots behind the leader Jason Day of Australia. In the first round on Saturday, Tianlang shoots nine over par. He won't win, but that's ok. He's doing great. We'll keep our fingers crossed for him.

TWO PENALTIES

Tianlang's Friday score included a one-shot penalty, incurred on hole 17, for 'slow play'. In golf, you get penalised if you play too slowly; in California, the DMV penalises you for driving too slowly.

Tiger Woods was penalised by two strokes for making an 'illegal drop' (Rule 26-1-a) on the par-five 15th hole. His third shot had hit the flag pin to ricochet into the water. He could have dropped the ball right there (one-shot penalty), to be played from the edge of the hazard (a difficult steep shot with little place to stand on), but he chose a second option: he walked back to re-play the ball (also one-shot penalty). Inexplicably, he dropped the ball two yards behind the original spot, while the rules of golf require a drop 'as close as possible'. He signed his score card after finishing the round, sealing his fate.

Did Tiger Woods know what he was doing? According to the *Rules of Golf*, he could have been (or should have been?) disqualified.

Here is a Multiple-Choice Test:

Question: Why did Tiger Woods get off lightly, with only a two-stroke penalty?

(a) Because he is Tiger Woods.
(b) Because of rule 33/7 (waiver of disqualification by committee).
(c) Because of rule 26-1-a.
(d) All of the above.

Answer: All of the above, but principally because of Rule 33-7. That rule saved Tiger Woods' hide: the local committee decided he was in breach of etiquette, but it was not a serious enough breach to warrant disqualification.

The rules of golf are nothing but convoluted. The rules book is an impenetrable nightmare mixture of pseudo-legal over-precision. For every rule, there are half a dozen amendments. Not surprisingly, a committee is always in charge to determine, interpret, and rule on the rules of golf in every tournament. Quite obviously, the original book of the *Rules of Golf* could not have been written but by a committee of Englishmen some centuries back, or maybe by a clan of Scotsmen.

Some of Tiger Woods' less successful competitors on the PGA tour called on him to disqualify himself. Obviously, here was a chance to have a shot at a superior golfer: it's payback time.

Golf is the gentleman's game. But you still want to win, says Phil Mickelson.

SATURDAY–SUNDAY, 13–14 April

On Saturday evening, Xiaofang, Bill and Brianna come down from LA. They arrive very late, as Bill had to work, delivering the mail to the good people and businesses of Torrance, California.

Sunday is Brianna's birthday, and we celebrate by going to SeaWorld. The weather is rather miserable for the first time since we arrived in Southern California, there is a permanent drizzle all day. That doesn't dampen the spirit of the kids, though. We play 'Drop the Ball in the Water Glass' and Max manages to score a hit and win a prize. He chooses a giant soft toy turtle.

THREE VICTORIES

Victory No. 1: Bill reports that the US Congress has upheld the law that orders the US Postal Service to maintain Saturday mail deliveries. A victory for the mailmen of America!

Victory No. 2: When we come home from SeaWorld, we hear that Australian golfer Adam Scott has won the Masters. Lina sends an email from Sydney: 'Adam Scott today, Max next.' Yeah: Aussie, Aussie, Aussie – oi, oi, oi!

Victory No. 3: The seal rope is to stay permanently, says Superior Court Judge Joel Pressman, endorsing the San Diego Council decision to separate seals and humans at the Children's Pool beach. This is a victory for the seals, say the animal advocates of La Jolla: 'Three cheers for the judge!' But the Friends of the Children's Pool, who advocate beach access for humans, counter: 'We're not done yet!' The challenge to Mayor Filner's order to close the beach temporarily will be heard in court next week.

MONDAY, 15 April

Today is National Tax (Return) Day in the US. The timely news is that President Obama has paid his taxes in 2012, a total of $112,214, at an effective federal tax rate of 18.4%. Obama reported an adjusted gross income of $608,611, most of this from his salary ($394,840), the rest from sales of his books. Royalties are declining, however. The household income of the Obamas has continuously decreased since 2009 when he was first elected. That year their income was listed as $5.5 million, in 2010 as $1.73 million, and in 2011 as $790,000. What does that mean? Is being president a risky financial business, a slippery slope of downward social mobility? I suppose he will quickly recoup his losses with a new volume of his autobiography after his final term ends in 2017. The Obamas' tax return also indicates that the First Family made substantial donations to charities, almost one-quarter of their gross income, thus lowering their tax rate in an entirely proper and praiseworthy manner.

I wonder whether the American public will get to see Mitt Romney's tax return. Fat chance? Romney was under some pressure during last year's campaign to release details of his tax returns, and he didn't, so why would he now. Anyway, who cares. He's history.

Obama is a brilliant writer. I remember reading his *Dreams of my Father* a few years back. There is a moving passage where he describes a theatre performance he witnessed while working as a community organiser in Chicago: a group of local Afro-American women, all amateurs, presenting their life stories in words and music, song and dance, stories of sadness and pain and loss as well as of exuberant vitality and joy. I quoted this passage once in a lecture at a conference on contemporary theatre in Germany, and the audience of scholars and professors were visibly impressed by the emotional impact of this piece of writing, and then hugely surprised when I told them who the author was.

MONDAY EVENING, late news

Today is also Patriots' Day in Massachusetts. It's the day of the annual Boston Marathon, the oldest continuously run marathon event in the world, first run in 1897, inspired by the race in the first modern Olympics in 1896.

On late night TV, we see pictures of an explosion at the finish line.

TUESDAY, 16 April

MOTTO OF THE DAY

On the shopfront window of the La Jolla Salt Room, next door to the dentist, I find an A4-size sheet of paper taped to the glass; across the top it reads, in big letters: *Today I'm grateful for...*, and then the text continues with some select choices, typed vertically on a few strips of paper meant to be torn off and taken away: ... *my friends, memories, my pet, the moment.* You rip your chosen strip off and take it home and ponder the words for a day or two, and if you forget where and why you got the thing, you'll find the name and phone number of the business and its website on the back.

Meanwhile, on other salty business news, I find that a new shop just opened on Fay Avenue stocks Himalayan salt blocks. It's a fancy kitchenware store with all the latest gadgets and gimmicks, and prices are accordingly. I buy a rectangular block, some eight by 12 inches and one inch thick. It costs $39, not exactly budget-priced, but it comes with a convenient metal frame that makes it easy to carry when it's hot. It works very well, and it gets a good work-out in our kitchen: grilled strips of beef and lamb, fillets of fish, vegies like asparagus and zucchini, no oil or salt needed. Great buy. I heat up the slab in the oven, put it onto the frame with my oven mitts and then onto the table: bingo, indoor barbecue ready.

BOSTON MANHUNTT

All of Tuesday, there is live TV coverage of the hunt for the Boston Marathon Bomber Brothers, Tamerlan and Dzhokhov

Tsaarnaev, aged 26 and 19, respectively. There is a wild story of a car-jacking, hold-up of a 7-Seven Eleven store, killing of an MIT security guard, police car chase, fatal shootout: breaking news, real-time reality television, brought to you by…

THURSDAY, 18 April

BLAZE OF GLORY

There is again all-day coverage of the Boston Lockdown on CNN and seemingly all other channels as well. Everywhere you see the same images and bits of fragmented news in headlines. Endless repetition of photos, video footage, the uncle of the two brothers making a statement repeated ten minutes later and then throughout the whole day, pictures of police, state troopers, FBI agents, press conferences on site, interviews with God-knows-who.

One female reporter keeps repeating, *ad nauseam*, that the first terrorist, the older brother Tamerlan, went down in a 'blaze of glory', meaning he was killed by police in a shootout. She asks some 'specialist' about the likelihood that the younger brother, who is the subject of the present gigantic manhunt, is also likely to go down in 'a blaze of glory', and then she wants to know about the background psychological motivation of people intent to 'go down in a blaze of glory'.

The *U-T* runs a cartoon on its editorial page, showing a crumpled old newsreader sitting at the news desk in front of a wall of TV sets with a headline that reads 'Boston Terror News'. The captioned quote runs: 'That concludes our inaccuracy and conjecture. Up next, sensationalism and fear-mongering!'

LA JOLLA MUSEUM No. 1

Boston is far away, on the other side of the continent. Here in La Jolla, on a Wednesday or Thursday, you could go for a peaceful, leisurely stroll around lunchtime along sunny Fay Ave to the Merrill Lynch Building, at the corner of Fay and Silverado, and take the escalator down to the lower courtyard to have a look through the wall-sized windows at the attractive, slim and exceedingly well-coiffeured young ladies in their tight-fitting gym outfits, doing their stretching and bending in what seems to be the women's pilates room of an up-market fitness studio.

Of course, this pleasant sight is not the goal of my stroll, but rather the suite next to the studio, the small but very fine Map and Atlas Museum of La Jolla, admission free, open on Wednesdays and Thursdays, between 11am and 4pm. Michael Stone, the founder, is a wealthy collector who made his money as a 'financier'; a third of his private collection is exhibited here, including some very rare pieces. It's a beautiful space, exquisitely lit with a focus on individual items.

On display are cartographic works from five centuries. The earliest piece is the famous 'T–O' map of the world by Isidore of Seville, dated 1472, the first printed map of certain date. There is a copy of the *Rudimentorum Novitiarum*, printed in Lübeck in 1475, which contains a map of Palestine. A good selection of maps document the discovery and colonization of the Americas, including a map showing Sir Francis Drake's attack on St. Augustine, Florida (1589), a couple of maps showing California as an island (a belief that persisted until the early 19th century), and a bilingual map by German immigrant D.F. Stotzmann of the early North American colonies (*Grafschaft Fairfield* in a map of Connecticut). A curious piece is a 'map in a suitcase': a three-dimensional map of San Diego County mounted in a display case used as a promotional tool by the Folsom Brothers around 1900 to promote their real estate business. The map shows the distinct settlement patterns of San Diegans around the beginning of the previous century. There is Old Town and the core area of Downtown SD, Pacific Beach and Point Loma are already well developed, the southern suburbs and La Jolla are just dots on the map. What is today a densely populated urban conglomeration offers itself to the real estate agent of the early 20th century as a landscape of unlimited potential: pockets of empty, sub-dividable land and freeway corridors everywhere.

The map museum also holds temporary exhibitions. Presently on show, and that's how this subterranean gem came to my attention, is a collection of historical pictographic maps of California by Jacinto 'Jo' Mora. Born 1876 in Uruguay, the son of a Latin American artist father and a French mother, Mora grew up in New York and New Jersey after his family immigrated to the US; he worked as a book illustrator and cartoonist before moving to California in 1903. He lived for two years in Arizona, drawing and photographing the Hopi and Navajo Indians with whom he lived, learning their language and working as a translator for the US Army. Later, he travelled on horseback up and down the California coast, retracing the route of the early Spanish missionaries on the *Camino Real*, and writing about the early settlers (*Californios*) and *vaqueros*, the forerunners of the cowboys of the American West. Eventually, he settled in Monterey and opened a studio in Carmel Mission. He created many public works, murals and sculptures, in San Francisco and Los Angeles. He died in Monterey in 1947.

Mora's *cartes*, as he called them, demonstrate his love and his fascination for the state that became his home. There are colourful maps of the state, of the cities of Los Angeles and San Diego, of Catalina Island, the Monterey Peninsula, or Yosemite national park. They are finely drawn and very detailed, geographically very accurate, surrounded by strips of cartoons on all sides of the image, dotted with numerous small vignettes that show historical scenes and personalities, architectural landmarks or other features of geographical or historical interest. There is a great deal of humor in these *cartes*: they are lovely to look at and great fun – scientific and magical, whimsical and precise all at once.

Some of the cartoons can be read like comic strips, like the one across the top of the map of the City of San Diego, dating back to 1927. It depicts the historical development of the modes of transportation characteristic of the area. Read from left to right, the frames show *Indios* walking on foot, Spanish *conquistadores* on horseback, the pioneering *gringos* with their covered wagons, then railroads with a plane overhead, and, finally, the automobiles that began eating up the freeways of California as early as the mid-1920s. In San Diego Harbour, Mora has inserted an old Spanish galleon, Cabrillo's no doubt, with the skipper looking out over the bay from the top of the mast, exclaiming (in a speech bubble): 'Caramba! You'd never know the old place now!'

Another highlight of the show is a poster, 'Evolution of the Cowboy', with two map vignettes of Salinas and Monterey framing the centrepiece 'Sweetheart of the Rodeo'. Mora depicts the metamorphosis of the local *vaqueros* of old into the modern professional rodeo riders who travel the county fairs to perform their tie-down roping stunts and show their skills in steer wrestling and bareback bronco riding. When The Byrds released their 1968 album, *Sweetheart of the Rodeo*, perhaps the hottest country-rock album ever made (with their terrific cover version of Dylan's 'You ain't going nowhere'), they chose Mora's poster as their LP cover. Thus, millions of rock music fans around the world would have seen Mora's art, and here at the La Jolla Map and Atlas Museum you can see the original.

The Reading Room at Wall Street and Girard Avenue, about 1899

LA JOLLA MUSEUM No. 2

La Jolla is a small town, but it has some truly wonderful cultural icons. On my afternoon walk back from Mr Stone's map museum, I pass by the La Jolla Athenaeum Music and Arts Library at 1008 Wall Street, around the corner from Girard Avenue, to buy tickets for a concert that evening. On a whim, I decide to become a member (for a modest annual fee of $40), which entitles me to borrow from the library – books, sheet music, CDs and DVDs – as well as to reduced prices for tonight's event, and any future to come. The library is another of La Jolla's treasured civic institutions; one of only half a dozen membership libraries in the country still in existence (and the only one west of the Mississippi). It is a museum and a library that specialises in music and the visual arts, and it is a gallery that organises exhibitions featuring local and regional artists, as well as lectures and concerts. The library dates back to 1894 when it opened as a modest reading room. Today it is housed in a lovely Spanish-Renaissance style villa, built in the 1920s with funds – it almost goes without saying – provided by Ellen Browning Scripps.

Tonight's concert at the Athenaeum is part of an Acoustic Evening Series, hosted by Jefferson Jay, a local musician who runs a popular 'open mic' show at a pub in downtown San Diego. Jay opens proceedings with a modest little song of his own about the tranquil pleasures of friendship. The next performer is a singer-songwriter and guitarist, a psychology major in real life, whose intense facial grimacing while singing makes him hard to understand. Maximilian promptly falls asleep.

He wakes up when we move to the foyer for the intermission. There are only about 25 people in the audience, and everybody is invited to cake and ice cream. An excited Jefferson Jay blows out a bunch of candles: it's his birthday. We sing 'Happy Birthday' and toast with a glass of SauvBlanc. After cake and intermission, Susan takes Max home. He is tired. I stay, and I'm glad: Wes Davis is next.

Davis, whose day job is teaching science to high school kids, plays a lively, finger-picking delta blues on his National Steel Guitar; he has got the sly sense of humour of the bluesman and the easy lyrics of the urban storyteller. I'm not surprised to hear that Davis and his 'No. 1 Blues Band' have just released an award-winning first CD (nominated for Best Blues Album at the San Diego Music Awards).

The final artist is Matt Fleischling, a good singer/song-writer with an already established following. Fleischling is the featured performer of the evening, but my money would be on Davis.

When I get back home, Max is sound asleep in bed. There is more live TV coverage of the hunt for Boston Marathon Bombing Suspect No. 2. It eventually transpires that younger brother Dzhokhov has been captured, alive, covered in blood. He had been hiding in a boat in a backyard of Boston suburbia, of all places, where he was found and reported to police by the boat's owner. Using high-tech long-range infrared detection devices, security personnel were able to confirm the brother's location from a safe distance before moving in. There was another exchange of gunfire. Police announce Dzhokhov is in a serious condition.

The people of Boston are cheering. America has new heroes. Fortunately, this time nobody went down in a blaze of glory.

FRIDAY, 19 April

In the afternoon, back to Colina Park and coaching with Todd Smith. He is just back from Punta Mita, near Puerto Vallarta, Mexico, site of a super-luxury golf resort on the Pacific coast. Todd was invited to the 'Third Gourmet & Golf Tournament', a *haute cuisine* event: some of the best chefs from around the world flown in for the weekend to cook for a select few players and resort guests. There are celebrity sommeliers, international wine writers, local tequila experts, cigar appreciation seminars for tobacco aficionados. The Glenmorangie ('16 Men of Tain') Lounge at the St. Regis offers a suitable ambience for a late-night sip of selected single malts.

And then there is golf: Todd and his partner shoot the lowest scores, only to lose on handicap. But you could be forgiven to think it matters: everyone is a winner here, wining and dining. This is the absolutely trendiest trend in luxury golf: after all, who wants to spend a few hours driving a cart along the fairways chasing a little ball, and then eat a hamburger and drink a coke?

In real life golf, at Colina Park, Max plays very well initially, shooting pars and a birdie on the first four holes. He is excited by the present Todd has brought for him from Mexico (ball marker with cap magnet, inscribed 'III Gourmet & Golf – Punta Mita'). But then he loses focus, interest, concentration. Todd is seriously annoyed: 'You're wasting your time, your parents' time, my time.' The coach abruptly turns his back and walks off the course: end of lesson. Max is shocked, but remains quiet.

SATURDAY, 20 April

Golf tournament at Solana Beach, Lomas Sante Fé South (Executive) Golf Course. No spectators are allowed on the course. Dragon Mom insists on caddying. Max is less than enthusiastic. His friend Kenny is playing in the group before him. Max does not know the players in his group, all older than himself (he plays in the eight-and-under age category). Max's lack of discipline infuriates Dragon Mom, and she resorts to pinching him on the arm.

Max misses a few easy putts and shoots ten over par for nine holes. He comes in seven, just beating Kenny. The score is hardly reassuring considering that, according to Dragon Mom's master plan, he will play an upfront role in the upcoming so-called World Championship. By contrast: the winner of his age group scores 27, one under par. Dragon Mom keeps up a stiff upper lip. Max is the youngest, after all. He has the skill but lacks discipline. We'll have to work on that, she says.

I learn why a nine-hole course is called 'Executive Course' around here. It's because, these days, the busy business executives don't have the time to play 18 holes anymore. Golf is a time-consuming business.

COFFE CULTURE

There was a time in America, and I remember it quite well, when it was impossible to get a decent cup of coffee, except perhaps in some ultra-ethnic neighbourhood in New York City or Chicago or San Francisco. The only thing you would get was a lukewarm brew that had all flavour and aroma percolated out of it while sitting on some hotplate for the better part of the day, and that was so bitter you needed double doses of sugar to make it somewhat palatable. Hence, I imagine, the standard dosage for artificial sweeteners: equal to two teaspoons of sugar.

Today, of course, all this has changed. Starbucks are as ubiquitous as McDonalds, specialty coffees are all the rage, and baristas are on the march across the country. The newest trend, originating from California boutique coffee brewers, is cold-brewed coffee. The term is somewhat of a misnomer, because it's not exactly about brewing, it's more like soaking. Does cold-soaked coffee sound perhaps a bit off-putting? Anyway, here's how it goes: you take the coffee of your choice, preferably free trade of course, grind it to a coarse grind, then put it into a container, add water, give it a good stir, and leave it to soak for a few hours, or preferably overnight. The next morning you fine-filter the brew a couple of times into a clean jar or cup or pot (depending on the quantity you made), and *voilà*: cold-brew coffee is ready. Supposedly, it is extra smooth and aromatic, and it is perfect for iced coffee, as it does not need to be cooled down. Add milk, soy, sugar, cream, half-and-half, ice, liquor, artificial flavoring, whatever: according to individual taste. With summer coming up, here's your new California Signature Drink: Happy Happy Hour!

Apparently, the Vietnamese invented the technique of cold-brewing coffee some decades ago.

SUNDAY, 21 April

It's the annual 'Day at the Docks' at Point Loma, the home of the sport fishing fleet on San Diego Bay. There is a carnival atmosphere: lots of people strolling about, kids fishing for mackerel in pens suspended in the harbour (success for Max, yeah!), music and beer, boat trips across the bay for two bucks a head. Sport fishing is big business here. There are plenty of big and still bigger charter boats to inspect, demonstrations of the latest fishing gear and boating equipment, casting competitions, all sorts of clubs vying to angle (terrible pun intended) new members; there are stands that sell hats and T-shirts, so-called marine art, newspaper and magazine subscriptions; surfboard, SUP and paddle board vendors all offering special deals. My favourite T-shirt has a simple slogan that betrays the hard-core all-American fisherman: 'Fillet and Release'.

We watch a demonstration by a guy with Asian background who fillets a 90-pound tuna: very neat, professional job. He works for a company that do these things for you: you call them up when your charter boat is on the way back to port, they meet you at the dock, take the fish you have caught (no matter what size), and prepare and deliver it to you at your home, ready for the BBQ.

We have lunch at the Point Loma Fish Market Restaurant and Café (fish and chips, sashimi, crab cakes, with one glass of wine for the driver). The place is very busy, but the self-service operation is briskly efficient and not too pricey (except for the five morsels of tuna sashimi for eleven bucks that remind me of Sydney prices). It's not really a fish market of course, but they have a retail counter that has quite a good selection of fish that look reasonably fresh. As we are sitting on a first-floor balcony overlooking the bay, with the SD skyline in the distance across the water, munching on fish and chips and crab and watching the boats coming and going, it feels a little bit like a sunny lunch at the Sydney fish market at Blackwattle Bay. I wonder whether people come here by boat, like we used to in Sydney. Probably not: the landings seem all tightly controlled by the sport fishing operators.

In the afternoon, we drive to Colina Park to meet Tim and his dad, Chuck. The kids play 18 holes, with Max way out in front on the first nine, but the less experienced and younger and smaller Tim much better on the back nine. For Max, it's a repeat of last Sunday's tournament: dwindling concentration, lack of discipline, loss of focus, declining motivation. Of course, Max wants to win against Tim, and he gets frustrated if he does not do well. Then he does worse.

Later we sit on our balcony eating a take-away pizza from Sammy's downstairs. The kids run around the flat, chasing and jumping, fighting over the giant stuffed toy turtle that Max has won at SeaWorld. For Tim, it's probably a welcome relief from his daily routine: American school in the morning, Chinese school in the afternoon, followed by abacus, piano, chess. Chuck tells us that Tim now plays golf twice a week at Torrey Pines with a Chinese coach, Jenny, one of the teaching pros at Torrey Pines. Tiger Dad Chuck insists that she speaks Mandarin to his son.

In the evening, when Max is asleep, Dragon Mom is in crisis mood. What to do with Max's golf? He is not making any progress. A new strategy is required. Maybe we should try Torrey Pines, I suggest.

MONDAY, 22 April

It seems that Max has finally got the hang of speed mathematics. Today he reports that he not only passed the math test in the time required, he also finished first in the class. Practice (*Kopfrechnen*, maths games, mental arithmetic) in the evenings and while driving is apparently paying off.

After school, we drive to Torrey Pines and meet Jenny Liu. She's a pro who specialises in working with kids. She loves coaching children, she says: kids just want to play, adults have issues. (Jenny has no children of her own – that may be part

Max and Dad at Hole Six, Torrey Pines North

of her story.) We immediately like her. She is straightforward and very polite. She thanks Max every time he does what she says (not easy sometimes with very technical instructions), and she says 'thank you' every time he does a good shot. Our job as parents, Jenny says, is to encourage Max, make sure he follows a pre-shot routine, does his practice swings in a relaxed, unhurried manner. We make a deal with her to coach Max once a week. Dragon Mom breathes a sigh of relief. There is still two months to go to the Callaway.

I am glad we're back at Torrey Pines after all these weeks at Colina Park. Late in the afternoon, you can watch the red-golden sun going down over the watery horizon while colourful hang gliders are flying back and forth along the cliffs facing the Pacific, and it's beautiful. Wow, says Max.

We get a player's card for Max. It costs $35 a month; for that he can get unlimited play at Torrey Pines after 3pm Monday to Friday, as well as every day on the other municipal golf courses in San Diego. We decide to focus on Torrey Pines from now on. We'll still go to Colina Park once a week, for coaching with Todd Smith.

TUESDAY, 23 April

Today is the day when Shakespeare was born and died. It's also the day Cervantes died. It is World Book Day, and in the USA 25,000 volunteers will be distributing 500,000 books in 6,200 towns across the country. Good on them, I say, and walk over to the La Jolla Library to borrow some new books for Max. For myself, I take out *Burr*, by Gore Vidal: I want to read a little more about American history. I also pick up a Patrick O'Brian volume of his Aubrey/Maturin novels: have yet to finish the series. This particular item, *The Reverse Side of the Medal*, sees Capt. Jack Aubrey badly burned at the London Stock Exchange. The machinations of financial speculators, inside traders, gullible investors, corrupt officials and lawyers in early 19th century London seem only too realistically contemporary.

WEDNESDAY, 24 April

I meet Axel Best, CEO of the *Schlaraffians*, for lunch at the La Jolla Shores Hotel, overlooking the beach. It turns out we have one rather exceptional thing in common: on 16 July 1969, we were both at the Kennedy Space Centre on Merritt Island in Florida, watching the launch of Apollo 11, the first space flight to land a man on the moon. I was with a group of students from the University of Minnesota sitting in a VIP stand, courtesy of the then US Vice-President and ex-US

Senator from Minnesota, Hubert Humphrey. We were about a mile away from the launch pad, while Axel was hunched in a bunker much closer to the action, watching the fiery, explosive lift-off together with his colleagues from the North American Aviation Co. (located at Seal Beach, near San Diego), the company that had built the second stage of the Saturn V carrier rocket. Best, an engineer and physicist specializing in semi-conductor technology, had come to California to work on the rocket some years earlier, part of the huge brain drain that brought thousands of German scientists to the United States in the 1950s and '60s. He finally retired and settled in La Jolla, where he is now looking after the *Schlaraffia* chapter *Am Stillen Meer* (should read: *Ozean*), playing golf and, generally, enjoying life. I suggest we might like to play a round of golf with Max, and I tell him about Dragon Mom's dream. I also tell him about my *California Journal,* not certain whether he is going to like what I have written about the *Schlaraffians.* He asks me to send him the piece by email, and I do. There is no response. Too bad.

THURSDAY, 25 April

John Rouse invites me to a theatre production at UCSD. It's a new play, written by one of the graduate students in the Master of Fine Arts playwriting course, and directed by one of the PhD students working towards a degree in directing. John says that he usually does not go to these productions, but this one is supposed to be a lively little play. He has heard good things about it. Unfortunately, after sitting through a boring first half, we both agree that his informants were in error, and we leave during the intermission.

We drive to La Jolla looking for a place to eat, but it's late and most places have closed already. We finally end up at the Milano Café on Pearl Street, opposite our house, while the last costumers are leaving. But the patron welcomes us in, and he is happy to stay open. John and I talk about the pitfalls of college theatre, and of theatre in general, and about America and the world. After watching half a play with an incoherent plot that made little sense, with stilted dialogue and wooden acting, with a leaden lack of communicative interaction between stage and audience, we have a pleasant late-night Italian meal. Talking about theatre can be an agreeable experience, watching it can be a pain.

John enlightens me about the proper way of paying a restaurant bill in the USA, including the tricky questions of splitting a bill and how much to tip. Here is how it goes, in five easy steps. Rule No. 1: In California, the sales tax is 8%, so the fool-proof way to work out the tip is to double the sales tax amount, meaning you pay a 16% tip. Other states have different rates, so adjust accordingly. Rule No. 2: Don't pay a tip based on the final amount on the bill (that includes tax), but rather on the pre-tax amount. The reason: you don't want to tip the government. Rule No. 3: Splitting bills is no problem (unlike Australia where restaurateurs cannot handle such outlandish requests). Just give the waiter two (or three, or more) credit cards and ask him/her to split the bill. Any proportion is ok. Rule No. 4: Keeping in mind rule No. 1, split the tip you agree to pay and write your part of it on the invoice (or leave cash on the table). If you want to pay more (or less) than your eating companion(s), then do so, by all means. Rule No. 5: There is no law that requires you to pay a tip. But you might get dirty looks if you don't. Or a waiter might follow you out on the street to remind you to pay.

SATURDAY, 27 April

SAILING IN SAN DIEGO BAY

I get a call from Wallace 'Wally' Cook who has read an ad I placed online on the website of the San Diego Yacht Club: 'Casual crew available for social sailing, weekends most anytime.' Wally asks whether I'm interested in sailing with him this coming Saturday. He's got a 30-foot boat, and there will be a race out of his yacht club on Coronado Cays. I say, of course, I'd be delighted, thank you very much for the invitation; but I also tell him that I'm not really into racing, that I have only done some twilight races (no spinnaker). Over the years, I have done a lot of recreational sailing with friends and on my own boat, in Sydney Harbour and along the coast, up to Broken Bay and the Hawkesbury River, and down to Port Hacking. This will be different, he says, but never mind, you're welcome if you like to come.

There's one problem: On Saturday, I'll need to leave the car for Susan and Max to play golf, so I'll have to get there by public transport. It will take close to two hours: Bus 30 to Old Town, Green Trolley to Imperial Transit Center near Petco Park, then another bus across Coronado Bridge and along the long tombolo known as Silver Strand Beach. I'm supposed to give Wally a call once I get to the bus stop at Coronado Cays, and he'll pick me up from there. No worries.

When I finally get off the bus, it's close to starting time and Wally sends one of his crew to pick me up. We race to the club, park the car and run to the jetty, hop onboard and we're on our way. No time for formalities. I shake hands with Wally who is on the helm, exchange 'G'days' all around with the crew, there's about ten people on board. The skipper tells me I'm in charge of the mainsheet, and we're already near the starting line, jostling about for position in the middle of a bunch of other boats mostly bigger than ours. Wally orders a few sharp tacks to time his approach to the starting line, and off goes the cannon.

Wally is about my age and size, with a stubbly beard and a washed-out cap on his head, while the crew are much younger, in their late twenties and early thirties, all very fit and enthusiastic. I quickly realise this is serious racing. There's a pretty stiff breeze blowing, some twenty knots, and the spinnaker comes out after the first tack for a downwind run across the bay. The fleet quickly spreads out, with some boats taking a very different course. It's hard work to control the mainsheet, there's a lot of shouting. Wally turns out to be somewhat short-tempered, he constantly monitors his course on a laptop mounted on the stern rail, and swears and yells if things don't happen as quickly as he wants. He is very competitive. Winning is not the most important thing, it's the only thing – as the saying goes.

I'm seriously out of my league here, and Wally soon orders another guy to help with the mainsail. Eventually I'm asked to change position and use my weight to sit on whichever high side for balance. I don't mind; it gives me a bit of a chance to look around and enjoy the exhilarating ride, although there's not much to see, except the sky-high Coronado bridge and city skyline below. The southern part of the bay where we are sailing is quite featureless, surrounded by bland industrial sites and navy dockyards on the eastern side and low sand dunes with condos on the other. We're not here for sightseeing, though, we're supposed to win a race, and Wally is relentless.

Two hours later we're back in port. We came in fifth, apparently not too bad considering the opposition, though we could have done better, says Wally. But he also acknowledges the crew, adding 'you all did very well, thank you, guys.' At the clubhouse, the crew relax over a few beers; they make jokes about Wally's temper, but it's clear they like him and have great respect for him. He's a very good skipper, is the universal judgement. Everybody seems to be settling down to a long afternoon of drinking. I have to tell our story of where we're from, how we got to Southern California and what we're doing here, and I get the reaction I'm used to by now: laughter, and 'Wow! Great! Good luck!'

Wally seems a little bit disappointed when I tell him I must leave. It's a long way back. He gives me a lift to the bus stop. I enjoyed this, I tell him, thank you very much. If you ever need me again, let me know. Sure, he says, I'll give you a call. We shake hands, one last smile, and he's back to his mates at the club, and I get on the bus.

MONDAY, 29 April

Jenny tells us we should work on Max's golf fitness. Golf fitness? Max really hasn't done much for his fitness, golf or otherwise. We have largely forgotten about the exercises that Todd taught him, early on. In Sydney, there was golf and the Ian Thorpe Pool in Ultimo. Max had a swimming lesson once a week, and we would go there quite often after school. At school, there is PhEd once a week, but fitness is not really a priority at All Hallows. Recently, Max and I have been going to the recreation centre, and we usually spend an hour or so playing basketball or hitting a tennis ball against a wall marked with the lines of a proper half-court. We should be doing more.

Jenny recommends a special program at the Del Mar Grand, reputedly the best golf course and resort in the San Diego area. It is called The Grand Junior Golf Academy, also known as the Titleist Performance Institute. They charge $50 for a session that lasts ninety minutes, but first you must pay $250 for an assessment procedure. According to the blurb, 'certified experts instruct junior golfers in an innovative, first-of-its-kind program held exclusively at The Grand Golf Club. This unique approach to golf and golf fitness instruction helps develop rotational velocity and teaches golf in a fun and engaging format.' We sign Max up, and the assistant pro (Christine, a friendly young woman from Madison, Wisconsin) shows us around and explains what they do: special exercises to develop lower and upper body strength, hip rotation, as well as swing and general technique. The program, owned by Titleist, one of the big manufacturers of golfing equipment, was developed in Del Mar, and it is now being marketed by the company around the world, most notably in China, says Christine. Todd Smith tells us later that he, too, is a certified TPI instructor.

TUESDAY, 30 April

ACROSS THE BAY WITH KAY, ON AN E-BOAT

Wally Cook has passed my name on to Kay Wittmann, a Berliner and a fellow sailor in his yacht club, and Kay sends an email asking whether I'm interested in a little excursion across the bay in his e-boat to a waterfront restaurant that has a lobster special on Tuesdays. I give him a call, and he gives me directions. He has a house near the yacht club on Coronado Cays, on one of the canals of this man-made waterfront development. I need to go by public transport again, but I don't mind. I can read, don't have to worry about drinking & driving (DUI, as it is known here: 'driving under the influence'), and Kay will pick me up at the bus stop.

Kay is a physician, aged 70; he is slim and fit. He has been practicing medicine for 42 years, and he still works a few days a week in his specialty area, anesthesiology and pain management. He and his wife Lotti have an ultra-modern house right on the canal. From the living room, you step out on to a deck that leads down to the water; a *Bénéteau 38* is tied up on one side of a jetty and a little 12-foot canopied runabout on the other. This is the e-boat.

Kay opens a bottle of white wine and explains that Lotti is at a book club meeting, so it's only the two of us for the trip. He has a great passion for lobster, and he does not like to miss the Tuesday specials at the South Bay Fish and Grill at Chula Vista Marina. His preferred method of transport is by boat, not only because it only costs a few cents of battery-driven electric power or because it's some ten miles by car around the bay and less than two miles across by boat, or because you can tie up directly in front of the restaurant's dining room. It's simply the fun way to go. This is something I can easily relate to. I tell Kay about my regular Sydney trips with my friend Wolfgang, usually on a Friday, sailing from Point Piper Marina in Rose Bay down the harbour past the Opera House, under the Harbour Bridge, past the glitter of Darling Harbour through the old revolving Glebe Island Bridge (now no longer in operation) and underneath the New Anzac Bridge, and docking at the pier of the Sydney Fish Market in Blackwattle Bay, for a lunch of oysters and sashimi and maybe a few prawns or fish and chips, followed by a leisurely sail back. When I am asked what I miss about Sydney, this is near the top of the list.

We take the bottle of wine and go down to the jetty to board the e-boat. We disconnect the cable that keeps the battery charged, undo the mooring lines, pull in the single fender, the motor purrs into action, and we're on our way. There is a steering wheel at the stern with a seat behind it, and benches along the sides. The engine is not quite as silent as I would have thought, but it is a machine built in the 70s, and I am surprised to hear that these electric boats were already around at that time. On the bay, the wind freshens up. It gets a bit choppy, and Kay changes course a few times to take the waves on the bow. When we get to the marina, some 30 minutes later, it is almost dark. The bottle is empty, and we're ready for another one over dinner. The whole lobsters come boiled, served with butter and some veggies, and they are a wee bit small, but so is the price: $16.95 each.

Kay has been in California since the 1960s. He and Lotti have two grown-up children who live in San Francisco. Kay is not from Berlin originally, as Wally wrote. He was born in East Prussia, but the family lived in Berlin for a short time after the war before moving to Bavaria where his father opened a medical practice and where Kay grew up. There is a special connection to Berlin, however: the Wittmanns like it there. It's their preferred city in Germany, and they have bought two little flats in the Hansaviertel of the Tiergarten district. It's a small world: the Hansaviertel is where my favourite Berlin theatre is located, the GRIPS Theater, and I have spent a considerable part of my life there. Kay knows about GRIPS ('...on the left, just when you come up the escalator from the subway station Hansaplatz'), but he has never been inside. When they are in Berlin, he and his wife often have breakfast in the restaurant at the edge of the little shopping plaza next to the theatre, and indeed, I have been there quite often myself, for lunch or after-theatre drinks. It is thus entirely possible that our paths have crossed, literally, in the past, both of us city-dwellers of Berlin from two different corners of the other side of the world.

'PAPA DOUG'

The Grand del Mar, where Max has his weekly fitness training, is a $300 million hotel extravaganza in pseudo-Tuscan postmodernist simulacrum owned by local real estate baron and developer Douglas Frederick Manchester. Reportedly, he has spent a whopping $110,000 for a set of custom-made SONY plasma TV sets, the biggest in the world, to fit out the Sports Bar in his hotel. It goes without saying that Manchester is fabulously wealthy. In 2009, his bank accounts supposedly held more than $56 million in cash.

Aged 69, Manchester is staunchly Catholic, anti-tax and anti-Obama. He insists on being addressed as 'Papa Doug', and everybody does, including Mitt Romney. Papa Doug is also how he signs his cheques; he had his name legally changed. Papa Doug is a generous philanthropist, but he is better known by San Diegans for a few other things:

1. He owns the two landmark hotels on the San Diego waterfront, the Grand Manchester Hyatt and the Marriott, along with other inner-city high-rise buildings, and is generally regarded as the developer who has single-handedly revitalised the city's harbour front district. That's not to say it is a very pretty or lively area, in my opinion.

2. His personal lifestyle is flamboyant, to say the least. He spent $200,000 on his 65th birthday party at his eponymous hotel, followed by a week-long cruise out of Costa Rica aboard a 165-foot yacht. For the opening charity gala of the Grand del Mar, Papa Doug wore a deep green tartan dress jacket with a smart red accented tux shirt and bow tie.

3. He spent $125,000 to fund the successful campaign for 'Proposition 8' in 2008, a measure to ban same-sex marriages in California, defining marriage as between man and woman. Manchester's stand earned him the wrath of the San Diego gay and lesbian community who called for a boycott of his various businesses. Manchester countered by saying that he was not anti-gay ('some of my best friends...'), but merely of the opinion gay people should not marry. In an interview

with the *NY Times*, Manchester claimed his motivation arose out of his 'Catholic faith and his longtime affiliation with the Catholic Church'. His aim was to 'preserve marriage'.

4. Manchester's own marriage of 43 years to wife Elisabeth ('Betsy') ended in a widely-publicised divorce two years ago. Details of the financial settlement between the parties remain secret, but the San Diego public was offered some tantalizing tidbits of gossipy information during the early sparring of lawyers before the family court. Elizabeth Manchester petitioned the court to guarantee she was granted exclusive use of the couple's La Jolla ocean-front residence (which Papa Doug had evacuated), that he hand back mail destined for her (which he allegedly had stolen; it was returned), and that he be ordered to pay temporary spousal support so she could meet her monthly expenses of $131,625.

5. Papa Doug is also the owner of the *U-T,* my trusted local newspaper that proudly proclaims on its first page banner 'The World's Greatest Country & America's Finest City'. He bought the paper at the bargain basement price of $110 million in 2011, after it had fallen on hard times during the Great Financial Crisis, a story not too dissimilar to many print publications that have been struggling to keep up with the advent of digital media. In January 2006, the *U-T*'s Sunday edition was a substantial 288 pages, with weekly book and technology sections, a separate children's feature, pages of stock exchange listings and real estate ads that seemed to go on forever. Three years later, the Sunday edition was down to 118 pages, the staff had been cut by half, and the local Copley family, who had owned the paper for three generations, was forced to sell. It was snapped up by a private equity firm based in Beverley Hills in 2009 and, after another regime of cost cutting, this company managed to turn the paper around and back to black figures.

When Papa Doug presented himself as the saviour of San Diego's flagship print medium, the public remained sceptical. There has been a great deal of speculation as to why exactly he invested in a business that is quite distant to his normal activities. Critics have noted that Manchester not only bought a publishing concern but the real estate that came with it, a valuable thirteen acres in Mission Valley that could easily be developed into hotels and office blocks, or shops and condos. Papa Doug insists he has no such plans. At this stage of his life, he says, his main ambition is to be the 'chief cheerleader' for San Diego.

The Grand del Mar is Papa Doug's prized possession. Over the last ten years, he has added a host of improvements to the resort hotel. Rumour has it that when his Russian girlfriend, somewhat younger than Papa Doug (well, quite a bit younger, actually), had indicated that she wished to learn how to ride a horse, he had an equestrian centre built, followed by a horse trail. He also added three acres of parking lots to the resort (involving the clearing of natural habitat), and a helicopter landing pad ('Touch down. Check in'), all of this without bothering to obtain the necessary development permits. Not surprisingly, there has been ongoing litigation. The City Council has issued several fines for permit violations, but Papa Doug just does not like to pay fines. He sends his lawyers in to battle, wearying down his opponents to eventually reach an out-of-court settlement, and the story starts all over again. The unauthorised building of the helipad seems to have been the straw that broke the camel's back, however. Council officials insisted on a court decision, and Judge Timothy Taylor ordered Papa Doug to remove the pad and pay a fine of $87,000. He also sentenced San Diego's chief cheerleader to 150 hours of community service.

As far as I know, the *U-T* has kept mum about this story. It seems perhaps banal to comment that the fine imposed on

Mr Papa Doug amounts to little more than a limp slap on the wrist. The hotel and media mogul will pay it out of petty cash, if he decides to accept the verdict. But Judge Taylor's penalty of community service is a stroke of genius. Hopefully, an appropriate service activity can be found for the former Mr Douglas Frederick Manchester. A job in the hospitality industry comes to mind, perhaps making up the beds and serving soup to homeless people in a shelter in downtown San Diego, in walking distance to the hotel on the waterfront that carries the name of the offender.

SATURDAY, 4 May

RAMONA BOWL

Max will play another tournament in the Downey suburb of Los Angeles on Sunday, so we decide to stay overnight again at Bill's and Xiao Fang's place. This time we make a detour to stop at the small town of Hemet in the San Jacinto Valley to watch a memorable theatre show. The annual *Ramona Pageant* at the Ramona Bowl is the 'Official California State Outdoor Play' and the 'Longest Running Outdoor Drama' in the whole of the country, now in its 90th year: 'Inaugurated 1923 by the people of Hemet-San Jacinto.'

The Ramona Bowl is an amphitheatre built into a picturesque boulder-strewn hillside with a canyon dramatically descending into a valley at the foothills of the San Jacinto mountains, home of the play's fictional *Moreno Rancho* set at the time of the American takeover of California. This is community theatre with a cast of hundreds, all local amateurs in costume as Mexican villagers, noble Indians and gun-slinging cowboys from Gringoland. There are lots of children, brown and white and of mixed colour, *padres* on the wallaby, itinerant Indian sheep-shearers, immigrants arriving from the East in covered wagons, ranch-hands, domestics and a freshly-appointed sheriff, with *Señora Moreno* as the tyrannical matriarch and her sickly but well-meaning son *Don Felipe* as heads of the local hierarchy.

The plaza outside the theatre's entrance is decorated as a Mexican village, and before the show begins, volunteer performers dressed in historical outfits of the mid-19th century sell popcorn and ice cream, margaritas and tacos and burritos, and a band of musicians serenade everybody from the balcony on top of the souvenir shop. It's the kind of popular communal theatre I like: show and food, a feast of theatre, obviously not in the same league as Ariane Mnouchkine's *Théatre du Soleil* in Paris, but in a spirit that is not too different.

The play is half romantic melodrama and half historical pageant, with a hearty dose of Broadway musical thrown in for good measure. At the end of act one it features a Mexican fiesta, giving the locals a chance to sing and dance to a Mariachi band. At the end of act three a band of Indians, young and old and apparently 'authentic' from the neighbouring Soboba Reservation, perform traditional dances and ceremonies. The *gringos* play a less artistic role; they basically just gallop through the scenery on their horses, shouting 'giddy-up' and shooting in the air.

The show drags on for nearly three hours, Susan and Max soon get bored, but my interest is kept awake by the bits of realistic social-historical commentary embedded in the melodramatic pageant. The beautiful Ramona, the heroine, is a half-Indian, half-European orphan; she is a ward of the señora who hates her for the simple reason that she is 'an Injun' but nevertheless forbids her to marry Alessandro, the Indian foreman on the ranch and son of the local chief. When Ramona finds out that her mother was Indian, she and Alessandro flee the ranch to join Alessandro's tribe; they have a child, poetically named 'Eye in the Sky', but not before, as the script takes pain to establish, they are joined by holy sacrament in a mission church in San Diego. Under pressure from the invading *gringo* farmers who are armed with rifles and title deeds to the land they begin to occupy, the Indians take to the mountains where they mourn the loss of their land and time-honoured way of life. The 'days of old' are gone forever. Eventually, Ramona's daughter dies, and Alessandro is killed by a low-life farmer who shouts 'I'll learn you damn Indians to steal my horses!' – a crime of which the poor Indian is of course entirely innocent. The grimmest scene in the play occurs when the notorious bad man has a not too subtle go at Ramona, trying to rape her. At the end, the evil señora has died, and Ramona and Don Felipe meet at the ranch. They decide to pack up and lead an exodus of villagers back home, to Mexico.

This is popular theatre, and the audience love it. There is a great deal of cheering when the cowboys gallop across the stage, the spectators mostly vividly applaud the singing and dancing, and at the curtain call the señora is booed as in a good old melodrama. It is show business framed by the usual American display of patriotic sentiment. At the beginning, an announcer asks the US soldiers and veterans present on the day, men and women, to stand up to be recognised and thanked for their service to the country. Similarly, the law enforcement personnel, first responders, fire fighters and other such role models who supposedly lay their lives on the line to protect us from all evil, are asked to stand up and be acknowledged. Then the play proper begins with a trumpet flourish, and a lone rider with an American flag (31 stars) gallops across the stage while the audience, previously told to show their respect, rise as one to a standing ovation.

When Helen Hunt Jackson wrote her novel *Ramona* in 1884, her aim was to advocate the cause of the Indians in a similar way to what her colleague Harriett Beecher-Stowe had achieved for Black Americans in *Uncle Tom's Cabin*. *Ramona* was one of the most popular novels in 19th century America. It certainly contributed to raise awareness among readers about the prejudice and mistreatment suffered by native Americans, just as Jackson's non-fiction treatment of the same topic in *A Century of Dishonor* proved influential among American political leaders. In the long run, however, the novel's popularity made more of an impact on the romantic-historical imagination of readers, creating a touristic interest in Southern California with people travelling to the San Jacinto mountains in search of the real-life scenes of the amorous encounters between the fictional characters Ramona and Alessandro. The tourist boom continues to this day.

MEDIA CONCENTRATION

I find out more details on the business interests of Papa Doug Manchester, chief cheerleader of San Diego. He is also the owner of the *North County Times*, the other major daily newspaper in San Diego County, bought in September 2012 for a mere $11.95 million ($6 million less than what Manchester got for his La Jolla home during divorce proceedings). The *North County Times* has a circulation of 75,000. It consolidates Papa Doug's hold on the print medium industry in the San Diego area. At the time of the take-over, Papa Doug had announced that he would take a hands-off approach to running the paper, but he also made it clear he wanted more 'positive stories', showcasing the good things that San Diego and its local business community have to offer.

Then there's the other media: the *U-T* has recently opened a TV channel to complement its offerings to the people of Southern California. *U-T TV* broadcasts daily from 6am to midnight, on HD channel, via cable and online. There's sports, the usual rubbish entertainment ('best birthday videos'), a 'watchdog program' to scrutinise local government operations, and lots of San Diego news and social and business affairs. It is expected that feel-good stories will dominate.

So here we have a mini-Murdoch in the making, or, as Rob Davis of the independent news website *Voice of San Diego* puts it more site-specifically, 'our little Murdoch-by-the-sea'.

I also find out that Papa Doug sold his waterfront hotel and favourite watering hole, the 'iconic' twin towers of the *Manchester Grand Hyatt*, for around $560 million in 2009, presumably to pay for divorce proceedings. One interesting detail in the sales contract: the hotel's name Manchester Grand Hyatt cannot be changed for twenty years. But hey, isn't this is contradictory? Douglas Frederick Manchester changed his name by deed poll to Papa Doug. So, should the hotel then not also be called *Papa Doug's Grand Hyatt*?

And now something positive:

Papa Doug also owns the Hotel La Jolla, at the corner of La Jolla Shores Drive and Torrey Pines Road, a few blocks away from the beach. To make up for the lack of beachfront location (monopolised by the La Jolla Shores Hotel), the Hotel La Jolla offers some tantalizing innovations: movie nights by the pool on the roof of the building with drinks and tapas and the 'first-ever World Cocktail Day Dinner': a 'seven course meal paired with seven global cocktails from each of the seven continents' for $77 per person. How could we ever miss this? There's also the ultimate happy hour every Wednesday, imaginatively called 'Veuve around the Click': a glass of *Veuve Cliquot* bubbly (*Witwe Klicko*, for Wilhelm Busch fans) will set you back $4 between 4pm and 5pm, $5 between 5pm and 6pm, $6 between 6pm and 7pm, and so on. Great idea! I'd say, 'Well done, Papa Doug! Get there early, folks! Happy Happy Hour!'

A VISIT TO BIRD ROCK

Max has become good friends with Vera who is in his class at All Hallows. Usually the eight boys in grade one stick and play together, and so do the 14 girls. But Max is open-minded. In Sydney, he was very good friends with his best girlfriend Chantelle.

For Saturday morning, we organise a play day with Vera, and we drive to their house in Bird Rock, near where the owner of the ocean-front home has generously supplied a public shower ('Dear surfer…') to passing bathers, surfers, windsurfers and SUP boarders. Vera has three older brothers, and that helps to explain why she and Max play together very well. The two of them climb down the steep cliff to the rocky shore and explore the guano-covered bird rock, a giant boulder and local landmark that you can reach at low tide.

Frank Lord, Vera's dad, has bought some muffins for breakfast, and he makes a decent cup of coffee. The Lords, Mary (originally from Ireland, with relatives in Sydney) and Frank and four kids arrived from South Africa only about a year ago, so they are relative newcomers, like ourselves. Susan and Mary have become good friends by now.

Frank tells us that he was in the wine business in South Africa; he owned a winery in Stellenbosch that he sold when the family could no longer tolerate the life over there. He is from an *Afrikaner* family. I recall my visit to South Africa some years ago, to Johannesburg, Stellenbosch and Capetown, and remember the feelings of insecurity experienced by the well-to-do white minority. I'm intrigued about the story of the Lords' immigration to the US. I had always assumed that a business migrant had to invest in a company of their own and employ some workers for a prescribed period of time in order to qualify for a residence permit. But Frank explains that this is not necessary; there are special funds set up for a kind of passive economic activity, with a choice of diverse portfolios available.

Frank is in great shape; he has never felt better in his life, he says. He has not worked since they arrived here. He plays tennis, goes sailing at Mission Bay Sailing Club and does a lot of windsurfing. Recently, he wind-surfed from Mission Bay up the coast to Bird Rock and went ashore near his house, dragging his board and mast and sail across the rocks and up the escarpment to his garage. But now he is getting restless, he says. He wants to get back into business, and he is travelling along the California coast, inspecting vineyards and wineries. He wants to set up a winery, initially perhaps in partnership with an existing operation, most likely in the wine area of North San Diego County. He will probably buy grapes from Northern California, the Napa and Sonoma Valley areas, and maybe from Mexico. He wants to make his own wine again.

Frank offers to put me in touch with his immigration lawyer. Hmm – interesting proposition.

GREEN CARDS

Trying to get a Green Card? Easy. Get an EB-5 Immigrant Investor Program Visa. You only need to invest a minimum of $500,000 in an approved regional fund, and you and your family (spouse and children under 21) can enter the USA almost immediately. Many of these funds focus on environmentally sound 'green' projects, and they usually pay approximately 3% interest per annum. You'll also need to pay a specialised immigration lawyer who will charge roughly $20,000. The whole process will take about two years, although some lawyers promise to do it in as little as six months. You don't need to be involved in the administration of the fund. There are no age or language requirements. You must leave your money in the fund for at least five years, and after that time you become eligible for US citizenship.

LA JOLLA MUSEUM No. 3

If you walk down to the end of Draper Avenue and turn right into Prospect Street, you are facing a gigantic black kinetic work of art, a seven-metre-tall silhouette sculpture of a worker holding a length of metal in one hand and a hammer in the other. The piece is constructed out of Korten steel and features a hidden electric motor that moves an aluminium arm holding the hammer up and down. This is Jonathan Borofsky's *Hammering Man*, the universal worker, slowly hammering away eight hours a day. It is one of the many identical pieces (of different height) that the artist from Boston has installed in cities around the world – at Seoul, Korea and Frankfurt, Germany, at Lillestrom, Norway and Basel, Switzerland, and at Dallas, Denver, Los Angeles, Minneapolis, New York, Seattle and Washington, DC, in the United States.

In La Jolla (not exactly an industrial city), the *Hammering Man* stands in the middle of a semi-circular plaza in front of the San Diego Museum of Contemporary Art. The museum is housed in what was originally the 1915 oceanfront residence of – who else? – philanthropist Ellen Browning Scripps. It was substantially rebuilt and enlarged by postmodernist architect Robert ('Less is a Bore') Venturi in 1996, and Venturi's building does not reveal a trace of the original, at least not to the uninitiated eye.

At the moment, the museum features an international group exhibition entitled *Lifelike*. It's all about art and reality, the perception of everyday objects and situations, the familiar as art in unexpected materials, dimensions, surroundings and framings; there's photorealism, pop art, video installations.

It's not exactly cutting-edge, but there are some interesting pieces and a few well-known names: Jasper Johns, Gerhard Richter, Edward Kienholz, Robert Rauschenberg, Charles Ray, Chuck Close, Ai Weiwei.

My favourite part of the museum is the sculpture garden overlooking the coastal promenade towards the Children's Pool and the ocean. The signature piece at the back of the building, complementing the *Hammering Man* at the front, is Nancy Rubins' *Pleasure Point*, a cluster of nautical vessels (aluminium dinghies, canoes, fibreglass catamarans and surfboards, etc.), all tied together with stainless steel wires and precariously suspended in the air off the roof of the museum. Looking up from the beach below, it offers a dramatic, enigmatic spectacle. Of course, boats belong to this place here on the Pacific Ocean, but hanging in the air? What's going on here? The counterpart to this airy installation is Andy Goldsworthy's rock-bottom solid, perfectly egg-shaped cairn of natural stones held together only by their own weight, located on a piece of lawn in front of the building. It's about three metres in height, a down-to-earth memorial, supposedly suggesting and tracing the route of the Scottish artist across America.

Then there's Roman de Salvo's *Liquid Ballistic*: a mysterious name for a sculpture that is a wooden cannon with large timber wheels, its undercarriage made of some plastic industrial tubing attached to a pump, the rear end of the barrel resting on a worn-out tyre half-buried in the ground. The cannon faces the sea, as if ready for action to foil an invader coming across the ocean. Obviously, this must be an ironic take on all the superfluous coastal fortifications around the world, from antiquity to the present. But is the timber cannon entirely useless? The pump suggests that it might be a water cannon, and could the handle on the barrel double as a seesaw, something for kids to play with? Finally, there is one of Niki de St. Phalle's famous *Nanas*, this time in the

Hammering Man, San Diego Museum of Contemporary Art

shape of the Hindu elephant god of happiness, good luck and success: *Grand Ganesh*, a colourful giant pachyderm, standing and dancing on one leg, decorated with glittering automotive paint. It is looking at a little companion: a mouse, as in the fable of old.

I like it that the individual pieces here are not isolated and unique works, but that they are members of larger groups or families. Similar cairns by Goldsworthy are located in New York and Iowa, and there is a counterpart to de Salvo's wooden cannon on the East Coast, in Brooklyn. Along with Niki de St. Phalle's *Nanas* and Borofsky's *Hammering Men*, they constitute interconnected landmarks that reach around the globe.

THE *SCHILDBÜRGER* OF LA JOLLA SHORES BUILD A LIFEGUARD TOWER ON THE BEACH

The good burghers of La Jolla Shores are justifiably proud of their lifesavers who do such a great job keeping people from drowning in the surf and from being eaten by sharks. So, they decided to build them a new observation tower, to replace the unsightly old concrete platform with a state-of-the-art piece of structural engineering, and it did indeed turn out to be an architectural masterpiece, completed just in time before the swimming season. It cost $2.8 million to build. Hello? $2.8 million for a lifeguard tower? Yep, that's about the sum of it.

The only problem with the fancy tower is that it seems to have made the beach less safe. That's because the lifeguards cannot see very well through the windows of the observation platform. Their views are being obscured by glare and distortion, apparently because the wrong type of glass was used in the installation. The problem is worse during certain times of the day, especially in the afternoon with the sun going down over the water in the West. Furthermore, the windows at the side of the booth are not correctly sloped. 'The sun at certain times of the day acts like a projector, taking people on the south side and projecting their image on the northernmost observation glass,' says Ed Harris, spokesperson of the San Diego

Lifeguard Union. Apparently, it's not unlike watching TV. 'In addition, a blur exists in corners where the glass meets, creating distortion akin to wearing eyeglasses with the wrong prescription.'

MOTHER'S DAY, 12 May

It's Sunday and Mother's Day, and Max and I go fishing. Susan does not want to come: she's staying home to watch The Players PGA Tournament on TV. While Tiger Woods (who eventually wins: $1.7 million prize money) is stalking the fairways at TCP Sawgrass, Florida, Max and I are boarding the *MV Dolphin* at Fisherman's Landing, Point Loma.

We are armed with rented rods and a one-day California Fishing Licence. Half a day's fishing (from 1pm to 6pm) costs $34 (senior concession for me; otherwise $44), plus a One Day California Fishing Licence ($14.40) plus rod/weight/hook rental ($12.00), all up $60.40, including tax. How much would I have to pay for something like this in Sydney, I wonder. At least twice that amount? During the month of May, there is a promotion: kids under 15 fish for free. Some 30 people are on board the 70-foot ship, mostly men, a few couples and a couple of kids. No teenagers. There's another boy called Max, aged nine; but the kids are not really interested in playing together, they want to catch fish.

We head outside of the bay, past the old Point Loma lighthouse. About half a dozen white herons try to make a meal of the live bait, anchovies swimming in small tanks mounted at the stern of the boat. The big birds fly in and land on the tanks' rim, balancing precariously with flapping wings, and take off when somebody shoos them away, only to be back a moment later having another quick peck at a helpless little fish. The herons fly away for good when the boat enters open waters and the wind picks up. About a mile offshore the skipper settles the boat to drift over some kelp beds. We bait up with cut-up squid and start fishing. Max is the first one to reel in a fish, a decent-sized Spanish Mackerel. Wow! He is greatly excited and all smiles. Of course, I left both mobile phone and camera at home: there won't be any pictures. Sadly, it's also going to be Max's last catch for the day.

I ask him what he wants to do with the fish. The crew on board will fillet it for him (for a dollar a fish), but he wants me to do this and cook it for us at home. He will take the whole fish home to show Mom, as a mother's day present. (The other present is a cut-out silhouette of himself, made by one of the mothers in his class at All Hallows after a digital photo, and framed by the kids in school: it's a quite well-executed *Scherenschnitt*.)

Fishing is rather slow, there's a 15-knot wind blowing and two-to-three foot waves, so the skipper decides to move back inside the bay. We take up position near the bait cages that have been taken over by sea lions, but nobody has much interest in looking at the wildlife or the scenery. We are told to bait up with the live bait: slimy and squiggly little anchovies, the size of your little finger. It's a tricky business, first to catch one with your hand and then thread the hook through the tiny fish head, just below the eyes. More often than you'd like, the slippery little things wiggle out of your hand just after you managed to get hold of one. I don't get to do a lot of fishing because I do the baiting for Max as well. As soon as my own rod is ready for action, Max comes over to me and says: 'Fish took my bait.' I give my rod to him and he continues angling while I re-bait his rod. And so on, again and again.

One of the crew has been watching us and decides to lend me a helping hand. He catches an anchovy and hands it to me, saying: 'Here, I got a good one for you.' I ask: 'Good one means big one?' 'Yeah,' he says. 'If you ain't gonna catch nothing with this one, there ain't no fish 'round here!' I take the rod to the other side of the boat, to get a break from Max. The monster anchovy is dangling and wiggling from the hook, and almost immediately I drop it in the water there is a sharp bite. I pull up the rod and reel in the line as quickly as I can, but there's nothing: the bait is gone. Another proverbial big one that got away. And there's Max again: a fish has taken his bait, for the umpteenth time. It's quite amazing that Max, despite a continuing lack of success, has the patience and the energy and focus to go on fishing the whole afternoon. That kind of determination is what he needs more of on the golf course, I think. Or in school, for that matter.

It's halibut season, and I'd be extremely happy to land one of the sweet flat fish that are supposedly down there, hiding and feeding on the sandy bottom; but they remain elusive. The skipper is not happy, and we change spots a few times. When moving to another area, the rods are left standing against the rail, some with bait attached to the hook, and the seagulls that follow the boat occasionally take a dive to attack the anchovies fluttering in the wind. One super-sized gull manages to catch one and gets hooked on the line, wildly thrashing its wings in a desperate struggle, almost pulling the rod over the rail. A crew member who is standing nearby, cigarette in a corner of his mouth, can catch the rod at the very last moment; he gets hold of the big bird by the neck, pulls out a pair of pliers and prizes the hook out the gull's beak. Then he firmly holds the beak closed with one hand, and with the other hand he takes the big bird under his arms, folds in the wings and lets the kids who have been watching the action pet it, before releasing the poor feathered thing, a victim of its own greed. The gull flies away just skipping over the waves, no doubt shaken but apparently not much the worse for the experience.

Back home, I clean the fish, wrap it in foil with a bit of ginger, shallots, coriander, soy sauce and sherry, and steam it in the oven. It tastes ok, a little fishy, but Max does not want to try it. He does not like the look of the dark meat. Since it's Mother's Day, we have Chinese dumplings and a pizza from Sammy's downstairs. Max's new favourite: Hawaiian, ham and pineapple with lots of mozzarella.

LA JOLLA TENNIS CLUB, FOUNDED 1917

Susan and I have joined the La Jolla Tennis Club. It's a two-minute walk from our house, and the annual membership fee for unlimited play is only $130 per person. There are nine courts. Two are usually reserved for coaching, three (across the street) can be booked in advance, and four are available on a first-come, first-serve basis. To play on one of those, you'll need to wait your turn if someone is already on the court, and you do this by sitting on a bench and wait till the players have finished their set (or two sets in case of doubles). You just ask the players what is their score and wait until the set is over. Then the court is yours until the next players appear. And so on.

Susan and I play an hour or more every morning, after taking Max to school, from 8.30am to around 10.00am. And sometimes I play with Max in the evening, after coming back from golf. We used to hit some balls against the wall in the adjacent recreation centre, now we play on a proper court, and I teach him the basic strokes. Max quickly gets the hang of it: forehand, backhand, volleys, even the occasional smash.

I am a little concerned regarding my level of fitness, particularly after the arthroscopy that ended my previous tennis career, not to mention my high blood pressure. But the knee is holding up well, against expectations, and I generally feel very good after a sweaty tennis workout before breakfast. In the morning, the temperature is usually in the mid-70s, so it's the best time of day to play tennis, there is no danger of becoming overheated.

Déjà vu: The last time I played tennis in the US was in 1996, in Ann Arbor, Michigan, where I spent a semester as visiting professor at the University of Michigan. It was in the middle of winter, two feet of snow on the ground and temperatures well below freezing point. My partner was a Chinese-American I met through my daughter's school; he lived in Ann Arbor and drove every day to work in downtown Detroit. He and I played once a week late at night in one of the all-weather courts on the campus, dome-shaped inflatable structures that were being held up by the warm air being pumped into the tent. It was an eerie scene walking across campus at midnight, red-faced and hot and sweaty after a 90-minute session of competitive tennis, wearing a bulky down anorak against the cold and a woolen balaclava against the bracing wind. We had to wear safety goggles fitted with prescription lenses; university policy did not allow normal eye glasses to be worn on the courts of UM. There are no such prohibitions in Southern California.

TUESDAY, 14 May

DRONES: HISTORY AND HEROES IN THE MAKING

The San Diego-based Northrop Grumman Company proudly announces a breakthrough in naval aviation: for the first time, its unmanned aircraft X-47B has been launched from an aircraft carrier and safely returned to an airbase on land. A spokesman for the company compares this to the first manned flight off an aircraft carrier in 1910. In navy-speak, the X-47B is a UCAV (unmanned combat air vehicle), a drone in other words, designed like a bat-shaped stealth bomber with an impressive wingspan of 19 metres.

Drones are very popular in San Diego because this is a navy town, and drones mean a revolutionary development in the art of war. They are also big business. Two of the country's largest defence contractors and manufacturers are located here: Grumman and General Atomics. Grumman employs nearly 4,000 workers, and GA over 7,000 in various facilities around San Diego county. GA made history when, on 4 November 2002, a Hellfire missile launched from one of its Predator drones over Yemen killed one of the al-Qaeda leaders allegedly responsible for the attack on *USS Cole* two years earlier. Since then, there have been numerous similar strikes, over countries from Iraq and Syria to Pakistan and Afghanistan, conducted by cyber warriors with extensive experience in PlayBox technology. These soldiers are often barely out of high school; they are armed with a joystick and sit in front of a monitor in some air-conditioned office building in an armed forces base somewhere in America or overseas. The US air force base in Ramstein, Germany, where Rudy Duran learned to play golf during the more peaceful times of the Cold War, is suspected to be the operational centre for drone attacks in the Middle East and the Persian Gulf area. If this is so, it would be in breach of German law.

The American Government likes to use drones in its 'war against terror'. The generals prefer not to employ US ground troops in countries like Yemen or Pakistan. Soldiers on the ground could become casualties. Drones can do preparatory surveillance work, for missions such as the one that took out Bin Laden, or go in for the final kill. That way, says Barack Obama, drones save lives. American lives to be exact.

The drone pilots are the new American heroes in the age of digital warfare. But how do you recognise the bravery of soldiers who control unpiloted aircraft on missions thousands of miles away and who kill people by clicking on an icon on a computer screen? Drone pilots don't go down in a blaze of glory, as the Boston TV lady would have put it. The Pentagon recently announced it would introduce a new medal specifically for drone operators. Unsurprisingly perhaps, not everyone felt that was the right thing to do. The plan drew heavy fire from some American veterans who protested against the idea that a combat decoration could be awarded to somebody who had never met an enemy in battle. The plan was quickly shelved after members of Congress introduced an amendment that would have ranked any such medal beneath the Purple Heart, the medal given to all American soldiers killed or wounded in action.

Eugene Ely was the American Hero who made history on 10 November 1910: he was a high school dropout from Iowa, a car-racing enthusiast and daredevil pilot who flew a wooden Curtiss bi-plane off a specially constructed flight deck on *USS Birmingham*, at anchor in Hampton Roads, Virginia. He almost plummeted into the water and just managed to land on a beach nearby. Two months later he reversed his stunt, landing his plane on board *USS Pennsylvania* at anchor in San Francisco Bay, and nine months later he crashed during an exhibition flight in Macon, Georgia, and died, aged 24. So it goes, according to Kurt Vonnegut.

SUNDAY, 19 May

Final Tournament US Kids' Golf Spring Tour, LA Region, at Lake Elsinore, just north of Temecula off Interstate 15. It's a new course in the middle of a planned community that is still in the process of being built, in a treeless hot plain. Max is happy: all the friends and fellow-competitors are there. He scores 39, three over par: a very good result. Still, the competition is ahead: Jack scores an incredible four under par, and Nathan as runner up comes out even at 36. Jack is declared 'Player of the Year' and gets a trophy, Nathan and Max get a silver plate each. Max is very proud: for the next couple of days, he takes the plate along with him wherever he goes. A few days later, he receives an invitation to play in the US Kids World Championship at Pinehurst, North Carolina. Dragon Mom wants to go, but I veto the idea. It's in the middle of nowhere, too far and too expensive, and it's only ten days after the Callaway World Championship. Maybe one world championship a year is enough. In any case, our return flight to Australia is on 3 August. Changing the tickets would be very expensive. Forget about Pinehurst.

On the way home from Lake Elsinore we take State Road 74 through the mountains, a twisting two-lane highway not for the faint-hearted but favoured by thrill-seeking motorcyclists. We stop at San Juan Capistrano and park the car to have a look at the mission, one of the oldest in California, and home to the famous swallows.

It's Sunday, ok, but still: to say this is a quiet little town is a bit of an understatement. On the main street, there is one pub where all the action seems to be: a blues band is playing, three huge guys with Stetson hats and huge beards belting out some great numbers. While Susan walks ahead, Max and I listen for a while through the open door and watch the people dancing. The scene reminds me of some quintessential American road movie, but I can't recall which one precisely. The dance scene in the bar where the Blues Brothers are impersonating The Good Ol'Boys? No, that wasn't it.

We decide to visit the mission first and come back to the pub later. The mission is only two blocks away, but when we get there, it is closed, it's just past 5pm, we can only peek over the wall to see some of the ruins of the original church building and the courtyard of the monastery that is still intact, its arches covered in bougainvillea and wisteria. On the way back, we find that the band is in the process of packing up. They seem in quite a hurry, probably they are booked for another gig at a more exciting location. One of the guys is coming out of the door with his guitar case in one hand and an ice bucket overflowing with dollar bills in the other. Tips for the band, I presume.

The main street is utterly deserted. The only other place open is a Starbucks. Susan and I have an iced coffee and Max a hot chocolate.

MEMORIAL DAY LONG WEEKEND, 25–27 May

On Memorial Day, Americans remember their soldiers who died in battle. It's a federal public holiday traditionally observed on the last Monday of May. Just like long weekend holidays in Australia, it is an excuse for backyard barbecue parties, picnics in the parks or on the beaches, short holidays, and shopping, shopping, shopping. It's a holiday, but all the shops are open for business. If you need a new car, or furniture, or clothes, or household appliance, or anything at all, you are well advised to wait until Memorial Day to visit your local mall or your Car Mile Centre out on the next freeway. Newspapers are full of full-page ads, TV stations run endless commercials spruiking Memorial Day Specials. On TV, suave voice-overs express an offer of thanks to 'our boys who gave their lives for our freedom' and implore buyers not to miss unmissable opportunities. There are always American flags flying in the background.

We decide on a short holiday, combining a scenic trip to Palm Desert (next to its sister city Palm Springs) where Max will play a golf tournament on Sunday, and a detour on the way back to the historic gold rush town of Julian on Memorial Day Monday. After Temecula, State Road 79 leisurely meanders across the central valley through lush farming country, ranches and orchards. It is a pleasant change from the frenetic freeway, but soon we're back on Route 74 that is as mind-bogglingly breathtaking here as the stretch between Lake Elsinore and the coast. It is a spectacular road up the mountains and down into the desert valley, one hairpin bend after another, with the road precipitously clinging to the mountainside.

At the Rancho La Quinta tournament, Max finally shows some consistency. He is on par until the last hole when he gets impatient: he is eager to finish the round and shoots a triple bogey. Again, he finishes third overall.

On the way to Julian, the GPS screws up my itinerary. I had planned to drive straight south to Salton Sea and then cut west through the Borrego-Anza State Park to Julian. But I forgot to tell the GPS, or rather to program in the waypoints, so the GPS directs me straight back to where we came from, the perilous road across the mountains with its killer reputation and attraction (for bikers). Before I notice what's going on, I'm already in the foothills and too upset and angry to re-direct my route. I should have had a good old-fashioned road map to have a quick look, but I don't, so I continue, cursing the GPS lady under my breath. We'll have to discover the Borrego Desert some other day.

In Julian, we stay overnight at the Apple Tree Inn, a run-of-the-mill motel despite the fancy name, and have dinner at the old-authentic Julian Café with its homemade specialties, chicken pie and turkey burger. We take one of their yummy apple pies with crumbles back to the motel, it will be our breakfast the next morning.

On Monday morning, we walk around the four streets of Julian, one tourist shop and café or restaurant next to another, all very quaint and friendly, full of historical bric-à-brac. Plaques on the old houses tell the stories of the original builders and owners, miners and tradesmen, immigrants from Italy and Austria and China, and internal migrants from the eastern parts of the USA, and presumably from everywhere else as well.

We take a guided tour of the abandoned Eagle Gold Mine. There is a lot of broken-down equipment lying around, rusty old trucks without engines and wheels, bits and pieces of heavy machinery. Our guide is a giant lumberjack-kind of a man with a willowing white beard flowing down to his chest, soft spoken and with a quiet sense of humour. People expect to be able to try their hand at panning for gold, he says, so the tour begins with a gold panning demonstration in a trough purposely built in front of the mine office that functions as a museum now. Then the guide tells us that panning was never done here at all, unlike on the gold fields of Northern California where the precious metal could be washed out of the sands of the alluvial riverbeds. But never mind, he says: the tourists expect to pan, so pan they will.

Digging for gold in Julian was altogether a different operation. The metal had to be extracted out of the veins embedded in rock in underground mining. It was a laborious, back-breaking process that involved cutting up the ore-bearing rock, bringing it up to the surface, crushing it and then extracting the gold by a chemical process involving liberal applications of mercury. Later, cyanide was used. The guide shows us the huge rock-crushing machine that must have made a hellish noise at the time it was running, from 1870 to 1924, 24 hours a day. He then takes us into the mine, down narrow, twisting shafts where you constantly worry about hitting your head against the low ceiling. In the old days, before pneumatic power drills came into operation (called widow-makers, as they tended to spin around, out of control), the workers had to break up the rock using tools like pick-axes, club hammers and hand drills, and they worked by the gloomy light of candles made of tallow mixed with sawdust. The most impressive aspect of the tour is when the guide switches off the electric light to give an idea of the darkness underground. The blackness of the space is quite overwhelming.

Today, Julian is all about apples. It is the self-proclaimed 'Apple Pie Capital of the USA', and given that Americans like to think that there is nothing quite American as apple pie, it is easy to understand why the town is a popular destination on the tourist trail of Southern California. Apples rule the local food economy. There's apple pie in all shapes and variations, to eat in or take out or for shipping home; there's apple juice, apple cider, apple jam, apple sauce, apple butter, apple chips.

Apple chips? Yes, here's the recipe: you'll need two table spoons of lemon juice, one sweet, crisp apple (like Fuji or Gala), and two teaspoons of confectioner's sugar. Slice apple into very thin slices (mandolin) and let soak for five minutes in a medium bowl filled with ice cubes, water and lemon juice. Line a baking sheet with non-stick baking paper and place apple slices on sheet, sprinkle with sugar, and bake in a pre-heated oven at 200 F for about 90 minutes, until crisp and dry. Cool and serve.

On our way back to La Jolla, we retrace the road to the Warner Springs glider port that we had passed the day before. I had promised Max we would go back to do a flight in a glider, if they would accept him at his age, and they did. This is a highlight for Max: the two of us sit next to each other in the little plane, a wee bit cramped for lack of space, the pilot in front of us, there is a camera mounted on the starboard wing, and up we go. An old Piper workhorse tows us up to 6,000 feet altitude (from 2,900 feet at ground level), I pull the tow release, and we're on our own, flying over the mountains quite close to a few of the peaks, the pilot banking for some steep 40-degree turns and asking Max whether his tummy is all right. It is, and Max is happy. We see the forests and the farmland down below, black-and-white cows the size of flies, and we can confirm that the earth is not flat. Then we cruise over a small settlement that turns out to be, as the pilot tells us, a women's prison, a low security facility where the inmates work during the day with the area's fire crews.

Later, back in La Jolla, we hear that there was a big brush fire just south-east of Julian, covering nearly 1,000 acres, apparently started by people doing practice shooting.

The Earth is Not Flat: Flying a Glider at Warner Springs, CA

MEMORIAL CULTURE 1–3

1. Americans love memorials. You can find them anywhere, in many a shape or form. People put a sticker with an obituary notice in the rear window of their car. Pavers are a universal favourite, you can find them pretty much anywhere: in the foyer of clubs, on the side of buildings, in public parks, along the oceanfront promenade. Wherever there is a brick pavement, it seems you can purchase a paver with your name or the name of a loved one inscribed and have it placed on the pavement, next to the ones already in place. In Pacific Beach, I saw trees planted on a sidewalk with a plaque at the bottom, surrounded by a miniature fence. In Colina Park, there is a similar site, a pine tree planted in memory of a member of the ProKids golf team, a boy who died aged 12.

You can also adopt a highway and have a sign erected with your name on it (in return for services like litter clean-up and vegetation control, either by yourself and your friends as volunteers, or by a company that you pay for their services). Public roadways often carry the name of a dear departed, and quite a few are named after firemen or police officers who presumably died in the line of duty, such as the stretch of State Highway 74 named after 'CHPO [California Highway Patrol Officer] Michael O. Brandt' who lost control of his patrol car while in pursuit of a drunken driver and went down the side of the mountain in one the hairpin bends on this hair-raising roadway.

2. While President Obama is laying a wreath at Arlington National Cemetery on Memorial Day, members of the San Diego military community and their families have gathered at the Veterans' Memorial under the Easter Cross at the top of Mt. Soledad, around the corner from Max's school. Two black granite plaques are being added to the memorial: inscribed are the names of two former Navy SEALs based in San Diego who were killed during the recent attack against the American consulate in Benghazi, Libya. A lone trumpeter blows 'The Last Post', and a Navy SEAL Captain invites the grieving family members and other attendees to reflect on the 'ultimate sacrifice' of the two soldiers. He assures the audience that the two heroes 'were the kind of men this country is proud to produce.' They 'ran to the sound of gunfire,' the captain says, when they 'knew that Americans were in need of assistance.' He adds that both men had no 'interest in living a common life,' and: 'We should all look to live like them.' Then four Navy fighter jets perform a fly-over at low altitude, creating a deafening roar over the mountain top.

During the ceremony, there is no mention of the partisan controversy in Washington where the Obama administration – Secretary of State Hillary Clinton, in particular – is being accused of not acting appropriately during the Libyan crisis and for trying to cover-up her alleged mismanagement afterwards. There is no mention also of the constitutional dispute regarding the appropriateness of the Christian Cross in state-sanctioned public events.

3. The block between Eads Avenue and Draper Avenue, adjacent to the La Jolla Tennis Club, is occupied by a US Postal Service carrier station. It has a huge parking lot where all the funny-looking, blue-and-white box-shaped delivery vans with their oversized rubber bumper bars and five large outside mirrors are parked overnight. In one corner of the lot, there is a little garden of succulents and cacti, an area of perhaps six square metres. It is a very neat and well-tended space, with some beautiful flowering plants. In the middle of it you will find a simple, oval-shaped plaque made of sandstone. It reads: 'In loving memory of Steve Mediano, his friends and fellow letter-carriers, July 2012.' I ask one of the posties who is just climbing into his delivery van about the memorial. He tells me that Steve was a good guy, friends with everybody. Last July Steve did not show up for work five days in a row and did not answer his telephone, so his colleagues finally called 911, and the police went to investigate. They found the door to Steve's home locked, and when they forced their way in they found him dead. He had lived alone and had died of a heart attack. He was 55 years of age, an American hero of everyday life. Steve Mediano had chosen a common life, or maybe it had chosen him.

TENNIS AT LJTC

Susan and I have started playing tennis with a group of regulars at the Tennis Club. They are four guys: Brian, Marv, Irv and Don, and four ladies: Val, Hettie, Karin and Ivonne. We met on the tennis court where they usually had the two adjoining courts next to us, and one day after play they walked over and asked whether we would like to join them to play doubles. They said they had been playing together for years, three times a week, but now it seemed they were frequently one or two persons short, and so, after watching us play quite regularly, they would be pleased if we would accept their invitation to join their group. Susan and I had noticed them as well, registering our surprise at the apparent age of our neighbours and commenting – to ourselves – about how 'the oldies' were playing, i.e. somewhat slowly.

Susan and I look at each other – yeah, hmm, well, why not? We would be delighted, I say. We shake hands all round and introductions are made.

Soon, a tennis routine has set in. Since Susan discovered there is free yoga on Mondays and Fridays at the recreation centre, she will play tennis only once a week. We agree to play mixed doubles on Wednesdays on two courts. On Mondays and Fridays, it's boys' play. We usually change partners after every match. After warm-up, we play two times two sets in two hours, from nine to eleven.

The remarkable thing about our tennis partners is their age.

They are:

Brian, aged 67, the youngest. He has retired after working as an administrator of an apartment complex for many years. He likes classical music, volunteers at the La Jolla Library, and drives a Toyota Prius (the earliest version of the first hybrid on the market). Brian is very quick around the court, he runs down just about every ball, plays conservatively, good to have him on your side of the net.

Don, aged 77, a retired high school sports coach. He is a competitive tennis player, grunts and swears (mildly) and gets upset with himself for missing a shot. He openly expresses his preference to be paired with Brian. Winning is everything, as they say. He is watching a lot of pro-sports on TV, and he seems disappointed when I tell him I don't follow the NFL. Don is a native of Southern California; he now lives in Arizona but still spends much of his time in La Jolla.

Marvin, aged 94; he is a child of the Great Depression, as he says. He served in the US army for nearly 40 years, survived combat duty in Korea, then became a heavy weapons specialist and instructor, travelled the world on various missions as military adviser and retired as lieutenant-colonel ('could have become a general, if I had served another year'). After the army, he ran the tennis pro shop at the US Open in New York for 20 years or so; he knows all the tennis greats and has the anecdotes to prove it. Marv is quite amazing on the tennis court. He's got a keen return of serve, seldom misses a volley, and he knows all the shots. He is no longer very mobile around the court, but when a ball comes into his reach, he usually hits it back, and not infrequently for a winner.

And then there is Irv, aged 97. Irv played with us a few times at the beginning, then he was away at hospital, and now he is back, on and off, after a hip replacement. He has recovered remarkably. Irv manages all the pairings and court bookings for the group. It is quite a sight to observe him play tennis at his age. True, there is not much of a spring in his step when he shuffles to the base line, and he cannot lift his head easily so he prefers to play with the sun in his back and not to change sides. But he doesn't give up, and if he returns a ball it's rarely wide or long or in the net.

Marv and Irv used to play competitive tennis for many years. As a double's team, they regularly competed in the US Amateur Championships and apparently did quite well in the seniors' division, taking home their share of trophies and titles. Even today, they are still pretty good players.

Tennis is important to all the oldies, but especially to Marv who is always the first on the court, parking his little

Mercedes SLK roadster right outside the gate. During change-over breaks, he sips from a bottle of Gatorade and recalls stories about the Korean war or about his meetings with champions like Ken Rosewall, the 'true gentleman' tennis player from Australia. He had breakfast with Rosewall once at a hotel during a tournament in Mexico City, and he recalls how Rosewall appeared with a freshly ironed white shirt and tie and sharply creased slacks, while the other players all walked in wearing their practice outfits and sneakers. By comparison with a gentleman player like Rosewall, says Marv, the American tennis players like Connors or McEnroe are all 'bums'. Marv is no fan of Andre Agassi either. He holds him responsible for introducing the embarrassing habit of blowing kisses to the crowd.

It's not easy to play with guys that old. Their speed and movement are obviously somewhat restricted, and you feel it's not quite proper to hit sure winners that they can never reach. On the other hand, you don't want to make it too easy for them (for one thing, they don't give you a second chance either), so you sort of try to hit the ball not too hard or not too far into a corner, somewhere near where they stand, and then you get the surprise of your life when they hit a winner back at you without mercy.

SURVIVAL STORIES

Marv is Jewish. His (second) wife hid in the basement of a farm in Poland for four years during WWII, and that's how she survived the Holocaust. She passed away a year ago, and Marv tells us he is still finding wads of money stacked away by her in all sorts of places. The last surprise find was $1,300 stuffed into a pair of gloves. It's hard to live by yourself, Marv says. He shops in the army PX and works as a volunteer in the army cemetery at the Miramar base.

He has five children and 10 grandchildren. They live all over the country, none in La Jolla.

Marv regularly rails against the federal government, saying that they have been ruining the country for the last five years. But later, during the government shutdown, he proudly announces that he got an email from Washington telling him not to worry: his pension is being paid, on time as usual.

MIXED DOUBLES

On Wednesdays, it's mixed doubles at LJTC, usually Susan and myself versus Brian and Karen, and Marv and Val against Hettie and Don (or Irv), or any such combination. Yvonne only shows up a couple of times. We play two sets, after which the winner plays the winner and the loser plays the loser. It's all very friendly and competitive at the same time.

Naturally, we are too polite to ask how old the ladies are. Val is the youngest, probably in her early 60s, and she is a very strong player, quick around the court and a hard hitter. She lives with her husband in a house at La Jolla Farms, a fancy neighbourhood overlooking the ocean on the way to Torrey Pines. They have their own tennis court, next to the pool, where we sometimes play when the courts at the club are used for league matches. Val used to be a nurse, but then she had a second career, making her hobby (collecting Persian carpets) into a business. She now repairs carpets and is an expert consultant for antique rugs. Marv tells me that she is married to a famous scientist who had a stroke a few years ago and is now house-bound in a wheelchair, with Val looking after him. She is a passionate gardener, too, and she grows all sorts of fruit and vegetables that she proudly shows off to me on an inspection tour. Next to her orchard is a row of solar panels, set on the ground at an angle to catch the sunrays that heat the water of the pool, among other things.

Then there's Hettie, from Holland originally, also a strong player with powerful strokes from the baseline. I suspect she is a few years older than Val, but I cannot really be sure. Why did I not ask, silly me? Karen, on the other hand, is clearly the senior of the group. She tells me she was born in Berlin, of Jewish background, and remembers growing up in an affluent family in a *villa* in Dahlem, and she remembers meeting some eminent persons from circles in the arts and the university, until she emigrated with her family in 1938, just in time before the Nazis made it impossible for Jews to leave the country. She must have been born around 1930, which makes her 80 years or more today. Like Marv and Irv, she is a wonderful tennis player for her age, and she never quits. Karen prefers speaking German to me. She is planning a visit to Berlin in the summer of next year, and she is excited to hear that we are planning to be there. I give her our address in Wilmersdorf, around the corner from Dahlem as it were, and she promises to call on us.

THE GOOD CLEAN-UP NEWS: END OF 'POOP DAY'

San Diego Mayor Bob Filner came almost good on a promise to have the rocks area of La Jolla Cove, just north of the Children's Pool, cleaned up by Memorial Day. The cliffs are inhabited by hundreds of birds, cormorants and pelicans, and by seals. Unlike the smallish harbour seals that call the Children's Pool beach their home, the pinnipeds here are the much larger California Sea Lions.

To say that the cliff stinks would be an understatement. The mayor had promised to find a solution to remove the smelly guano and feces deposited by the animals, and on 28 May, a day after the deadline he had set for himself, the company finally selected to do the high-tech job, Blue

Mixed Doubles at LJTC: Brian, Karen, Hettie, author, Marv, Irv, Val (from left; Susan behind camera)

Eagle, began working on the site, applying naturally occurring bioactive agents, including non-pathogenic bacteria, that literally eat up and digest the animal waste that has been accumulating since the last clean-up over a year ago. This is the theory, anyway; the proof of the pudding is in the eating, as the saying goes, and whether the bacteria will really and effectively consume the waste remains to be seen. The mayor has not ruled out a secondary campaign to use industrial-strength vacuum cleaners, if Blue Eagle fails to deliver. He had famously proclaimed, on a previous occasion, that if no other solution could be found, he would hoover the rocks himself.

Cleaning the cliffs is indeed not an easy matter, given the ecological sensitivity of the area. A complex set of regulations to protect the marine environment and bird rookeries had created a veritable bureaucratic stalemate that up to now had prevented any concerted clean-up action. The Mayor finally decided to cut through the red tape by issuing an 'emergency finding', declaring that the evil smell had become a public health hazard.

Residents and local business owners have long been complaining about the stench hanging over the rocks. Supposedly, it was driving visitors and potential customers away in droves. But even now that a serious attempt at clean-up has begun, not everybody is happy. One new complainant has protested that the work should have been postponed, since the spring nesting season is currently in full swing and the cormorants have chicks in their nests.

We can attest to the powerful stench emanating from the Cove. I always ask Max and Susan, on our way back from golfing at Torrey Pines, whether we should make a little detour to have a look at the cormorants, the pelicans and seals, and the indignant answer is always a prompt: 'No! It stinks!'

On a related matter close-by: it seems that the harbour seals on the beach at the Children's Pool have finally won. The Friends of the Children's Pool citizens action group have all but conceded that they will not be able to reclaim the beach for what it was originally intended, a safe swimming area for children protected by the man-made breakwater wall. The rope barrier along the beach will remain in place indefinitely, to separate human from beast, meaning that the pinnipeds are here to stay. Their number has been constantly increasing; at present, they have taken over the beach completely.

TUESDAY, 4 June

BLUEGRASS MUSIC

Tonight, there is a lecture/concert at the Athenaeum; the topic is bluegrass music. It is the third in a series by a group called 'The Virtual Strangers', but we missed the first two. The lecture part consists mainly of name-dropping anecdotes and video clips by some early bluegrass artists whose names are mostly unfamiliar. The most interesting part is the information about the local bluegrass scene, which apparently is alive and well and thriving. There is an annual summer bluegrass festival in north San Diego County. The venue, at Vista, is very appropriately the Antique Gas & Steam Engine Museum. It features live performances by nationally known artists and bands as well as by international guests. Some of the overseas performers, from countries like Japan and Slovenia, apparently don't speak any English, but they sing in perfect Bluegrass American. There's also music workshops, hands-on instructions for the kids, raffles, the lot. Unfortunately, it's in August, and we won't be around.

The second part of the evening is a concert by the four-piece band, which brings back a lot of my own name-popping memories of the music I listened to and the eclectic collection of LP records I bought years ago: Doc Watson, Mississippi John Hurt, Pete Seeger (he with the fretless banjo), Taj Mahal, Lester Flatt and Earl Scruggs, and of course Bob Dylan and John Lee Hooker and Muddy Waters. And not to forget Leo Kottke who sat in for a while in my class when I was teaching at St. Cloud State University, Minnesota, and who performed in a little coffee club on campus.

During the intermission, I chat with the Virtual Strangers. I ask them about the origin and meaning of the term 'breakdown' in bluegrass music, as in 'Foggy Mountain

Breakdown', something I wonder about every time I hear one of these fast-paced banjo-and-fiddle tracks, but they don't have an explanation: 'It's just a fast instrumental.' The guy who plays the mandolin has a beautiful instrument, and it turns out he made it all by himself. The concert ends a little bit like in school, with the lyrics of a song passed around on a handout and the audience asked to join in. The *finale* is that old chestnut, 'Will the circle be unbroken' (of which my favourite version is the one by Jerry Lee Lewis that I used to listen to on CD – *Best of JLL* – while driving my Toyota in Sydney, Australia).

Coincidentally – and this is surely one of those moments that could give any person an attack of vertigo – the very next morning my sister Doris, from Berlin, writes in an email about a Belgian film she just saw and was greatly impressed by. It is called *Broken Circle Breakdown* and has an American country music soundtrack. It is the story of a young couple, she the owner of a tattoo parlour who falls in love with a singer in a Belgian bluegrass band and becomes a bluegrass performer herself, both in search of the freedom that apparently can only be found in American country music. The film has won a swag of awards in Europe, including the Berlin Film Festival, but is not likely to be widely shown in this country (there is sex, full-frontal nudity, and the dialogue is in Flemish).

HOW TO DISPOSE OF YOUR AMERICAN FLAG, PROPERLY

In a letter to 'Dear Abby' in the *U-T*, an incensed garbage collector and 'patriot named Daniel' complains about the insensitivity of his American compatriots who unthinkingly throw out their old and tattered Stars and Stripes with the week's rubbish. 'Don't these people know,' asks Daniel, 'what our flag means, and how many men and women have given their lives for what it stands for?' The garbos wonder, rightly so I suppose, 'what kind of a person would do such a thing?'

Abby – ever the gracious observer of human folly and frailty – thinks it's probably a matter of ignorance rather than intentional and provocative disrespect, but she concedes the letter is timely given that the Fourth of July is just around the corner. Thus, the pre-eminent albeit near-anonymous commentator on the nation's social mores provides readers with a succinct primer regarding proper flag disposal. According to the U.S. Flag Code, says Abby, flags that have become unusable should be destroyed, 'preferably by burning'. This, of course, should be done discreetly, so as not to arouse the suspicion of neighbours who might suspect that something subversive is going on, an act of 'protest or desecration', as the American Legion's pamphlet *Flag Etiquette* puts it. An alternative to a secretive private cremation of your old flag in your backyard is the public 'Disposal of Unserviceable Flag Ceremony', presumably a bonfire, conducted by your local American Legion post every year on 14 June, which is National Flag Day. The Boy and Girl Scouts of America also conduct these ceremonies. Just hand in your unwanted old Stars and Stripes to the boys or girls when they come around during their annual cookie sale, and they will take care of it for you.

In case you wonder what patriot Daniel does whenever he and his fellow garbos discover an American flag in an American trash can: why, of course, they would respectfully pull it out of the rubbish and dispose of it properly.

Johnny Cash, the late great country singer and good friend of several presidents (from Nixon to Clinton), once observed that he thought 'one of our freedoms' included burning the flag as a public protest. But then again, in one of his songs, Cash was 'mighty proud of that ragged old flag.'

MORE MEMORIAL CULTURE

Driving back from Max's Grand Del Mar's golf fitness session, Freeway 805 is choc-a-block full of cars, it's the rush hour in the afternoon, and I hate the idea of moving forward at a snails's pace on an *Autobahn* that seems purpose-built for cruising along at a relaxed 90mph (like in Germany on the A5 Frankfurt-Basel, in the good old days). We get off 805 at the first ramp, hoping to find the coastal highway somehow by driving west towards the setting sun, but instead we get lost in an industrial area called Carroll Canyon.

This is where the San Diego Animal Memorial Park is located, an unexpected discovery of an oak-studded pet cemetery surrounded by companies with names like Turbine Components, Truck Covers USA or Rhino Linings Corporation. The pet memorial is a full-service cemetery and cremation centre. It offers a free pick-up (conditions apply: fee charged after hours) and a burial service on supposedly beautiful landscaped grounds with an on-site chapel for viewing your deceased pet, 'carefully groomed' and placed in a cedar box for the memorable occasion. It also provides a variety of cremation and 'inurnment' services. If desired, the pet's pet, e.g. a favourite toy companion or chewable cow-hide bone or whatever took the animal's fancy while alive, can be buried or cremated alongside its dead owner.

The Pet Memorial company sponsors a free grief support group, the 'Hug Club'; it meets every Saturday between 1.30pm and 2.30pm. A 'Bereavement Package' is also available, at additional cost and individually tailored to a client's emotional needs. It includes therapy classes, Tibetan sound healing, author events, and, for the spiritually inclined, a pet psychic and medium.

The Limpus family, Bob and Dory Limpus, who founded the park as a 'living memorial to all companion animals', were instrumental in setting up the National Pet Remembrance Day, first observed on 11 June 1971, the anniversary of the day the park was inaugurated in 1962. I am not entirely sure why a pet cemetery would qualify as a 'living memorial', but so it goes.

It occurs to me that perhaps the management of the Pet Memorial Park could extend their services to provide flag cremation and flag burial ceremonies as well. After all, it's all about proper disposal, isn't it? Your favourite hamster that has reached its use-by date or your beloved old flag that has become a terminal weather victim – don't both reserve respect? The boy and girl scouts provide a free service, to be sure, but why shouldn't good old American Free Enterprise have a role here to play as well? I am quite convinced that, with all their experience, the caring people of Pet Park would do an excellent job of laying your flag to rest in a dignified manner.

FRIDAY, 7 June

Today is National Donut Day.

Max has to do a 'demonstration speech' in class. The topic of his choice is 'how to make apple chips', an outcome of our trip to Julian, the Apple Pie Capital of the USA. Yesterday, after nine holes of golf at Torrey Pines, Max and I spent the afternoon baking the chips, and I helped him make a poster (a visual aid is required for the demonstration), then rehearse his speech. He should be all right, if he can for a couple of minutes forget about jumping and fidgeting around.

At 11am I get a call from the school: Max has a stomach ache, he is in pain and crying, can I come pick him up? When I get there five minutes later, there is no sign of tears, he tells me that he feels already a 'little bit' better, and by the time we get home, the pain is gone and forgotten. I buy him a slice of pizza for lunch, and then we discuss what to do next. It turns out he is happy to go back to school and give his speech.

When I pick him up after school he reports that he did well, everyone liked the chips, and Miss Higgins wants the recipe.

NEWS FROM THE PRINCIPAL, ALL HALLOWS ACADEMY

The Principal of All Hallows sends an email: 'Today is a day for celebration!' The school just underwent a routine accreditation check and was cleared for a six-year period until July 2019. The principal wishes everybody a great summer and does not forget to exhort parents to make sure their children continue 'doing educational things' during the holidays, like reading or practicing maths: 'It is most beneficial to the students if they have a continuation of learning during the summer.' The principal also informs parents that the school has been nominated for a 'Best of La Jolla' award, run by the *La Jolla Light* free local newspaper, and she exhorts all parents to vote in the on-line voting competition. To enter a valid vote, you must click for a candidate in at least 75 percent of the dozens of categories on offer. You cannot simply vote in the one category you are interested in! Just about all and sundry business activities in La Jolla are covered, from every imaginable restaurant category to dentists, real estate agents, bank, formal wear, dry cleaner, florist, art gallery, senior living, financial planner, fitness clubs, credit union, cosmetic surgeon, in-home carer, pilates studio, and Best Happy Hour Location – to mention only a few. So, I dutifully click one box after another to enter a valid vote in the 'Best Private School' category. Good luck to All Hallows, and thumbs up! It's almost the end of the school year.

We are going on a *Summer Holiday*, as Cliff Richard used to sing. Our destination will be a wintery Sydney. But first

Max will be competing in the Callaway Junior World Championship.

SATURDAY, 8 June

Today, the odometer of my trusted, murky-green-coloured Mercury Grand Marquis '97 reads 107,389 miles; if we add the 1,400 miles or so that we drove in the rental Mitsubishi before buying the Mercury, we've covered some 5,500 miles since we landed at LAX exactly 120 days ago: an average of approximately 45 miles a day.

It feels like we have been living here, at Pacific Beach initially and now at La Jolla, much longer than that. We feel quite at ease. A routine has set in. Life is predictably good. Most importantly, Max is happy in his school. He still is quite keen to play golf.

WEDNESDAY, 12 June

Today is the last day of the school year. The summer holidays begin at noon with a pool and jacuzzi party at the house of two of Max's school mates, twins Bobby and Mary. The hosts have hired a lifeguard for the occasion. There is plenty of pizza for the kids, and the *Veuve Cliquot* is bubbling freely.

Yesterday evening, while brushing his teeth, the first of Max's milk teeth had fallen out. There was a bit of blood and a bit of crying, but the promise of a visit by the tooth fairy soon convinced him to go to bed and sleep, in anticipation of the five-dollar bill that we said he might find under his pillow the next morning, and he did. I'm surprised to hear him say he does not believe in the tooth fairy. Still, he holds on to the bill the whole day and puts it under his pillow again for the night.

The next morning, we have an appointment at 8.30am for Max at the La Jolla Family Dentistry, which is downstairs, right below our flat. The dentist, Dr Su (abbreviated from her overly long and complicated Tamil name), is from Sri Lanka originally. She trained in Canada. We are a little concerned about Max's teeth, because there are two prominent incisors coming out behind the one he just lost, the space there is fairly crowded, and the one remaining front tooth should be a bit wobbly by now, but is solid as a rock. Dr Su suggests that the tooth should be extracted. She takes some x-rays, administers a local anesthetic and takes out the tooth while Max plays 'brave little boy'. We have no insurance, so we pay by cheque: $50 for general examination and x-rays, $100 for the extraction. In two weeks Dr Su will see Max again for a check-up: no charge.

Before she goes to work on Max, the dentist makes me sign all sorts of waivers and disclaimers. I agree that I understand everything that is happening here today, and that the procedure may not be successful.

I mention that I hope Max will not have the same crooked teeth that I have, and I show her my pearly whites. She has a look and says, yes, she hopes so too.

DEATH AND BURIAL OF AN INDIAN MATRIARCH

Ida Brown, a revered elder of the Kumeyaay Nation of American Indians in Southern California, died on 11 June after complications from a stroke. She was 90 years old. The Kumeyaay Indians are the original inhabitants of San Diego. They were the Native Californians who greeted Juan Cabrillo when he sailed into San Diego Bay on 28 September 1542.

Ida Brown experienced three distinct life cycles in her time. She was born in 1923 to a semi-nomadic existence in what is today Mission Valley, a densely populated area of criss-crossing freeways, motels and shopping and office malls. In the 1920s the area was still undeveloped land, with grass three feet high, deer and wild pigs running freely. The Kumeyaays practised hunting and gathering as well farming, animal husbandry and fishing. In the 1930s, the government forcibly relocated the tribe to make way for the El Capitan Reservoir. The Indians' traditional habitable land was submerged, and a new reservation was found near Alpine, along both sides of the old US Highway 8. The tribe fell on hard times, having to struggle in the new, harsh environment of the highland winters. Eventually, the tribe members pooled their savings to buy the land from the government to create what is today known as the Viejas reservation. Ida was one of the founding members. The reservation takes its name after the Spanish name of their land, 'El Valle de Las Viejas' ('Valley of the Old Women'). Today, it is a sovereign tribe governed by an elected tribal council.

During WWII, Ida Brown worked as a riveter. In 1951, she met and married her husband, a fire fighter. They had two sons and a daughter and eventually more than 20 grandchildren and great-grandchildren. The couple always lived on the reservation, but unlike some people of the tribe, they always worked (Ida mostly as a home aide nurse) and led a modestly comfortable life. This did not change when the tribe became rich after a change in US policy: from forced assimilation to tribal economic independence. Gambling, or gaming as it is euphemistically called in North America, was the salvation. It was introduced in the early 1980s, starting with family-friendly bingo sessions. In a series of court cases, the tribe fought the State of California to win the right to conduct full-fledged gaming facilities, resulting in what is today a Las Vegas-style palace, the hugely popular and immensely profitable Viejas Casino and Resort just off the Kumeyaay Highway, some 30 miles east of downtown San Diego. The Viejas Outlet Centre, a mall with 57 shops, is nearby. The tribe owns a number of other businesses as well, including a bank.

Ida Brown always tried to instill in her children and grand-children a sense of their cultural identity, driving them to weekend pow-wows and traditional ceremonies. One of the important Kumeyaay traditions is the burning of personal belongings after the death of a tribal member. The Kumeyaays believe that a dead person's spirit will stay on earth for a year, and sending material belongings to the sky as smoke will make the afterlife more welcoming for the spirit. The purpose of the ceremony is also to prevent disputes about inheritances and helping the family to say goodbye to their loved-ones. It is a practice that has been around for some 10,000 years, as long as the tribe has been living in Southern California.

Thus, following Ida's burial, a deep pit was dug near the house of her daughter. Family and friends gathered, singers and dancers performed, and a fire was lit. First into the flames went Ida Brown's green sofa where she used to sit and watch TV (the Court Channel), then her tupperware and other cooking utensils, her motorised wheelchair, her books and jewelry, her bed and her refrigerator where she kept the pork chops that she loved to fry. Finally, her clothes went up in flames, including her favourite outfit: pink blouse, black pants and soft grandma shoes. Pink was her preferred colour, and dancing at tribal ceremonies her life-long passion.

Las Viejas Arena is the name of the sports stadium of San Diego State University. The Kumeyaay Indians are paying the university $6 million dollars annually for naming rights. I think it should be the other way around.

JUNE GLOOM

'Seems it never rains in Southern California?'

Well, not very often, but we have been experiencing an unfamiliar weather pattern for a few weeks now. In the morning, you wake up to low grey clouds hanging over the ocean, it's rather cold, and it looks as if it's going to rain, though it never does, but there is moisture and fog in the air. It's June and it's supposed to be summer and getting warmer, but it isn't. Then, if you drive up the hill to Max's school on top of Mount Soledad at 8am, you have brilliant sunshine and it's easily 10 to 15 degrees warmer. If you drive further inland, it's getting hotter and hotter still, until you reach the extreme summer temperatures of the desert only a few miles to the east. There is a heat wave going on at present, with temperatures reaching 120 degrees in the Borrego-Anza desert, only a few miles east of Julian, but it remains pleasantly mild on the coast at La Jolla.

We are told that this is the 'June Gloom' of Southern California, the typical weather for this time of the year. It's the result of a coastal inversion, clouds of cold air rising from the ocean and pushing towards the bluffs of the shore by the prevailing westerly winds. In the LA Basin, this weather pattern is partially responsible for the notorious smog that covers the metropolitan area. In La Jolla, the shallow cover of marine stratus clouds is usually broken up by the sun around noon, and the rest of the day is mild to warm. This is the time of the year when the rents in La Jolla shoot up sky-high with the influx of tourists and the well-to-do residents of the desert states of neighbouring Arizona, Nevada and New Mexico who are seeking relief from the searing heat that relentlessly burns down on the gated enclaves of their own shadowless communities.

GRADUATION MONTH

In California and everywhere else in the USA, June is graduation month. Students are saying goodbye to their professors and their mates. University presidents and deans thank their wards for their perseverance and their brilliance, and congratulate themselves for having successfully graduated yet another generation of young Americans, releasing them into a future of their own (or their parents') choosing after the kids spent four years or more doing time within the walls of state-sanctioned education, be it public or private.

Graduation ceremonies, with all the trimmings of academic gowns, processions and valedictory speeches, are being conducted across the country in both middle schools and high schools as well, so that by the time students get to college, they have already graduated twice. We somehow manage to miss the event at Max's All Hallows Academy, proof of how unfamiliar we still are with the system.

On Friday, 1 June, the *U-T* runs a full page of excerpts of graduation speeches from different schools around San Diego County. The astonishing thing is that these are previews, available along with the names of the speakers and their respective schools before the orations are actually delivered. Does that mean that graduation speeches must be submitted to the school authorities before the event? Seemingly yes. Some schools even hold auditions to pick their valedictorian, as at Carlsbad High where students must present their speech in front of a selection panel made up of the principal, a counselor and two English teachers. I wonder whether Amanda Mickelson, daughter of local golfing legend Phil, who was honoured to give the graduation speech at her Carlsbad Middle School, had to undergo the same procedure?

Am I the only one who thinks this is weird? Are we not in the land of free speech? What does it mean if school principals need to authorise their students' thoughts? Is this censorship? Are the school authorities afraid that something subversive or critical might be voiced? Perhaps even a bit of light satire on such a serious, momentous occasion? And can they not trust their disciples after years of schooling to deliver something that is mature, independent and perhaps even original?

Reading through the excerpts in the newspaper I find very little of the above. There are the usual clichés about hard work, learning for life, great teachers, making a difference, bringing out the best in everybody, dreaming big, working hard. There are authoritative quotes by the usual suspects (dead white males, of course), from the Dalai Lama (ok, well, he's still alive) to the 'late, great football coach'. Aristotle is cited twice in the 12 excerpts (must be near the top of some Google list).

But these are excerpts of speeches. Perhaps the more interesting, quirky, unconventional bits did not strike the editors at *U-T* as print worthy. And a live speech is something else altogether different. People are known to have experimented with their approved scripts, all in the name of the First Amendment, of course.

As did a high school student in Texas, who reportedly had his microphone turned off the moment he deviated from the script of his speech (that had been previously authorised by the school principal). The weirdest thing about this incident is that the speaker did not plan to say anything critical about politics (neither at the school, local, state, federal or global level), but rather he wanted to insert a word of 'Thank you' to Jesus and the Almighty Lord for having helped him through high school. Would that have violated the neutrality clause of the US Constitution?

The incident raised the ire of Texas Senator (R.) and devout Christian Ted Cruz who publicly warned the school principal to 'back off' and respect the student's right to free speech. Cruz, who has ties to the Tea Party movement, came to national attention recently when he was proclaimed 'Stooge of the Night' on David Letterman's *Late Show* for having voted 'No' on gun control reform, after having received $16,000 from a gun lobby organization, and despite 85% of voters in the state of Texas being in favour of some form of gun control legislation, including background checks of prospective buyers of certain types of firearms. Letterman had a photo of the immaculately coiffeured senator shown on the full screen for what seemed a whole minute at least, and then suggested that Cruz' barber should be subjected to a background check.

THURSDAY–TUESDAY, 20–25 June

FAMOUS HOUSES IN CALIFORNIA

Max has been invited to compete at yet another tournament, the California State Junior Championship at Livermore, in the Bay Area east of San Francisco. Since it's some 450 miles north of San Diego, we decide to make a holiday out of it. Along the way, we will be visiting some of California's top tourist sites: Hearst Castle, Pebble Beach Lodge, San Juan Bautista Mission, Winchester Mystery House. We leave Thursday afternoon and stay overnight at Torrance. Brianna is excited as ever that Max has come to visit her.

The next day we drive up north on the old Highway 101. We stop at San Simeon on Morro Bay and take the guided tour of the Hearst ranch and castle. I've been here before, and it is mostly as I remember it, except the super-efficient new visitors' centre *cum* souvenir shop *cum* restaurant/café where you can eat steaks and hamburgers made from beef raised on the ranch, butchered and barbecued on the premises. The *casa grande* built by the original media mogul is still the perfect showcase of America's imperial emergence as the world's superpower after WWI, when a spoiled American kid with his mother could travel through war-ravaged Europe and buy up all the antiques and artworks they could lay their hands on, and have them shipped across the Atlantic to the other side of the continent to be assembled, somewhat incongruously, in a phallic pile that looks like a Franco-Italian renaissance mansion with design references to the architecture of Moorish Spain. It is perhaps the prototypical pre-postmodern building, created fittingly by the inventor of yellow journalism and the celebrity magazine. What is more, the fake European façade cleverly hides its original core: the house is constructed out of state-of-the-art, earthquake-proof, steel-reinforced American concrete. It is an impressive achievement, to be sure, and the two pools are jaw-droppingly stunning, simply beautiful. The unbelievably blue indoor Roman pool is my own personal favourite.

There are a few things I don't remember from my previous visit, for example the style of William Randolph Hearst's social events, described as 'California casual' by the guide. The blue willow-patterned china in the formal dining room, laid out on what must be the world's longest refectory table, looks like it's straight out of Costco; there are silver napkin holders with paper napkins; there is plenty of cutlery but no fish knives. Did they only eat beef? I had forgotten about the private cinema theatre, too, and the five-minute black-and-white home movie shown to visitors: there are shots of Hollywood producer and host W.R. Hearst wandering around the place in cowboy gear, visiting celebrities like Mary Pickford and Douglas Fairbanks Jr., Charlie Chaplin playing tennis and fooling around in front of the camera, and the corrupt mayor of New York (name forgotten) who had to leave office in a hurry and in disgrace shortly after his visit to California.

From San Simeon, we join Highway 1 towards Big Sur, hugging the coastline, up and down, twisting and turning, spectacular vistas over the Pacific, one of the world's great ocean roads. This is the fifth time I have driven this road, and it is as exhilarating as the first time. As the sun goes down we reach Monterey where we stop for two nights, exploring the area where I used to live and work for two years in the early 1970s, trying to retrace my steps: from what was then the Monterey Institute of International Studies (and is now the Graduate School of Middlebury College) on the corner of Franklin and van Buren streets down to Fisherman's Wharf, along Cannery Row and the coastal drive to Pacific Grove, and finally Carmel Village via the 17 Mile Drive. I remember our weekly excursion to Salinas to buy ice cream at a Baskin-Robbins (until we discovered, much later, that there was another B-R outlet a few miles up the road, in a little mall off the road towards Carmel Highlands).

I try to remember what it was like forty years ago: long lunches over the water at Fisherman's Wharf, watching the otters at play and chatting over the roar of the sea lions, walking over the flowering ice plants along the seafront to Pacific Grove in spring, our rented house on 17 Mile Drive (rent paid by the college) where the raccoons came to visit in the evening to try to knock over the rubbish bins, and the deer who came early in the morning to eat the flowers in our front yard. Quite a few things have changed. The little inexpensive restaurants on Fisherman's Wharf have gone (today it is choc-a-block full of tacky tourist shops and upmarket eateries), the hippie cinema on Cannery Row (where you could lie on old sofas and bean bags to watch a movie while smoking a joint) is no more, but Carmel Village is quaint as ever, the coastline even more beautiful than I remember, and the seals and otters are still playing in the water, a few metres off the beach at Spanish Bay. I remember the drive around the Pacific Grove peninsula on Sunset Drive and along the Pacific Grove Links golf course with its fantastic views over the ocean. This is a visit to a previous life.

Since Dragon Mom and Little Dragon Maximilian are now serious golfers, we pay our respect to Pebble Beach, watching some Asian players trying to find the 18th hole that is laid out in front of the Lodge. We have a drink on the veranda, and I suggest to Susan that it is every golfer's dream to sit here. But she is not overly impressed. Nothing special about the building and the facilities, she reasons, and it's way too expensive. She has never heard of Bing Crosby – how could she have? – but to spend this much money just for the history? To play the links at Pebble Beach today, a visiting golfer needs to pay a green fee of $495. The cart fee is $40 and a (compulsory) caddy will cost you another $150 (including tip). From the spectators' area, you have a fantastic view over the course and the beach, taking in Carmel and the highlands beyond across the bay to Point Lobos. The views are free.

On the way to Livermore on Sunday we stop at San Juan Bautista. Memories of previous visits are flooding back. Nothing much seems to have changed. I vividly remember exploring the historic mission site, trying to identify the locations that Hitchcock used in *Vertigo*, and my first encounter with the Chicano farm workers' theatre, *El Teatro Campesino*, that forever shaped my ideas about what popular theatre should be all about. Today the Mission Church is holding a fund-raising garden party. The place is packed with visitors, the car park overflowing with pick-up trucks. We walk around the stalls, eat a freshly-made pulled pork sandwich while listening to a Mariachi band, and Max has a go at target shooting. I tell Susan and Max the story of *Vertigo*, and the film that was made around here. Max wants to know more about the shot from the top of the bell tower where Kim Novak's Madeleine falls to her death. (Or does she?)

At San José we pass a sign to the Winchester Mystery House that Todd Smith who grew up not far from here at Palo Alto had told us about. It is too late to visit, so we decide to come back later.

Stopping at the Lonely Pine on 17 Mile Drive: Hitchcock was here

LLL

Livermore is the home of the famous Lawrence Livermore Laboratory, where many of the scientists who worked on the WWII Manhattan Project – that produced the first nuclear bombs detonated at Hiroshima and Nagasaki in August 1945 –

went to work after the war, including Edward ('Dr Strangelove') Teller, its second director and long-time associate director. During the decades of the Cold War, the super-secret facility developed much of the United States' formidable nuclear arsenal, beginning in the early 1960s with a thermonuclear warhead for missiles that could be launched from submarines, to the multiple warheads carried on ICBMs in the 1980s. Today, it is commissioned to develop programs to safeguard America's nuclear stockpile that, in its heyday, could have been used to destroy the whole planet a few times over.

The good citizens of Livermore are justifiably proud of the work that has been and is being done in the sprawling lab just outside the town's gates. In a promotional tourist brochure extolling the beauties and civic virtues of Livermore, the discovery of a new element called *Livermorium* (No. 116 on the Periodic Table) is mentioned and credited to the Lawrence Lab (even though it was discovered by scientists in Dubna, Russia, who named it in honour of their Californian colleagues with whom they were competing in the nuclear arms race). Amazingly, the brochure has nothing to say about the ground-breaking work involved in designing and testing the atomic bombs that kept the world safe, if on the brink of an apocalyptic exchange of intercontinental missiles, while the Cold War between the two superpowers was simmering along until finally, slowly, after half a century of an ideological stand-off, the Soviet Union imploded upon itself.

On the other side of town is another nuclear facility, the Vallecitos Nuclear Centre owned by General Electric Hitachi. We stop there to ask for directions, and the security guard tells us that on this site was the world's first privately owned and operated nuclear power station. It was online from 1958 to 1963, producing a moderate amount of electricity that was fed into the local grid. Since its de-commissioning half a century ago, work has been going on to clean up the site.

SONGS

Which begs the questions that the residents of San Diego are currently asking themselves: how long will it take to dismantle *SONGS*, the San Onofre Nuclear Generating Station, in the northwest corner of San Diego County, right on the beach next to a popular swimming and surfing spot, San Onofre State Beach? How much will it cost? And who will pay for the de-contamination of the complex?

The nuclear power station, which had been providing electricity for almost three decades to some 1.5 million homes in Southern California, was closed permanently on 7 June. Previously, two of its reactors were shut down (in January 2012), due to radioactive leaks emanating from faulty tubes and pipes in steam generators after a major overhaul that was supposed to fix previous ongoing problems. There had been numerous citations for safety breaches over the years.

No one knows how long the de-commissioning, demolition, de-contamination and removal of the defunct plant will take. The planning stage alone, to prepare a detailed blueprint and timeline for the restoration of the once pristine coastal strip, could last several years. In other words, the residents of Northern San Diego County are likely to have a radioactive ruin on their doorstep for maybe a decade before even a single brick will be removed.

And who is going to pay for it all? Again, nobody really knows. The city of Riverside owns 1.9% of SONGS, San Diego Gas & Electric 20%, and Southern California Edison the rest. Edison announced that it has set aside $2.7 billion for decommissioning, which it claims is about 90% of the estimated cost. Everyone suspects, of course, that the final bill will be much higher, and that the customers will end up having to pay.

We have passed the plant many times now on our regular trips to and from LA, and it was always a somewhat ominous,

Destined for the Scrapheap: Passing SONGS on the I-5

unsettling encounter. Paradoxically, it was also a welcome milestone for us on the I-5. On the way north, passing below the high-voltage power lines strung across the freeway, the reactors signaled the end of the San Diego region and its dense traffic, with a pleasant stretch of less hectic freeway driving ahead of us. On the southbound journey, the egg-shaped twin domes of the cooling towers were a similarly welcome sight, telling us we were almost there, almost home, only a few more miles to go. Before we understood that the whole thing was destined for the scrapheap, the towering structures always seemed to exude an air of reliable solidity.

SUNDAY, 23 June

We arrive in Livermore in the afternoon and drive straight to Las Positas Golf Course so Max can play a practice round. Las Positas is one of the many beautiful golf courses in the plains of the Californian central valley, surrounded by vineyards with the distant mountains on the horizon. We meet a couple who have come all the way from India; they caddy their two sons. Beesh is the same age as Max, and the two get on very well together from the start, in a friendly competitive way. Max is soon on fire, shooting one eagle, a few birdies, half a dozen pars, and everybody is very impressed, particularly by his long tee shots. He can now hit a golf ball about 120 yards and more, although his accuracy and consistency need improvement, as ever. His tee shots on a par-three hole reach the green only about 60% of the time. He usually manages the next chip shot on the green, but then has got only one putt left to make par: not easy for anybody. He usually does better on the longer holes.

Still, things look good for tomorrow.

Later, we drive downtown to find a place for dinner. Livermore is a town of some 80,000 inhabitants and must be on the A-list of 'America's Tidiest Towns'. It's very pretty, neat as a pin, and equally boring. It's 8.30pm, Sunday evening in Middle America, and there's no one about, as Max Sebald used to observe of the quaint old seaside towns of East Anglia. There is a huge flagpole at the intersection of the two main streets that mark the epicentre of the town, and a plaque proudly states that the American flag has been flying here without interruption since 1905. The streets are lined with trees, there are pretty fountains merrily splashing along. Apart from three teenage girls hanging out on the plaza in front of the theatre (which is dark that night), everything looks deserted. Two Chinese restaurants are still open, we choose the one that has a couple of customers at one table, the other joint is empty altogether. When we walk in, the customers rise to pay their bill, and the waiter rushes over to tell us to hurry up with our order, the kitchen is about to close. The food arrives five minutes later while the kitchen staff is noisily shuffling out the door. It is not yet 9pm.

Driving back to our motel we pass by the theatre again, the teenage girls are still hanging out on the plaza, practicing some dance steps.

MONDAY, 24 June

Monday is the first day of the two-day tournament. We check in early, I get equipped with a funny looking caddy's apron and am told to observe the rules. Over-coaching is especially frowned upon, a point that is made three times on the poster pinned up behind the registration desk. Max's age group will play nine holes today, and the other nine tomorrow. We tee off rather late, at 3pm, and the waiting becomes a bit tedious. Max starts off nervously, then calms down to play solid pars and a birdie, but on the last three holes he loses concentration and interest. Final score: six over par, ok, but somewhat disappointing after his terrific practice round yesterday.

I am angry because Dragon Mom keeps on interfering from the sidelines. Susan is a spectator, and the rules do not allow her to say anything at all; she is not even supposed to be on the fairway. She says she is not happy with my caddying. She claims I let Max play without direction. That's complete bollocks, of course. Max is stubborn, and it is hard to make him listen to you at the best of times. No surprise then that later Dragon Mom and I have the usual non-productive argument about Max's golf.

TUESDAY, 25 June

Today, Max's starting time is even later, at 4pm, so we spend the morning driving back to San Jose to visit the house that (Mrs) Sarah (Winchester) built. Born in 1839 in New Haven, Connecticut, she was the wife of William Wirt Winchester, who had inherited his father's Winchester Repeating Arms

Company that sold hundreds of thousands of firearms to the farmers and pioneers, Indian and buffalo hunters who had set out on the great westward trek overland in pursuit of America's manifest destiny. It subsequently supplied arms to the US Army, as well as other armies around the world, and it is selling firearms to thousands of American gun lovers today.

Following the death of her only child shortly after birth and of her husband who only lived to 43, Sarah Winchester apparently went into a deep depression, and that's when she left the gloomy-greyish coast of New England for the sunshine of California. She arrived in San Francisco in 1881, started building her Victorian-style mansion in 1884 and never stopped until she died, peacefully in her sleep, at the age of 83. By then the maze of a complex had grown to some 160 rooms, not counting kitchens, bathrooms, gardens, outbuildings and the like. Sarah Winchester never remarried, she lived alone in her ghost-house for 38 years, surrounded by servants.

Even the Great San Francisco Earthquake of 1906, which reduced the seven-story complex to four, did not interrupt her building frenzy. She simply had the debris cleared away, the affected part of the house boarded up, and merrily went along adding rooms, staircases, kitchens, the latest in indoor plumbing and hydraulic elevator technology, stained-glass windows made exclusively for her by Tiffany's, and so on. She is said to have gone into her *séance* room, in the very centre of the building, every night at midnight to consult with her spirits, and she would emerge every morning with new plans to give to her foreman who would immediately direct the permanent crew of carpenters to get to work. Her preferred building material was redwood, except she did not like its colour so she had it all painted over and covered with made-to-order textiles. She was a little lady just over four feet tall, and much of the interior architecture reflects her personal size: low-rise stairs (she was also afflicted by arthritis in later years), or doors that would have knocked the heads off people less height-challenged than the eccentric landlady.

I am rather disinclined to believe the popular theory that Mrs Winchester felt haunted by the souls of the untold number of people (not to mention the animals) who were killed by the rifles manufactured by her husband's company, and that she followed the instructions of a Boston psychic to build a house never-to-be-finished and in such a way as to confuse and keep the ghosts at bay. Hence the doors that open into walls or lead to 20-feet drops into open space, staircases that go up to the ceiling and no further, corridors leading nowhere, windows that look out into other rooms, cabinet doors without cabinets. If Sarah really suffered pangs of conscience because of her involvement in the bloody family business, why did she not simply give the money to charity? Another theory claims that the building reveals her 'serious interest' in the theories and design features of Masonic Rosicrucianism, notably in a speculative fourth dimension (thus the Escher-like staircases going nowhere). But so what? Isn't what the Freemasons and Rosicrucians are all about not just another kind, not necessarily of a higher order, of superstitious mumbo-jumbo?

There is no doubt that Sarah Winchester was neurotically superstitious. The number '13' (not exactly a sophisticated kind of superstition) crops up everywhere in the house, as does her favourite design element, the spider web. She was also a religious fundamentalist: she owned a huge houseboat ('Sarah's Ark') on a marina in San Francisco Bay in anticipation of the Second Great Flood. Or was this because keeping a big boat is simply what rich people did at the time, no less than today?

So, the whole business of the Winchester Mystery House is one of myth and speculation and fabrication, heavily edited to a popular script designed to sell a tourist attraction that marries the spooky allure of a haunted house with the hard-luck story of a famous-name celebrity. Perhaps the only lessons that Winchester House might realistically teach us is that (1) extreme wealth offers no protection from silliness, and (2) living a socially isolated life without family or friends is not a good idea in the long run.

And this: in the 1880s, Sarah's estate comprised 160 acres of farmland in the middle of the entirely rural Santa Clara Valley, the house was surrounded by orchards. She had a thriving plum drying and packing business operating on the site, the prunes giving her a bit of extra income, not that she needed it. Today, the orchards are sold off and the house is entirely surrounded by the hustle and bustle of a suburb of San José, part of the urban sprawl that is the San Francisco Bay Area.

TUESDAY afternoon

This afternoon, it's Susan's turn to caddy; I stay in the background. Dragon Mom has promised to relax and let Max play his game, but she cannot help herself: from the first hole onward, she is all over him, lecturing non-stop in Mandarin and English, pointing, moving him around – a classical case of over-coaching. Dragon Boy, of course, does not like it; the two start arguing immediately on the first hole, and Max's game never takes off.

On the fifth hole it gets worse when he accidentally picks up a ball just off the green, and immediately drops it when everybody shouts: 'No! Don't!' Max was surprised that the ball had suddenly appeared seemingly out of nowhere. He had not seen that it was hit by a player in the following group who should have waited until the green was clear. A second later that player's mother comes running towards Max, screaming at the top of her lungs: 'What are you doing?' Max looks at her, bewildered, and starts crying. We try to cheer him up, telling him not to worry, it's not his fault. The people who have witnessed the scene are all very supportive. They tell him he didn't do anything wrong, he's doing well, and they applaud his every shot from then on. Everybody tells us we should lodge a formal complaint. But what's the point? Max picked up a ball that he shouldn't have but that shouldn't have been there in the first place, then he gets yelled at by some hysterical stranger, and his composure is gone. He puts up a brave face, but his focus and motivation are gone for the rest of the day.

The whole thing is so bloody pointless: Max dropped the ball a fraction of a second after he picked it up, and it pretty much landed exactly where it was before. There was no apparent loss or gain in the lie of the ball. Nevertheless, there is a whole lot of screaming and excitement: 'We need a ruling on this! Where is the marshall?', etc.

Hectic Tiger Parents, everywhere you look.

Of course, one is not supposed to shout on a golf course, particularly not at a six-year old child. Furthermore, that mother was a spectator, she had no business to be where she was and to interfere. At the following tee, I quietly suggest to her that she should apologise to Max for shouting at him, but she just snaps at me: 'My dad shouted at me, too!'

At the end of the day, Max comes in at seventh place. We tell him he did very well, but he is not a happy child. We immediately drive back home, 450 miles all the way on I-5, a straight four-lane freeway with little traffic at that time of late evening and night, mostly trucks carrying farm produce. Thankfully, Max is soon sound asleep. Passing through Delano, memories of my previous visit here are flooding back. One of the first articles I ever published was on the strike of the United Farm Workers Union, mostly Mexican immigrants, in the iceberg lettuce and table grape industries, and on the strategy of the powerful agribusiness people to import non-Hispanic immigrants, illiterate Egyptian and Yemeni labourers, in an attempt to break the strike. Oh dear, how long ago was that! I am tempted to stop and drive around to have a look, but it is dark and there is nothing to see.

We push on, and I make it to San Diego in just under eight hours, with one break for fuel and a coke at a truck stop near Bakersfield. I drive mostly around 80mph, 15 miles over the limit. Luckily, there's not a cop in sight.

We finally pass the twin domes of the San Onofre nuclear power plant just inside the San Diego County line, and I slow down. We're almost home. By the time I park the car in the underground carpark of Bella Capri it is 2.30 in the morning. I carry Max up to our flat and put him to bed. He does not wake up.

MR NICE GUY 2013

The *U-T* proudly reports that its owner and publisher, Papa Doug Manchester, has been named 'Mr Nice Guy 2013' by the non-profit 'Nice Guys' charity club of San Diego. According to the president of the organization, local businessman Skip Hodgetts, Mr Manchester was a clear favourite for the award, both due to his generosity as a philanthropist and his high profile that is supposed to help the Nice Guys' charitable work. 'Papa Doug stepped up to the community in a fashion that many people in this community may not understand,' Mr Hodgetts is reported as saying.

According to his own newspaper, Mr Manchester's proud history of giving to local causes includes endowments and scholarships to San Diego State University, Papa Doug's *alma mater*, as well as to the University of San Diego and Cathedral Catholic High School. He is known to have donated to the Child Abuse Prevention Foundation, San Diego Diocese ministries, YMCA, Scripps Memorial Hospital and the *USS Midway* Museum. This year, Papa Doug's attention is on cancer charities. He has set himself the ambitious task of raising $1 million. If the campaign should fall short of this, then the newspaper will make up the difference, according to Mr Lynch, friend of Papa Doug and CEO of the *U-T*, and himself a former Mr Nice Guy.

Papa Doug will be officially honoured at the occasion of the Nice Guys' annual black-tie gala event later this year, to be held at the Del Mar Grand Resort (conveniently owned, of course, by Papa Doug). The event is expected to raise between $200,000 and $250,000 for charity. In 2012, Nice Guys San Diego raised $1.24 million for different local charities, including $640,000 for its 'Victory Fund' set up to aid wounded marines, sailors and their families.

The motto of Nice Guys San Diego is: 'Offering a hand-up, not a hand-out.'

Who, according to the Nice Guys of the business community of San Diego, is in the habit of handing out hand-outs? Why, the government, of course.

MAX AT PLAY

We take Max to a birthday party at the recreation centre. There is a table (previously reserved for the party) with snacks and sodas, chips and ice cream, cupcakes galore and other paraphernalia of such festive affairs. The birthday kid is now seven years old and gets heaps of expensive presents from the boys in his class: computer games, hockey sticks, water pistols, Lego boxes and transformer kits. I wonder whether he will be very excited about Max's gift: two fancy picture books, age-appropriate and in hard cover.

Max is fascinated with the water guns, and he keeps on playing with them even after the other kids have gone on to the next piece of entertainment. At home, Max has pretty much no toys at all, except for the giant turtle he won at SeaWorld and his favourite soft toy pet parrot, and a few miniature cars and trucks; we left everything in Sydney. But it seems he doesn't need any toys either. His special activity at home is building cubby houses. He started doing this already more than a year ago in Sydney, and the antipodean experience has been inspirational, it seems. He uses the obvious material at hand: cardboard boxes from our shopping trips, sofas, chairs, doonas, blankets, pillows, magazines. He cuts up bits of cardboard and re-arranges them with sticky tape. The cubby house is always a work in progress, he keeps on re-decorating and doing make-overs, not unlike Mrs Sarah Winchester. One day a pool is added (with a blue doona for water, to jump in from a chair), then a reading room (I usually read to him before he sleeps, but now he started reading on his own), then the house becomes a shop (where we have to buy things from him), and then a bank (he manufactures little credit cards out of paper to insert into a slot between two pieces of cardboard transformed into a make-believe ATM), the next day it is a motel (with Vacancy/ No Vacancy signs).

Max's classmates who come to visit are all fascinated by Max's cubby-house play, and they readily join in to crawl along underneath cardboard boxes, between a sofa and a wall of chairs and pillows with a blanket as a roof over their heads, and they don't get tired. It's something they prefer to do, sometimes even the beach or the playground appear less attractive.

INTERNET FRAUD

A week before we are supposed to move out of our flat in Draper Avenue and into the (self-proclaimed) 'healthy life-style apartment' of L. in Alabama Street that we rented a couple of months ago through AirBnB, we get an email from the web-based company: 'Your host has cancelled the reservation.' This is very bad news. We had planned to share this flat, about a mile from Colina Park, with Ken and Jeffrey while they were in San Diego for the Callaway Tournament, and now we have no accommodation for either of us. And less than a week to find an alternative, at the height of the summer tourist season! L. sends an apologetic message, saying his flat was flooded and the damage could not be fixed at such short notice. He assures us that he'll do his best to find something else for us among his friends, but all he does is send a few names from the list of AirBnB.

I have no reason to doubt L.'s sincerity, but a lingering suspicion remains. We've read about similar experiences of other clients of AirBnB: they receive a cancellation notice a few days before their rental was supposed to start, and that's it. Eventually, they'd get the money back, often paid months earlier to secure their holiday accommodation, but that's cold comfort if you had a trip planned and you are given the boot two or three days before you were supposed to board a plane and arrive at the destination of your dream, booked – or so you thought – via a secure site on the internet.

So, it's back to the computer, endlessly searching websites for a place to live for a couple of weeks. There is not much on offer, and what is available is priced way over our budget. We face the prospect of shacking up in a cheap motel on El Cajon Boulevard. Then another offer pops up on AirBnB: 'modern luxury flat' at Bird Rock, panoramic ocean views, accommodates six, $280 a day. Could this be it? Similar deals go for much higher, up to four times as much. And it's available for the time we're asking about: too good to be true.

Of course, it isn't. By chance I find another website (of a reputable San Diego real estate firm) that advertises – lo and behold! – the same apartment at $600 a day, and it is booked out solid till the end of August. There is no doubt it is the same flat. The blurbs on both websites are virtually identical: same text, same pictures. Wow! What do we make of that? It is clear there are bad people out there in Cyberspace trying to do you in.

The 'host' of the 'modern luxury flat' has obviously copied the ad from the real estate company's website and posted it under their own name. Out of curiosity, I follow the link and register to express my interest in renting. I write that I'd like to pay via electronic bank transfer from an Australian account to an account in the US (suggesting this would save on banking fees/commission). A few minutes later comes the reply: yes, available, with accommodation for six, happy to have you, here's my bank details. I'm tempted to copy everything down and go to the police, but then I stop in my tracks: would I make a fool of myself? Surely there are hundreds of operators out there, bombarding people like you and me with news of fantasy lottery wins or with business propositions involving some grieving widow of an oil minister in some god-forsaken oil-rich African tribal state who allegedly died an untimely death in a terrorist attack, leaving behind an estate valued at a cool few hundred million dollars which the now merry widow wishes to entrust to a trustworthy friend (you, the email addressee!), only in order to avoid paying the unreasonably high taxes in her home town in Uganda or Liberia or wherever – in other words, the kind of email you get on a regular basis. Still, this one seems to involve a reputable operator. Or maybe not? With the internet, how does one know? Eventually, I decide it's all too much of a hassle. I don't have time to go to the police. I wasted enough time on the internet already. We need to find a place, urgently. We need to get organised for the Callaway Tournament.

SUNDAY, 30 June

HALFWAY MARK: FIVE MONTHS IN SOUTHERN CALIFORNIA

After breakfast, we check out of the apartment that has been home now for the last three months. We leave a few boxes of personal effects in the garage of our friends in Bird Rock. For once we can travel light. We drive up to Torrance and check in with Xiaofang and Billy. Brianna is over the moon to see and play with Max. I buy a surfboard for Max, and we spend the next few days checking out the local surfing spots: Manhattan, Hermosa and Redondo Beach. But the conditions are too rough, and we soon give up. I promise Max we'll go surfing at La Jolla Shores after the holidays, the waves are much safer there. Instead, we play tennis and soccer in the park next to Bill's parental home, visit the local library, and eat out at Chinese seafood buffets.

THURSDAY, 4 July

On the Fourth of July, we drive up to the Hollywood Bowl for the concert and fireworks. There is a park below the amphitheatre where we meet some friends of Bill's and settle down on the grass for a picnic. It's a fun, communal affair with shared food and drinks. The concert features the LA Philharmonics under the baton of Sarah Hicks, a most attractive young lady from Hawaii and a very accomplished musician. The program is largely the familiar nationalist-militarist brass and bells and whistles (Souza). One musical rediscovery is the 'Major Bogey March' (from 1914, by English composer Kenneth J. Alford who seems to have been a keen golfer). This is the organisers' only contribution to what was billed as an 'international' program (everything else is dinky-di American), and the tune is of course well known from the Hollywood blockbuster *Bridge on the River Kwai*. The pretty conductress invites the happy audience to whistle along to the Bogey March (in England during WWII, British soldiers famously used the tune to sing their own lyrics, 'Hitler has only got one ball'). Afterwards, Miss Hicks comments that we, the audience, if asked what we did on the Fourth of July 2013, could proudly proclaim that we performed with the LA Pilharmonics. Laughter and applause. Very cute.

The main attraction of the night is somebody I never heard of before, singer Josh Brogan, but Bill assures me that Brogan is a famous pop artist (who allegedly sold over 100 million CDs), and he is not a bad crooner either, though his band is much better than its frontman. And the dancing, swinging conductor of the Philharmonics, Sarah Hicks, in stiletto heels with tight-fitting satin top and pants, who brings the patriotic superhits to life under the multicoloured spectacle of floodlights, laser beams and exploding fireworks, is certainly someone worth revisiting, on any stage including this one.

FRIDAY, 5 July

We pick up Max's golf buddy Jeffrey and his dad Ken from LA airport. They have heaps of luggage. The house of Bill and Xiaofang and Brianna has become crowded like a refugee camp, and we organise our departure as quickly as possible. Ken has never been in America, and he thinks he does not need a car and can rely on public transport to get around, but on the available evidence he quickly changes his mind. We drive to LAX to rent a car, and then back on the I-5, going south. I insist Ken borrows my GPS, but he refuses. He says he'll just follow me. But I know better, so we check the route on the computer, and Ken meticulously writes down every turn and waymark between Torrance and our flat in San Diego. In Sydney, Ken drives a cab for a living, he thinks he can find his way around anywhere. But this is Southern California. He has no clue what it means to drive 110 miles down a busy freeway that is mostly eight lanes wide, with two extra car-pool lanes part of the way. Ken and Jeffrey arrive over an hour after us.

We finally did manage to find a two-bedroom flat just off I-8, five minutes by car to Colina Park. The deal is made again via AirBnB, and I cannot suppress a worrying thought that it might turn out another fraud or we might get again a last-minute cancellation. But this one turns out to be ok: it is a modest, pleasant enough apartment that belongs (again!) to a landlady of Chinese descent, so we have a communicative advantage. Max immediately re-arranges the furniture in the living room to build a cubby house for himself and Jeffrey. Meanwhile, Ken and I sit at the dining room table, and I explain the topography of Southern California. He takes detailed notes to plot his itineraries, from our flat to Torrey Pines and the golf course where Jeffrey will play.

The next morning we drive to Colina Park. Max is in good spirits to play again with Jeffrey. They start on the back nine, and Max hits par on the first two holes, then birdies the next one. But Jeffrey is nervous; he bogeys and double-bogeys and then starts crying. He has been practicing in Sydney every day for the last few weeks, before and after school. Now the pressure is getting to him. He was always better than Max, and now he seems afraid that his younger friend has caught up with him. Ken immediately calls off the game, he does not want his son to lose confidence. I'm at a loss to say whether this is the right way to go about it. Ken is adamant, and Max finishes playing nine holes by himself.

Not a very auspicious start, I think to myself.

SAN ONOFRE: END OF A NUCLEAR PLANT

On the TV news that night we hear that the cost of dismantling the San Onofre Nuclear Generating Station in Northern San Diego County is estimated at $4.1 billion, and removal of the plant is to last three decades. Or longer, considering that safety regulations are constantly evolving. The planning process for the decommissioning alone is expected to be from five to seven years. It's a huge job to exactly foresee and plan the sequence of events. Where do you start?

Plant buildings, turbines and cooling systems can be dismantled pretty much like any other non-nuclear facility. The steel-reinforced concrete containment domes, the huge egg-shaped structures that can be seen along I-5 from some miles away, need to be broken up and trucked away piece by piece. The dismantling and disposing of internal reactor components present the greatest challenge.

At this stage, it is not at all clear what to do with the spent nuclear fuel. Some is currently stored in cooling pools and steel-and-concrete dry casks. A permanent depository, to be decided by the federal government, has not yet been found. During the dismantling of the original Unit One, shut down in 1992, radioactive leaks were discovered. The possibility of leaks and underground contamination around Reactors Two and Three will further inflate the cost of removing the plant.

What will happen to the plant's electric transmission switchyard and the high-tension wires strung across I-5 is anyone's guess.

What will the place look like when it's all over? Like the beach that was there in the first place?

SATURDAY, 7 July

The last few weeks before the Callaway Junior, Max has played one tournament after another. The outcome has always been pretty much the same: he hits a few remarkable shots, lands a few wayward ones in rough territory or behind some trees, and finally gives a hole away with a careless putt. Too many double bogeys, too few pars, not enough birdies. He usually manages a final score of between six and fourteen over par: not good enough to earn him a medal.

Dragon Mom finally admits defeat a week before Callaway: she realises that very likely she will not see Max's name on or near the top of the leader board. The last straw for her is Max's performance at the San Diego Junior Masters tournament, held on the Thursday and Friday before the World Championship. It's at Colina Park, a kind of warm-up event for the Callaway. In theory, Max should have a good chance to win here, or at least come close. He has the skills, he knows the course, he has practised here for nearly half a year. If anything, he should have a kind of home advantage. He has played two holes in one at Colina Park (holes one and seven), and he has birdied all the holes at one time or the other. His problem is still the same: he does not focus, he does not care adhering to a pre-shot routine, he plays always in a rush. He gets too easily distracted. Some of the tee boxes at Colina Park are located right next to each other, and he's usually more interested in what's going on at the other tee rather than preparing for the next tee shot of his own. And it's clear by now that he hasn't quite got the single-minded passion to win. His dream is to play, not to win. Winning is an extra bonus, but not essential. Once Max has finished his round, he will be immediately running and jumping around and mucking about. He is only six years old. But so are his competitors who have internalised to be more serious about golf.

At the Junior Masters, Max scores 16 over par. Dragon Mom is thoroughly depressed, she knows that her vision for her son has not worked out. There is little chance that Max will miraculously improve his game to do better at Callaway. He is no Tiger Woods, as Rudy Duran had suggested at our meeting in Scottsdale, Arizona, half a year ago. I tell Susan she should not feel that way. Our son is doing all right. He has made a lot of progress. Golf is a game for life. He has learnt a lot and made lots of friends. Max has reached a level of play at his age where he can be confident of being a competent social golfer or even competitive club player for the rest of his life. That's no mean achievement.

Dragon Mom is anything if not resilient. The next day she tells everybody who wants to listen that kids' golf is all about having fun and making friends, that the score doesn't matter, that the kids really are too young to play 18-hole tournaments anyway, that learning to play golf well is a long shot, and so on. She even admits that we (she generously includes me in her public soul-searching) have made a mistake by pushing Max too much too early, that we'll make sure to take it easy from now on, the main thing is that he'll be enjoying his game. Any such mini-lecture ends with a reference, ironically, to Rudy Duran and his mantra: the kids must 'own' their game.

CADDYING MAX

Despite her newly professed conviction that the kids must manage their own game, Dragon Mom cannot help herself telling Max what to do. Whenever she's on the practice green or the course with him, she is coaching, lecturing, repeating the obvious things *ad infinitum* and *ad nauseam*, in English as well as in Mandarin, a waterfall of unhelpful advice: 'Routine! Behind the ball! Don't play into the bunker!' After each round she promises to be quiet the next time, but she can't help it. I tell Dragon Mom that Max has two worst enemies in golf: himself, and his mother.

Eventually, Max resolutely refuses to go on the course with Dragon Mom, so the job of caddying falls to me by default, not that I'm particularly keen on it. I know Max's golf, and I know what his problems are, but he is usually not interested in hearing about it. He is stubborn, to say the least. But the two of us get along quite well on the course. I might suggest something to him, and if he does the opposite I encourage him. Sometimes he is right, of course, like when I suggest a certain club and he prefers another, and if he does a good shot he goes, triumphantly: 'See? Told 'ya!' And he is more convinced than ever that he alone is in charge of his game.

But for Dragon Mom the matter is not quite settled, neither between her and Max and her and myself. It's personal, of course; she simply finds it impossible to give up playing the Great Golfing Guru Mom. Her last resort is a belief that a 'professional' caddie will do a better job than either of us and help Max to improve on his score. Behind my back she hires Xavier, a student from SDSU who has grown up playing golf at Colina Park. I'm furious, not only because of the manipulative way she goes about it, but I doubt whether a caddie who doesn't know Max at all and has never see him play will help. Again, an unproductive argument: Dragon Mom has made the deal ($50 a round for Xavier) and it's *fait accompli*. For a moment, I feel like walking out of the whole thing, but of course I can't leave Max alone.

Anyway, our son sees the whole business strictly through his own eyes, and he doesn't mind. On the contrary: Xavier is a veteran of the First Tee program, one of the 'cool' older kids at Colina Park who all play golf very well and know the course inside/out. Max, like all the kids his age, looks up to them in awe. Xavier is a quiet, well-spoken, likeable young man of Mexican descent, and Max is keen to play with him.

The evening before the tournament the two of them go on the course, and Max plays half a dozen holes with Xavier caddying. When they come back, Max is quite excited and clearly on a high: he has played well, and Xavier has taught him a new shot. It's a trick shot Max calls hop-hop shot: a short chip onto the green where the ball bounces twice, rather than once, and then – or that's the general idea – slowly rolls into the hole.

This is not good, I say to myself, experimenting with a new shot just before an important tournament? But I keep quiet. I speak to Xavier in private and try to impress on him what is important: slowing Max down, making him concentrate and focus, doing the pre-shot routine, the basics. Xavier nods. No problem, he says, Max will do very well.

SUNDAY, 14 July

OPENING CEREMONY, CALLAWAY JUNIOR GOLF WORLD CHAMPIONSHIP, TORREY PINES

Around the two putting greens in front of the pro shop of Torrey Pines Golf Course, exactly 99 flags are fluttering in the light ocean breeze that cools the ambient temperature of 95 degrees to just bearable. The flags represent 56 different countries, 42 states of the USA, and one huge Stars and Stripes that towers over all the other ones. Most of the 1,225 golf players between the ages of five and seventeen from around the world who have qualified for this tournament are running around in a beehive of activity, chatting excitedly, exchanging small gifts representative of their country with each other, or lining up for the putting competition (an 18-hole mini-golf course set up on the practice green with pine cones and twigs as hazards), or seriously rehearsing their putting skills. Meanwhile, the adults are elbowing their way through the crowded pro shop, looking for overpriced souvenirs with the tournament logo and the latest fashion items in designer golf apparel. Named after its principal sponsor, one of the leading manufacturers of golfing equipment (conveniently located nearby in Carlsbad, North San Diego County), the Callaway is the oldest and most prestigious event of its kind, held annually since 1968. It attracts a lot of customers.

We meet up with our friends from Sydney: dad Patrick and daughter Sophie, aged ten. They are staying at another resort and golf course where Sophie is playing in the girls' competition. Max, Jeffrey and Sophie used to play together at tournaments in Sydney, and there is great excitement about the reunion six months after we left for California. Everybody is very happy.

Next to the clubhouse, a raised platform has been constructed in front of a huge poster announcing CALLAWAY JUNIOR WORLD CHAMPIONSHIP 2013. To the left of the lectern there is seating for the official guests who will attend the opening ceremony, and in front of the podium a few hundred white plastic chairs have been placed for the parents and visitors who are eagerly awaiting the highlight of the opening show: the parade of flags. The kids line up behind their respective national colours and a sign announcing the name of the country. There's piped-in elevator music, and off they march, around the clubhouse and in front of the officials on the rostrum on one side and the assembled parents and spectators on the other. As the tournament chairperson announces the names of the countries, there is enthusiastic applause, and the children's march snakes around the back of the spectator area to take up position behind the adults. Finally, the Stars and Stripes arrive and everybody stands for the US national anthem.

It's all so cute, in an all-American sort of way: the California sun is sparkling, the blue ocean is glistening beyond

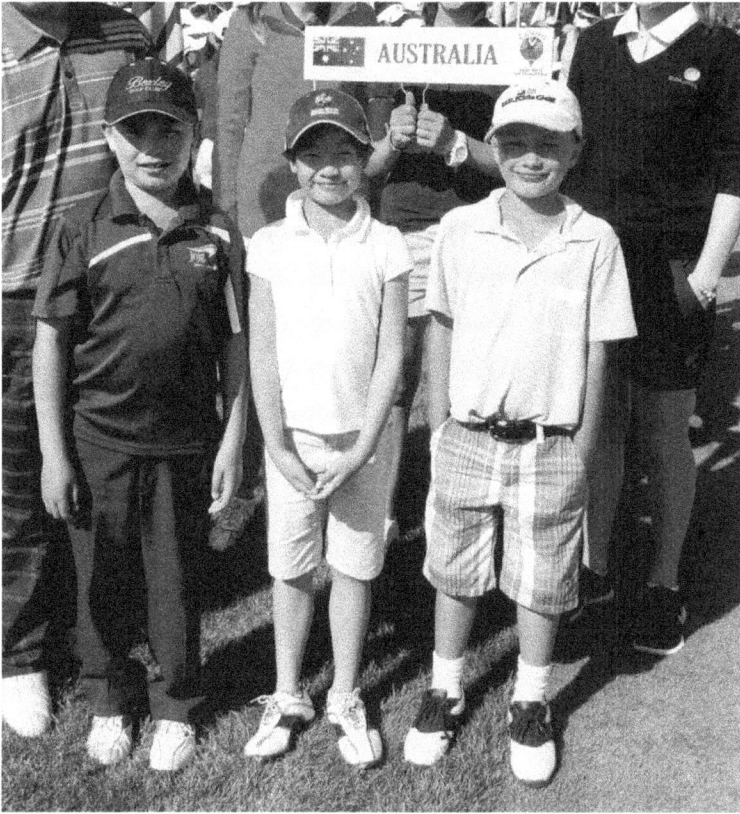

The Australian Contingent at the Callaway. Front Row (from Left to Right): Jeffrey, Sophie, Maximilian

the glorious Torrey Pines fairways, the child golfers are dressed up like mini-pros in their brand-new colourful designer gear. The competitors of some countries, like the Thai and the Japanese, sport a team uniform – the Japanese arrive in spotless white pants and caps and red shirts with a prominent yellow MacDonald sponsorship logo on their chest – but most others present a motley crew of fancy individual outfits. The parade is a little bit like the athletes' entrance at the Olympic games, something the organisers are proud to point out ('mini-Olympics'), but there is a slight difference underlined by the arranged staging: at the Olympics, the athletes are in the middle of the stadium at the centre of everybody's attention; here the players are paraded around in front of the adults and then to the back of the spectators' area, behind the adults, where the kids are supposed to line up and listen. Of course, they don't; they soon lose interest in the proceedings, and while the various speakers drone on about the illustrious predecessors of today's competitors, the kids chase each other across the lush lawn in front of the first tee of Torrey Pines South Course.

The staging of the ceremony makes it clear what this tournament is all about: the parents, the organisers, the sponsors. Not one of the official speakers addresses the children, the talk is all about thanking the parents, the officials of San Diego county and the Callaway organization, and about evoking the history of the tournament with its famous winners: Tiger Woods, Phil Mickelson and Ernie Els. Chinese teenager Tianlang Guan, who sailed with us on Sydney Harbour and is presently in San Diego for training, would have been the star participant, but he was only invited to make a cameo appearance for the media the previous day. The reason: he has refused to play in this year's Callaway, so he does not rate a mention anymore. He won in 2012. At age 14, Tianlang does not want to play with the kids anymore. And why would he? After being invited to the Masters as the youngest player ever, he is now preparing to compete in the Canadian Open against the adult pros. Instead, all the media attention is on Allan Kournikova, little brother of famous Russian tennis nymphet Anna, and on an unknown 15-year old from South Africa, Jovan Rebula, who turns out to be the nephew of Ernie Els and is being coached by Ernie Els' father. The organisers hope that history will repeat itself and that the youngster from South Africa will do battle against some promising local boy, as Uncle Ernie did when he won the tournament against a San

Diegan prodigy, Phil Mickelson. That was 30 years ago, when Mickelson and Els were teenagers.

Coincidentally – as I learn later – during the tournament's 60-years history, none of the winners in the youngest age group where Max is competing ever made a name for himself or herself in professional golf. There may be a lesson in there.

TUESDAY–THURSDAY, 16–18 July

CALLAWAY JUNIOR GOLF WORLD CHAMPIONSHIP, AGE GROUP SIX-AND-UNDER, COLINA PARK

So, this is it: the main event, the one we came here for, the one Max has been practising for since February. After the opening ceremony at Torrey Pines, there is two days of warm-up and practice for the competitors to get to know the layout of their courses, followed by three days of competition, three times 18 holes. Max plays in the youngest age group against 55 players from around the world. It will be an exhausting week, especially with the present heat wave in Southern California, with temperatures in the high 80s and low 90s.

On Monday, Max plays his practice round with Xavier and, unsurprisingly, he does not do better than usual: his score is 69, 15 over par. It's clear that Xavier couldn't manage Max's play better than either of his parents. On the eighth hole – one of the more difficult holes at Colina Park – the tee shot ends up just an inch short of the green, and only some six feet from the flag. It should be an easy two-putt for par, a birdie is within reach. Instead, Max decides to try his new hop-hop chip shot and misses badly. The ball shoots across the green into the rough, he chips it back and ends up three-putting for a triple bogey. Later Xavier explains to me that he had told Max to use his putter, but Max had stubbornly refused. Never mind, I say, he has to own the game.

But Dragon Mom is not impressed, and without ceremony Xavier is paid off. Sorry, she tells him; it was an experiment, it didn't work. To Dragon Mom, it's the American way: Xavier didn't deliver the goods. He is clearly disappointed but does not seem overly surprised. The procedure is not unusual; local caddies are only on stand-by, and they are used to erratic parents around here. The older kids at Colina Park are well trained in the etiquette of the gentleman's game. Like Xavier, they are unfailingly cheerful and polite. Of course, Xavier had expected to be employed for four days' caddying, and to earn a substantial tip afterward. But he does not show any anger or frustration. He smiles, wishes Max well and calmly says goodbye to us. I feel terrible, however, and I talk to Todd Smith and apologise. No worries, he tells me, it's ok; he'll get Xavier another job. Xavier ends up driving the club's VIP van for the duration of the tournament, probably for better money.

So, the job of caddying comes back to me. I find it hard to show any enthusiasm, but Max promises to listen this time, and he and I solemnly agree to have three great rounds of golf. Max will take his time, he will focus and not muck around. Promised! Word of honour!

But the question of who will caddy Max takes yet another turn. On Tuesday morning, while Max and I are preparing for the first round on the practice green, Dragon Mom runs into Todd Smith in the clubhouse, and he asks her whether she needs a caddy. It turns out that Shaun, another one of the 'cool' senior boys at Colina Park, had lined up a job to caddy for one of the contestants from Thailand, only to be unceremoniously sacked – just like Xavier – the night before. Apparently, one of the Thai pros accompanying the team had decided to act as caddy himself.

Shaun is one of the champions at Colina Park; he has played here for over ten years, and he has a record of 26 holes in one to his credit. Wow! When Max hears that there is another 'cool caddy' who wants to play with him, he is happy to ditch his dad. I'm beyond caring at this point, and I just repeat to Shaun that he should try to make Max slow down and focus. Don't worry, Shaun says, he knows his job, he knows the greens (26 holes in one!), Max will do very well.

Predictably, he doesn't. Max's score is 17 over on the first day, 14 on the second. By that time, Dragon Mom is resigned to her fate. We invite Shaun for lunch after the second round on Wednesday, and he suggests his favourite Vietnamese restaurant on El Cajon Boulevard. We have an excellent pho and an animated conversation. Max and I show Shaun how to prepare the paper wrappers of (soft-drink) straws to shoot darts out of the straw that becomes a blowgun, Amazon Indian-style: rip off one end of the paper, twist the other one into a sharp point, and blow hard). Whereupon Shaun show us what else you can do with the little white wrappers: tear off both ends, push the paper together as tightly as you can over the straw, then pull it off the straw and lay the crumpled, compressed piece of soft white paper on the table, drop a drop of water (or coke or whatever drink at hand) on one end, and – *voilá* – they wriggle like little worms. It's a very funny trick, and Max and I are quite impressed.

Shaun tells us about his immigrant background (his parents came as refugees, father is unemployed, mother working long hours as a cleaner to feed the family). After a while, Susan and I look at each other. We both find Shaun is trying remarkably hard to work on our social conscience, while at the same time going on about how inspirational golf and Colina Park have been in his career up-to-date: as prospective high school graduate, devoted child and model patriotic citizen.

We drop Shaun back at Colina Park, and while we drive home to our flat, he sends an SMS to Susan's mobile phone:

he demands more money for the last round. That was a mistake, because Dragon Mom only needed an occasion to fire him. To her, the matter is simple, again: Shaun has failed to deliver. Max has played at his usual level, if not below. Dragon Mom is not impressed by Shaun's soapy hard-luck story of childhood deprivation and boot-camp determination to succeed. This is America, it's the result that counts, dummy! Max is by now used to a last-minute change of caddies. He doesn't mind, he says. Anyway, he liked Xavier better than Shaun.

Again, I have the dubious privilege to caddy for Max. It's the final round, and he begins nervously, but I let him play and he gradually relaxes. He has promised to listen to what I say ('Slow down!'), but he still plays too rushed: too little focus, not enough concentration. The shot off the first tee goes wild and lands next to the adjoining fairway, some 80 feet from the green. But Max recoups with a brilliant chip that rolls to within four inches off the cup, and he manages a par. Great recovery! He's beaming, and we high-five. Next up are two bogeys followed by two pars. Then he misses some easy putts: there's a quadruple bogey on hole six (ouch!), a double bogey on seven and a bogey on eight. Too hurried, again! Once more, he manages to relax and scores a par on the next hole. Score for the front nine: nine over. He assures me he'll do better on the back nine: 'Don't worry, dad!'

In our group is a little boy from Mexico, six years old like Max, who plays very well on the first six holes, but then his play falls apart and he starts crying, softly but uncontrollably, while his father-caddy is swearing and muttering under his breath, gesticulating in desperation. On the back nine, Max is more consistent: five over, and he finishes first in his group. Total score for the last round: 14 over par, same as last round. The kids shake hands, sign their score cards, and while the Mexican boy is still crying Max jumps around, punching his fist in the air, acting as if he has won the tournament. He is happy play-acting, fantasising.

Max's final score lands him in 24th place out of the 42 players who finish the tournament. The winner is one of the boys from Thailand who comes in at two over par in the last round, and runner-up is a Canadian boy of Chinese descent who finishes his last round with five over par. During the award ceremony, tears begin to roll down the Canadian boy's cheeks, but he's not crying because he's a winner. He's crying, uncontrollably, because he came in second, meaning he's a loser, and he's devastated. His supporters try to cheer him up with shouts of 'Smile!', to no avail. He's standing there with a medal around his neck, a trophy in his hands, crying and crying.

Our friends from Sydney have done a little better than Max. Jeffrey has taken an equal 18th place against a much tougher opposition in the age group eight-to-nine, but his dad is not exactly happy. Ken had hoped for a better result, but he's philosophical: it's the first major tournament for his son. It was an expensive exercise but a great experience; it's good to find out what it's like playing in an international competition. They'll go back to Sydney with even greater determination, to train harder and to win, eventually. Only Sophie has done very well: she has taken fifth place in her group, a great result. She and daddy Patrick are over the moon: with this result, Sophie will be invited to play in every tournament around the world. And Patrick can afford it: he works for an airline company, as IT manager, and they can fly for next to nothing anywhere they like.

We had arranged to celebrate at our place, downstairs at Sammy's wood-fired pizzeria to be exact, but Ken does not find the way and gets lost, so the mobile phones go into action to decide on Plan B: we drive up to a shopping plaza near Jeffrey's course in San Marcos and find a Chinese restaurant that doubles as a sushi bar-cum-pizzeria. Everybody is happy now, the kids are having a great time chasing each other and playing hide-and-seek behind pillars and under the tables in the cavernous, almost empty restaurant, and the adults are shouting rounds of beer and swapping tales of the great tournament and making plans for the future.

We say goodbye, with no clear idea when we'll see each other again. On the way back, Max is soon sound asleep on the back seat of the Mercury. Susan and I don't say much, we're both very tired, it has been a long, exhausting day. I try not to fall asleep at the wheel.

Thus ends the Dragon Mother's dream, at least for the time being.

FRIDAY, 19 July

Email to Friends and Family in Germany:

'Am 2. August werden wir unsere Rückflugtickets nach Sydney in Anspruch nehmen, dortselbst bei meiner Tochter und Richie in derem neu gekauften Haus in Dover Heights mit Blick aufs Meer Quartier nehmen, am 22. August fliegen wir nach LAX zurück, von da aus direkt nach Washington, DC und New York City für 10 Tage Urlaub/Sightseeing, und dann geht's zurück in die alte Wohnung in La Jolla, wo für Max am 2.9. die Schule beginnt. Vom 1.2.2014 bis 31.1.2015 haben wir uns in einer 4-Zimmer-Wohnung in der Wiesbadener Strasse in Berlin-Wilmersdorf eingemietet, nächstes Jahr also Deutschland, Golf wird dann erstmal klein geschrieben oder ad acta gelegt, die Attraktionen der Hauptstadt müssen dafür kompensieren.'

We have made plans for the rest of the year and beyond: on 2 August we'll use our return tickets to fly back to Sydney, stay for a couple of weeks with my daughter and son-in-law in the house they just bought at Dover Heights, overlooking the Pacific Ocean, then we'll fly back to the US, from LAX straight on to Washington, DC, for a few days sightseeing, then by bus to NYC for ten days to explore the Big Apple, and finally back via LAX to our flat at La Jolla, corner of Draper and Pearl. We will arrive in San Diego on 1 September, Max will be going back to school the next day.

We have decided to move to Berlin at the end of January, so Max will have gone to an American school for exactly one year. We have found and reserved a four-room flat in Berlin-Wilmersdorf and signed a contract for a year. While in Germany, the priority for Max is to learn the language. Golf will be on the back-burner, most likely there won't be any at all. The attractions of the German capital will have to compensate. Max is excited: he knows *Fussball* is the big thing in Germany, and he wants to play soccer. The World Championship will be held in Brazil next summer, with the German *Nationalmannschaft* considered an outside favourite with a small chance to win. But Max is apprehensive, too. He realises he will have to attend a new school and will have to say goodbye to his friends in La Jolla. We assure him we'll stay in touch by phone and skype, and that they can visit us in Berlin. And he'll make new friends in Berlin.

Max and Susan at Times Square

PART THREE
LA JOLLA AUTUMN

SUNDAY, 1 September

We arrive back in La Jolla after an exhausting trip: Sydney, LAX, Washington, DC, New York City, LAX, San Diego. Four time zones, three distinct climates. We pick up our car from Xiaofang's and Bill's place in Torrance and head straight away for the I-5 South, Max's surfboard on the back seat. Southern California greets us with its freeways. The usual sunshine is waiting for us, warm days and silky, balmy nights.

MONDAY, 2 September

All Hallows Academy, First Day of School Year 2013/14.

Max is glad to be back in school, happy to be back with his schoolmates. He is in Grade Two now, his teacher is Mrs Merritt. She is more experienced than Miss Higgins, insists on discipline, expects homework to be submitted properly. If something is missing, or not in the right place, we get a note that we must sign and send back to her. She keeps reminding Max to form his letters and numbers correctly, i.e. legibly, and rightly so: his handwriting is not exactly pretty.

Soon the school routine takes over again. There is a new schedule, with some new activities: chess, tennis, German (Saturday school) to prepare for next year, and Chinese (Sunday school). Here's what Max's week looks like:

Monday to Thursday: school from 8am to 3pm

Friday: school from 8am to 1.45pm

Monday afternoon: free (golf, surfing, or playdate with friends)

Tuesday afternoon: tennis from 4pm to 5.30pm

Wednesday afternoon: chess club at school until 4pm

Thursday afternoon: half-hour choir practice after school, then tennis from 4pm to 5.30pm

Friday afternoon: free, same as Monday

Saturday morning: German School in Hillcrest from 9am to noon

Sunday afternoon: Chinese Academy at La Jolla Day School from 1.30pm to 4.30pm

SURFING AT LA JOLLA SHORES

On Mondays and Fridays after school, and sometimes on Saturday afternoons, I take Max surfing to La Jolla Shores. It's our favourite beach and ideal for learning how to surf. The waves are usually pretty flat, and the soft sand slopes very gently. We go into waist-deep water, Max takes up his position lying on the board, I turn him around to face the shore, we wait for a suitable wave, I give him a push and off he goes, scrambling to his knees, and soon he is standing up, balancing till the wave runs out. Max quickly gets the hang of it, and soon he doesn't want my help anymore. But I keep a close eye on him, and I don't let him go too far out, although that's where he would like to be, with the much older kids who are hanging around on their boards, waiting to catch a wave.

TENNIS AT BARNES

At New York, we had been to the US Open and watched Rafael Nadal make short thrift of a low-ranked opponent in a night match. Now, Max wants to play more tennis, and since golf is no longer the centre of Dragon Mom's universe, why not. He wants to join Vera who plays twice a week at Barnes Tennis Centre, which is to San Diego junior tennis what Colina Park is to San Diego junior golf, except at Barnes there are none of the 'underserviced kids' that hang out in the area around El Cajon Boulevard. But the teaching philosophy is similar: learning to play tennis is about learning life skills. The tennis centre is a great facility, with lots of courts, and they offer junior tennis for all age groups and skill levels. Barnes is on West Point Loma Boulevard, about half an hour by car from La Jolla on the other side of Mission Bay near the old hippie surfers' hang-out of Ocean Beach.

We enroll Max in the same group as Vera, and now it's 90 minutes of organised tennis coaching twice a week. It's great fun for the kids to play in small groups of four to six students, and Max takes to it like a fish to water. He quickly masters the basic strokes, and soon he and I play together after school or at the weekend, and he cleverly chases me around the court. He tries very hard to get a proper serve going, but that will take some time and lots of practice.

Surfing at La Jolla Shores

We're glad to be back after our long summer holiday. Nothing much seems to have changed, except golf: no more Colina Park, no more tournaments, no more coaching. But we manage to play at least one round a week, mostly at Mission Bay which is nearest to us, or at Torrey Pines, our favourite and certainly one of the most beautiful courses in the country. It's great just to walk along the fairways and look out over the ocean and watch the hang gliders when the sun is going down over the watery horizon.

CHESS CLUB

Max has joined the chess club in the school, one afternoon a week. It's run by a group of aficionados who belong to an adult chess club in San Diego and who hope to discover and to recruit new talented players. I taught Max how to play about a year ago in Sydney, but he was never really excited about the game (probably I should have let him win more often!), and we did not play on a regular basis. But he remembers the rules, and he is keen to join the club to play with his mates.

There are usually two or three instructors who teach the rules and basic strategy. The kids are given little exercises to work out, and then play against each other. They get points for everything, and all points are added up, so there is a daily winner and a champion at the end of the year. I usually arrive a little early to pick up Max so I can look around, peek over some young shoulders and give a tip here and there. The kids are eager to play with me because they get extra points for playing with an adult and super bonus points for winning against an adult. I'm not a hot-shot chess player so I have to watch out that I don't get run over by some clever nine-year old.

VOLUNTEERING

As parents, we are expected to do a certain amount of volunteer work at All Hallows. The lunch break suits me best, timewise, so I register for lunch hour supervision. The idea is to help the staff on duty to make sure the kids don't do anything silly during their break, like breaking their legs playing touch football or soccer or basketball or any of the other plays they devise for themselves. All the games seem to involve a whole lot of running around and frequently crashing in on one another.

But first it's assisting with food distribution. A long table is set up on the school yard, the boxes delivered from local fast-food suppliers are waiting to be opened, and then the kids come running out of their classes, form a line, drop their meal tickets into a box and receive their portion of lunch: Mexican (usually burritos), Italian (pasta or pizza), Chinese noodles or rice (with meat or veggies). There is a menu and the children (or their parents) tick the relevant boxes of their choice a week in advance. I hand out the little plastic or paper containers or plates, the pizzas are delivered in XXL-size cartons, and I need to put on plastic gloves and tear off one pre-scored slice for each customer. Some boys have double orders. Then the kids take a seat around the tables set up in one portion of the yard, they wolf the food down in a few minutes, throw the disposable plates and cutlery into a bin, and off they rush to play. The girls usually take a little longer than the boys, sitting and chatting. We, staff and volunteer, fold down the sun umbrellas, clear up the remaining rubbish and check what the kids are doing. They play a few more minutes, then the whistle goes and everybody shuffles back to take their place in line, one single file to a class, and the teachers arrive from the staffroom to pick up their flocks and lead them back to the classrooms. End of volunteer service for the day.

Much of the food is only half eaten before being thrown into the bin. I think Jamie Oliver would not like what I have seen.

MONDAY, 9 September

GERMAN PROJECT

Max has an assignment to do a project in school, a report on a foreign country. The favourite countries (Canada, Mexico, China, Italy, France) are quickly snapped up, so Max settles for Germany. Everybody in class is given the relevant copy of a book in a series entitled 'My country is...', and Max's country turns out to be '...West Germany.' I don't believe my eyes when I see the book. It's a British production from what seems like the early 1960s (no publication date provided). The authors seem unaware of East Germany (aka the German Democratic Republic; the map provided shows the outline of the Federal Republic with the names of a few cities, but the adjoining countries are not identified: *terra incognita*. Thus, the good children of All Hallows Academy in La Jolla will not hear about the Berlin Wall, nor – for that matter – that it came down in 1989, ushering in a new, re-unified Germany. In the book, the capital of the country is Bonn, and there is the usual stuff about a folksy people (beer and *Lederhosen*), along with some modern aspects (cars and *Autobahnen*). Oh, dear!

I take the book back to the school to have a word with the teacher and ask her, politely, whether Max can use his own material for the report as the book appears, '...ahem, somewhat out of date.' She is quite embarrassed and apologises profusely, saying she did not have the time to check all the books, and, yes, of course, Max can use any material that he wants and can find. The first thing I make him do at home is to look at a map of Europe and write down the names of all the countries surrounding Germany.

Max knows the map of the United States quite well by now, he also knows the names of the Great Lakes and of the American national anthem by heart, and he can recite the Pledge of Allegiance (something the whole school does every

Monday morning, when the flag on the playground is raised by a couple of senior students).

I'm not sure what to make of the teacher's explanation. I get the distinct feeling she has been using this book before, perhaps year after year, and I wonder whether she really understands my concern. Her pupils are second-graders after all; what do they need to know about foreign politics?

CHARTER SCHOOLS

Some of the parents we meet at the San Diego German School on Saturday mornings take their kids to the Albert Einstein Academy, a so-called charter school with a German-language stream. I'm immediately suspicious because of the ostentatious name (forgetting for a moment that my son's school calls itself an academy too). I never heard of charter schools before. Now I learn they are all the rage, and that there are quite a few around. They are private schools that receive regular government funding, and they must be approved by the local public school board. Some are entirely tuition-free while others charge only nominal fees. In the San Diego Unified School District, charter school enrollment is up dramatically this year, the second-highest rise in the nation. One in every 20 school students in America attends a charter school.

While some of these institutions seem to make a lot of sense (like Albert Einstein with its German stream, or similarly specialised schools catering to highly gifted students, or focusing on science or arts education, music, theatre and dance), other charter schools seem to target parents who are dissatisfied with the public school system in general. There seems to be a widespread feeling of malaise and mistrust with what the government has on offer, supported by widely-publicised test results like PISA that show the nation's educational performance is in decline and below average compared to other OECD countries. The government, on the other hand, seems to be only too happy to rid itself of its responsibility and grant licences to charter school operators.

'GUNS SAVE LIVES DAY'

Following the mass shooting (13 people dead) on 16 September 2013 at the Washington Navy Yard, the issue of gun control legislation has again become a hot topic. Some people are surprised to hear that the Second Amendment Foundation has proclaimed the 14th of December 'Guns Save Lives Day', and the organisation's founder and CEO, Alan Gottlieb, is immediately interviewed on CNN to explain. Alan Gottlieb describes himself as the 'premier anti-communist, free-enterprise, laissez-faire capitalist' of the USA. He is also an anti-environmental activist, gun-ownership advocate and author of 19 books, mostly on guns and the constitutional right of law-abiding American citizens to determine for themselves the kinds of firearms they think are necessary to defend themselves and their families against the government and other enemies. Gottlieb is no dummy; he has a degree in nuclear engineering (University of Tennessee) and a flourishing business advising politicians and other folk on how to obtain funding for their various causes. But he seems to have made a terrible PR blunder, as CNN's Piers Morgan points out to him, in choosing as the date for his day of gun promotion the first anniversary of the Sandy Hook Elementary School massacre in Newtown, Connecticut, where 27 people were killed, including 18 children in first and second grade. When Morgan begins reading a quote by one of the mothers who lost a child at Sandy Hook Elementary on her reaction to the coincidence of the dates, Gottlieb starts laughing, and

Morgan (almost) loses composure: 'How dare you?' The interview quickly degenerates into a shouting match.

So, was the choice of date an oversight? Not so. The way Gottlieb sees it, he and his fellow gun lobbyists have the same right to exploit the anniversary of the elementary school shooting for their own political agenda as do the proponents of gun control, people like Morgan and their ilk. His heart goes out to the victims' families, says Gottlieb, but his solution to avoid such massacres in the future is not restrictive gun laws (because 'guns don't kill people, criminals do!'), rather the way forward is to arm people, like teachers, school nurses, counselors (perhaps even the kids themselves?) so that they can protect themselves and fight back. I remember the TV ad for bullet-proof body armour, children's sizes and discounts for school orders available.

Gottlieb is a parent and a gun enthusiast, just like the mother of the 20-year old perpetrator at Sandy Hook. She owned about a dozen rifles and handguns and used to take her two sons to the shooting range where they both learned about gun safety. Before he went on his shooting spree, the son took his mother's life, shooting her with the same weapon taken out of her arsenal – an AR-15 semi-automatic assault rifle – that he then used to kill the children and teachers at Sandy Hook. The handgun with which he blew out his brains after being cornered by police also belonged to his mother.

Now, a new twist in the debate on gun control has arisen, as law enforcement officials at the Bureau of Alcohol, Tobacco, Firearms and Explosives have pointed out: plastic handguns made with 3-D printers. A Texas-based organization, Defense Distributed, is behind a campaign to popularize do-it-yourself firearms. The design of its prototype, a handgun appropriately named 'The Liberator', can be downloaded from the internet, and apparently more than 100,000 people did so in just two days before the website was ordered to be shut down by the government.

In tests conducted by ATF officials, it was found that the 'Liberator' had enough fire power to injure vital organs. These printed guns could possibly be slipped past metal detectors in airports or into schools, government offices or to sporting events. It is not expected that seasoned gangsters or other professional criminals will use them – there are plenty of more powerful, conventional guns around, after all – but that amateurs and gun enthusiasts might use the new 3-D technology to print their own armory on a desk-top printer to circumvent existing gun control regulations – such as they are. The 'Ultimaker 2', recently ranked No. 1 in a consumer test of 3-D plastic printers, sells for a reasonable $2,499 plus shipping. It is described as 'an aesthetically pleasing 3D printer with premium features and high-quality results' that is 'perfect for any skill level.'

In short: any dummy with a laptop will soon be able to print their own handguns to defend their families and property.

TUESDAY, 17 September

MAKING WINE IN SAN DIEGO COUNTY

In the morning, after dropping off our kids at school, Frank Lord and I drive to Ramona to help a friend of his with his winemaking business. Just out of La Jolla, Frank's car phone rings; it's an automatic call from his son's school, advising that the school is in lock-down mode, following a shooting in the village. There is no cause for alarm, the computer voice tells us: this is a routine procedure. Frank's son goes to the Bishop's School, on Draper Avenue, just a few metres from where we live, adjacent to the La Jolla Tennis Club.

This is right in the middle of our neighbourhood. Frank and I exchange a worried look at each other.

A few minutes later, Susan calls on my mobile to say that the same has happened at Max's school: All Hallows up on Mount Soledad is also in lock-down. We wonder what's going on. People are a little nervous right now: just days after the shooting spree at the Washington Naval Yard that left thirteen people dead. Later we find out that the shooting in La Jolla is related to a domestic dispute, and it happened in Bird Rock, not anywhere near the Bishops' School or All Hallows (where Max and Vera had remained blissfully unaware of the lockdown). There is nothing to be worried about.

When we get to Lenora Winery, winemaker Eric Metz is already waiting for us. He has brought a whole bunch of donuts and Danish pastries for breakfast, as he was expecting both Mary Lord and Susan to come with us, but the two had changed their mind, so it's only the three of us, plus Roberto, Eric's Mexican part-time associate. Eric and Roberto have hand-picked the year's cabernet sauvignon grape clusters over the last two days, and there are some 200 crates of grapes waiting to be processed. We're ready to do some volunteering to make wine.

For a one-person business, Eric's winery has an impressive collection of machinery, housed in a rather overcrowded-looking, sprawling industrial shed. You need to carefully navigate your way around the place. There are plastic fermentation tanks, oak barrels precariously hovering over you on some metal scaffolding, cartons of wine shakily stacked up five or six cases on top of each other, bits and pieces of equipment that I cannot identify.

And then there's the big machine: a state-of-the-art Milani Grape Separator from Italy, some 12 feet high, with a conveyor attached at one end and a long vibrating table at the other, all shiny stainless steel. So we get to work:

Roberto unloads the grape clusters onto the bottom of the conveyor belt, they travel up to the top of the machine where they are crushed and de-stemmed in one go, then gravity takes over: the cleanly picked stalks drop into a basket on the shop floor, the separated grapes are sorted over a grid that shuttles back and forth, grapes and juice are collected into a tube below to be pumped into a huge plastic tank, while the bits and pieces of stalk and grape that survived the separation process are moved along on the slats of the vibrating table. Frank and I, standing on either side of the machine that shakes and rumbles and makes a horrific noise, remove the remaining wooden bits. We are to make sure that not a single grape escapes on its pre-ordained path into the fermentation tank. Meanwhile, Eric keeps a close eye on the whole operation, monitoring and adjusting the various parts to ensure everything moves smoothly.

When all the crates have been emptied, we break for a late lunch, tasting one of Eric's reds, a nice, pleasantly mellow drop of merlot. Eric's name betrays his parental origins: Lorraine, France. But he is not a professional winemaker; he got into the business after retiring from his engineering job. He talks about the difficulties of winemaking in Ramona, an area that is still largely unknown to wine buffs. It was only in 2006 that the area, Ramona Valley, was designated an AVA (American Viticultural Area), a recognition of a quality *terroir* that promises prestige and brand identity. It's a breakthrough that bodes well for the future, though at the moment wineries here are in their infancy and struggling to survive. Unlike Temecula a few miles to the northwest that has managed to make a name for itself as a viticultural centre, Ramona is off the beaten track (meaning: not on a freeway) and only few tourists manage to find their way up the hills. But as it lies higher up, it has a cooler micro-climate, and the wine growers of Ramona are confident they will make better wines. Their problem is distribution.

Like Eric, the two-dozen winemakers of the valley are all self-taught, small-scale operators, fiercely independent and individualistic. Their output – mostly in the range of 500 to 600 cases a year – is not large enough to attract the attention of wholesalers, and they don't have the manpower and capital to promote the growth of their business on their own. Some, Eric says, prefer things the way they are, while he would certainly welcome a helping hand from bodies such as the county's Small Business Advisory Office or the Chamber of Commerce to advise on branding, maximizing business operations or reducing red tape. Eric sells his wines mainly through the internet and at weekend cellar door openings.

Looking at the cases of wine stacked up in Eric's shed, I begin to realise that making wine is the easy part; selling it is the challenge. It reminds me a little bit of desktop publishing which was all the rage when affordable laser printers came on the market a few decades ago. The idea was to avoid the exploitative stranglehold of publishers and short-circuit the cumbersome process of getting a book into print. At the end of the day, the desktop publishers found themselves with a lot of books sitting on top of their desks, and didn't know what to do with them.

After lunch, our job is to clean up, and this takes almost as long as processing the fruit. The machinery is taken apart, everything is hosed down and washed, and then re-assembled. We wish Eric well, and he gives us a generous supply of bottles to take home. On the way back to La Jolla, Frank and I speculate about his future as a winemaker. Eric is a very likeable guy, and we admire his enthusiasm and energy, as well as the know-how and the skills he has acquired. But Frank is not overly optimistic that Eric will be able to take his business to another level. Frank certainly knows that he himself will have to do things differently if and when he opens his own winery. But he is very determined to do so.

DREAM BIG, WORK HARD, AND OPEN YOUR OWN WINERY?

How much will it cost? Unimproved agricultural land is still reasonably cheap in the Ramona Valley, an acre will set you back some $15,000. You'll need at least four acres, plus some extra land to build your shed on. Or a house, if you prefer. Once you've got buildings in place and bought your winery equipment, you've probably spent between $200,000 and $250,000. Then you need to prepare the land: put in an irrigation system, pay for soil testing and improving, buy and install trellises and fencing. Grapevines cost about three to four dollars a plant, and you'll need about 600 per acre. If you do everything yourself, it'll cost you in the vicinity of $10,000 per acre, but that could easily double if you have to pay people to do it for you.

Once you have your soil prepared, trellises in place and rootstock planted, you must wait. You'll get half a crop after three years, and a full crop after five. If everything goes right and the weather is your friend, you'll harvest two tons of grapes per acre, and the yield will be about 100 cases per acre, 400 in total, or 4,800 bottles in a good year. You will drink some yourself and give some away to your friends, let's say 800 in total per year. That will leave you with 4,000 bottles to sell. If you make a high-quality wine that you can sell at $25 a bottle, you'll make a cool $100,000. After ten years of hard work and with a good business plan, you will have recouped your initial investment and can look forward to making a nice profit and a decent living. You've got it made! Dream big and work hard!

But hold on: there is a big IF here! You can sell your wine for $25 a bottle directly to the customer via internet or at the cellar door, but if you sell to a distributor or wholesaler, you will only get $12 or maybe – if you are lucky – $15 for your premium red. So, a net annual income of $48,000 seems much more realistic. Not counting your own costs, taxes, and what have you.

But it's all about the dream, isn't it?

THE COST OF LIVING WELL IN SOUTHERN CALIFORNIA

Driving back from German School in Hillcrest on Saturday mornings, we usually stop at *Ranch 99* Market on Clairemont Mesa to do some shopping, mainly for fish and meat and fruit and veggies, as well as Chinese staples: chicken feet, barbecued pork, various congee mixes, red bean paste, noodles, buns, assorted sauces and what have you.

Here's an example of prices for fresh fruit in September. We buy tangerines (99c per lb), sweet red potatoes (69c per lb), green asparagus ($1.99 per lb), Korean pears ($2.59 per lb), bananas (Chiquitas, 49c per lb), Fuyu persimmons (49c per lb), and a box of red papayas, four big ones for $9.99. There's boxes of mangoes, too, but I'm not convinced: they are from Brazil and too tough to the touch.

As I'm in charge of meat and fish and seafood, I check out the relevant counters and tanks with fresh and frozen and live protein. I buy some beef fillet mignon for the week to come ($4.99 per lb), and then move on to the seafood. There is quite a good choice: live fish, including good-sized turbots from Korea, lobsters and crab. I buy some fresh Atlantic salmon fillet as a stand-by for Max (8.99 per lb), and then decide to splurge out on tonight's dinner: red snapper sashimi (*Izumi dai*, half a pound at $ 4.50), a dozen oysters at 99c each, and a 2 lb. fresh lobster at just less than $12 (not live, but nearly; the live ones in the tank are $9.99 per lb, but it's hard to choose them because the tanks are out of reach and a bit murky, while with the fresh ones in the box I can have a good look and a squeeze, so I make sure to pick out the best one, with a solid weight in the hand, good-sized claws and legs all in place, a lively green colour and a nice, fresh smell).

This makes for a pretty good meal on a Saturday night. The sashimi is lovely, the oysters terrific. I don't know where they come from: they are roundish, fairly thin, flat and smooth, a bit like the French *fines de claires*, easy to open, with a clean briny taste, with just a hint of creaminess. And the lobster is very good, too: I just throw it into a pot of boiling water, let it turn red, then throw it into a pot of ice water to cool it down. We simply eat it with a bit of melted butter. And there's some green salad to finish the meal off. I have a bottle of a very nice, easily drinkable, fresh and citrusy Chilean SauvBlanc ($4.99 special at Grocery Outlet Bargain Store) to wash it all down with.

Max prefers Chinese noodles; he eats some sashimi and takes a couple of bites of the lobster, but can't be bothered eating more (he wants to get back to his Germany project). Susan eats half the tail and that's enough for her; besides, she does not like using a nutcracker at the dinner table, so I finish the lobster by myself, which I don't mind doing, I enjoy the cracking and sucking even though I mess up my new white T-shirt in the process (it ends up in the washing machine straight away).

With regard to liquor and beer, comparing the prices we pay here in California to what we had to pay in Sydney makes you want to cry with sympathy for our friends down under. At present, there is a special on a 12-pack of large cans of Asahi Super Dry, one of my favourite beers, at $ 7.98, so I stock up on a few cases. In terms of the International Standard Comparison Six-Pack Rate (courtesy of a highly respected German researcher, an authority in the field), this amounts to $3.99 for six large cans of premium beer: unbeatable. Add to this the inconvenience of having to buy alcohol in Sydney in a special store, known as bottle shop, whereas here you can load everything into the same over-sized supermarket trolley.

Summa summarum: We are not poor, and that's what we can afford for dinner in the Golden State, a land of plenty, California Dreaming. We don't eat like this every day, but in theory we could.

MORE ON COST OF LIVING: 'PRICE OF GAS MAY WORRY SOME …'

We pay around $3.50 for a gallon of petrol (or gas, as the Americans have it), that's about 95 cents a litre and probably more than a third less than current prices in Australia. With a coupon from our trusted retailer, Vons, we get a seven cents discount per gallon, which almost makes up for the state tax – but that's misleading, because unlike the state sales tax that you pay separately every time you pay at a check-out counter, restaurant or wherever, at a petrol station the tax is already included in the price. So, petrol is cheap, and it seems as if it's getting cheaper still. American oil producers pump 8 million barrels a day, more than Saudi Arabia or Russia. America has become the world's largest producer of energy. The country is in the midst of an energy revolution.

The miracle words are shale oil, fracking, and horizontal drilling. Much of the tremendous increase in natural gas production that's driving energy prices down comes from the vast resources in shale oil that are now being tapped all around the country. There's a huge boomerang-shaped arc of shale deposits that starts in Wisconsin, swings south-east to New York and Pennsylvania and further south across Texas to Louisiana, Alabama and back via Utah, Colorado and Wyoming to the Dakotas. The stuff has been around forever, but until recently it was either impossible or too expensive to get it out of the ground.

Now, fracking, or hydraulic fracturing has arrived, and it is hugely controversial. High-pressure pumping of huge amounts of water mixed with sand and potent chemicals down into underground rock formations to release the gas is not everyone's idea of safe energy production. But it is going on at full speed almost everywhere, despite local moratoria and a lack of consistent regulation. In California, over a hundred wells are currently being 'fracked', mostly in Kern County around Bakersfield that lies at the heart of the huge Monterey Shale Field, one of the country's largest deposits. It runs along the St Andreas Fault and covers a huge part of Central and Southern California. Fracking is also being used to exploit the off-shore oil fields in the waters off Santa Barbara, site of the infamous 1969 oil spill, as well as in wells in the LA metropolitan area. Critics of the fracking boom are concerned about the drilling impacts on the environment and public health. They are especially worried about the industry's high demand for water – in drought-stricken California! They are wary of spills and waste disposal polluting the groundwater. And what about the proximity to seismic fault lines: can fracking operations trigger earthquakes?

Traditional crude oil production is also rising rapidly, due to a technological breakthrough called horizontal drilling. This is more of a conventional method of bringing oil up to the surface. Near-horizontal drilling at an angle means more efficient coverage of fields that are close to being exhausted and the possibility to reach deposits otherwise not accessible.

So, is the USA – like Australia – a 'lucky country' that lives off its mineral wealth without paying much attention to other things, such as sustainability, innovation, energy savings, and diversification? Hardly so. For one thing, it is at the forefront of technological research and development. It also invests heavily on renewable energy and energy savings. The federal government is committed to triple its own use of renewable sources. It is the largest energy consumer in the country and must 'lead by example', according to President Obama. The federal government occupies about half a million buildings and operates 600,000 vehicles. At the moment, it uses 7.5 percent of its electricity from renewable sources; the goal is 20 percent by 2020. The state government of California, meanwhile, is heavily investing in alternative energy projects. It is about to spend $15 million to build hydrogen fueling stations across the state, although there are only about 200 hydrogen-powered cars on the roads in California today. The money is to be raised by way of a one-off $3 levy on car licence plates. There are, I remember, about 40 million motor vehicles driven by fossil-based fuels that emit considerable amounts of carbon-dioxide into the California sky.

Then again: California Governor Jerry Brown supports fracking, as does President Obama. It is one thing where conservative opponents in Congress are in agreement with the White House.

GOVERNMENT SHUTDOWN

Topic Number One in all current private conversations and public discourse is the spectre of a Government Shutdown, foreshadowed by a recalcitrant minority of Republican members of Congress and the Senate hell-bent on bringing the Obama administration to a standstill, no matter the cost to the national economy. Hundreds of thousands of federal employees will be furloughed or laid off, from astronauts at NASA to humble cleaners in the Smithsonian museums to civilian employees working for contractors in the many military bases across the country. People have strong opinions on the matter. Most seem to think that what is happening is downright stupid and infantile, and they tend to blame the Republican hardliners even if they may not be enthusiastic about President Obama and his policies. Simultaneously, an ominous deadline is looming: after 17 October, the Federal Government will not be able to pay its bills anymore unless Congress agrees to lift the debt ceiling or to extend the payment deadline. The US government has never defaulted on its financial obligations, both domestic and international, and expert economists of all persuasion predict dire consequences if this would happen: a homemade recession that could lead to a trickle-down worldwide economic downturn. A lot of people are beginning to get seriously worried where the country is heading.

Meanwhile, life seems to go on pretty much as usual.

SAN DIEGO COUNTY, *OKTOBERFEST*

'Let's have a party!' October is *Oktoberfest* month all over San Diego County. Pubs, casinos, grocery chains, hot dog stands, farmers' markets, micro-breweries and butcheries are all getting into the act: German food and beer. T & H Prime Meats and Sausages of San Marcos, self-proclaimed 'Oktoberfest Headquarters', announce their award-winning artisan *Bratwurst*, made by *Sausage Meister* Jacob Kappeler according to a 'family recipe from the 1600's' [sic], all natural, fresh, low fat, no additives, no nitrites: 'delicious!!' What to eat with your *Bratwurst*? Why, *Rotkohl* and *Saurkraut* [sic], of course. I'm pleased to see that German culture (minus proper spelling) is alive and well in Southern California, and that its popularity extends to other ethnicities. Our friend Minh for example, from Shanghai, mother of a boy who also attends the Saturday German School, confesses she is a great fan of German food. I don't mind *Eisbein* and a *Warsteiner* myself, on the odd occasion. Basically, though, I'd rather have *yum cha* and *Guilin* noodles and steamed fish with shallots and ginger or congee with scallops, anytime.

TUESDAY, 1 October

GOVERNMENT SHUTDOWN CONTINUED

The federal government has shut down, partially at least: essential services are still open, but no-one seems to know exactly what they are. President Obama says he refuses to be blackmailed, and House Leader John Boehner complains the president does not negotiate. Both claim the other is un-American. There are hectic activities, but no outcomes. There are bipartisan meetings on all levels, but nobody gives in. It's like a game of poker: everyone is waiting for the first person to blink.

I'm still trying to understand what this is all about. Apparently, a right-wing section of the Republican Party (aka the Grand Old Party, GOP) wants to derail Obama's ACA by what in Australia is called 'blocking supply', i.e. withholding funds. The Republicans' goal is to 'de-fund' Obamacare; they want to roll back a piece of legislation that has already been approved by the House of Representatives. Now the Senate is holding it up, with a bunch of die-hard conservative senators refusing to play ball, as the American say.

In San Diego, some 33,000 workers are laid off. Many more have been asked to stay on the job without pay. The Miramar Air Show was cancelled at the last minute. All national parks and monuments are closed. In some places where the government facilities are major tourist sites, like Mount Rushmore or the Statue of Liberty, local and state authorities have come to the rescue, paying the salaries of furloughed federal workers to keep the attractions open and the tourist dollar flowing.

Not so in San Diego. Here the Cabrillo National Monument at Point Loma, overlooking San Diego Bay towards the east and the Pacific Ocean towards the west, remains shut. We had been meaning to visit the place for some time, to walk around the old lighthouse and inspect the monument to the first European visitor to California. Max is more excited about the prospect of playing in the tide pools on the Pacific side of the park, looking for crabs. As the site is only a couple of miles from Barnes Tennis Centre, we drive up there after tennis practice to see whether there is anything to see. The road leads along the ridge on top of the narrow peninsula, with rows upon rows of neat white tombstones on neatly trimmed lawns on both sides. This is Fort Rosecrans National Cemetery, on the grounds of what used to be Fort Rosecrans, the old fortification built to protect the seaway into San Diego Bay. When we get to the entrance of the national park proper, the gates are closed and there is nobody around: no sign, nothing to see. We drive home, and I promise Max we'll come back another day, after the shutdown.

MONDAY, 14 October

COLUMBUS ON THE PACIFIC

The birthday party that had been planned at Point Loma to commemorate the centenary of the dedication of the Cabrillo National Monument by President Woodrow Wilson on Columbus Day, 14 October 1913, had to be cancelled. With the site closed due to the deadlock in Washington, D.C., what could be done? Well, you just postpone the festivities until next year.

Who is this Señor Cabrillo anyway? And what's he got to do with Columbus? To start with, there is some confusion regarding the name. *Juan Rodriguez Cabrillo* or *João Rodrigues Cabrilho*? Spanish or Portuguese? There is little that is known for sure about the man. Historians tend to agree that he was born in Portugal around 1499, went to Mexico with Hernan Cortes, and subsequently became an extremely wealthy *conquistador* by exploiting the gold treasures of Guatemala. In 1542, he was commissioned by the Spanish Crown to explore the California coast. Leading an expedition of three ships from Jalisco in Mexico, he landed in San Diego Bay on 28 September, then went on to 'discover' the Santa Catalina islands off present-day Los Angeles, continued north past San Francisco but missed the entrance to the Bay (just as many sailors did for the next 200 years, not unlike Lieutenant James Cook who had discovered Botany Bay but missed the entrance to Sydney Harbour a few miles north). Cabrillo sailed as far as the Russian River estuary where he was finally forced back by bad weather, only to meet an untimely death in a skirmish with natives on Santa Catalina, 'the island of romance', in early January 1543. Again, the story of Captain Cook's demise comes to mind.

That the cancellation of Cabrillo's anniversary celebration went pretty much unnoticed, certainly without any public protest, has probably something to do with the unremarkable history of the monument. In 1913, the San Diego city fathers had entertained great plans to build a legacy for the Portuguese-Spanish sailor. The superficial similarity with the story of Columbus (a Spanish-sponsored commission, an expedition of three ships, the 'discovery' of the other side of America) suggested a grand historical narrative waiting to be invented and exploited in order to put San Diego on the map. A huge statue was to be built, as a Western counterpart to the Statue of Liberty, to create an attraction at the 'Silver Gate' entry to San Diego Bay that would equal the hugely more famous 'Golden Gate Bridge' city to the north. It was to be a 150-feet tall landmark to guide mariners at sea and bring in swarms of land-locked tourists to the area.

Alas, nothing would come of it. The Federal Government donated a less than generous half-acre parcel of land as the site for the statue, and that put a damper on the project.

The financing and actual building of a monument was left to a civic organisation, the Order of Panama, which did not survive the First World War. Another patriotic league, the Native Sons of the Golden West, asked by President Coolidge to take over the project in 1926, did not fare any better. In 1935, a bronze plaque – better than nothing! – was affixed to the 19th century lighthouse, in a ceremony attended by the Portuguese ambassador; it commemorated the first 'Alta California Landfall' by 'Juan Rodriguez Cabrillo, distinguished Portuguese navigator in the service of Spain'. Four years later, the Portuguese government managed what the Native Sons of Southern California had failed to accomplish over two decades: it commissioned a sculptor, Alvaro de Bree, to create a sandstone statue.

Ironically, the work was not destined for San Diego; rather, it was meant as a contribution by the people of Portugal to the San Francisco Exhibition of 1939. However, the statue arrived too late for the show and was unceremoniously stored in a Bay Area warehouse.

Subsequently, the then California governor, Mr Culbert Olsen, promised to transfer the piece to Oakland, as a tribute to that Bay City's substantial Portuguese population, but he was thwarted by Mr Ed Fletcher, the state senator representing San Diego, who was outraged at the idea and simply decided to 'kidnap' the statue which was exactly what he did, later claiming he had acted on the time-honoured principle that 'possession is 90% of the law.' In a clandestine operation, the statue was 'spirited' out of the warehouse and shipped to San Diego by train. Subsequently, Mr Fletcher and his colleagues in the state legislature stalled all attempts by the governor to get it back. It was finally dedicated on its present site on 'Cabrillo Day', 28 September 1942, only to be immediately closed to the public during the duration of the war. In 1957, the bronze plaque at the lighthouse was

The Navigator's Chart, the Sword and the Cross: Cabrillo Monument at Point Loma

replaced with a new one on which the name of Cabrillo was changed to its Portuguese spelling, and in 1988 the monument itself, badly eroded by then, was replaced by a replica.

One hundred years later, when we finally visit the monument after the national park has opened for business again, the statue does not quite live up to expectation. It shows the Portuguese captain, armed with a sword and a navigator's chart and circle, standing in front of a column crowned by a cross. The city fathers had dreamed of a towering sculptural spectacle to rival the famous lady with the torch (or sword, if you prefer to follow Franz Kafka). At a height of 14 feet, the Cabrillo statue is somewhat larger-than-life, but – regrettably – it pales into insignificance compared to the monumental statue on Liberty Island (151 feet from base to torch, 305 feet if you count the foundation and pedestal). It is nevertheless a nice piece of work on a pleasant site with stunning vistas over city and ocean, and it is certainly worth a visit, even though you might frown at the traditional iconography that displays the familiar props – the sword and the cross – which the *conquistadores* had brought with them from their native Europe to take possession of what they thought was the New World, its lands and its indigenous peoples.

GOVERNMENT SHUTDOWN (CONTINUED)

As the government shutdown goes into the second week, the rhetoric heats up. Mrs Sarah ('Obama lies–freedom dies') Palin makes a re-appearance from nowhere to share the media limelight with prominent right-wing ideologues in their opposition against what they perceive is the creeping transformation of the US government into a socialist dictatorship. At a rally in Washington, the so-called 'Value Voters Summit', junior Senator Rand Paul from Kentucky (son of failed presidential candidate Ron) tells the enthusiastic crowd that there is a 'war on Christianity' being waged around the world, 'from Boston to Sansibar', and that the government doesn't want you to know about it. Not far from the White House, another speaker tells the President to 'put down the Q'uran' and come out of his besieged fortress with hands raised above his head and then 'get out of town.' Of course, there is also Mr Ted Cruz, the Tea Party's pin-up boy and 'Stooge of the Night' on the David Letterman show. Now the junior senator from Texas is on the news everywhere and around the clock, railing against Obamacare, describing it simultaneously as a trainwreck, a disaster, a nightmare and the biggest job killer in the country. Mr Cruz, incidentally, does not need to worry about his own health insurance. He is covered under the family plan of his wife, Heidi Cruz, an executive with Goldman Sachs, paid for by the giant banking and financial company (a value of some $20,000 annually).

In terms of anti-government rhetoric, it is the anti-politician Ben Carson, MD, who takes the cake. Interviewed on TV, he declares that 'Obamacare is the worst thing since slavery,' indeed 'it is slavery, because it makes us all subservient to the government.' Then Dr Carson goes on to quote Vladimir Lenin who said that socialised medicine is the cornerstone of a socialist society. Hmm, you say, and scratch your head? Dr Carson? Never heard of this guy before? Neither have I. Just as well that Mr Carson is not a politician, one might say. But he is a Black American, so he should know about slavery, right?

It stands to reason that the good doctor is not a dummy. Perhaps he read Comrade Lenin while doing pre-med at Yale? He is not just any old doctor, either. He is director of paediatric neurosurgery at John Hopkins University Hospital in Baltimore, Maryland, not far from the nation's capital. But first and foremost, Dr Carson is a religious man. He believes the world was made by God 6,000 years ago. His call for a tax reform based on the biblical principle of 'tithing' immediately generates a great deal of media interest and questions about a rumored career change: will Carson go into politics? The soft-spoken doctor, suave and eloquent, corrects the ABC interviewer: 'tithing' is not the same as a flat tax, and as to politics, he will deal with this issue as he dealt with all the decisions he has taken in his life, he will 'leave it up to God.'

THE FALL OF BOB FILNER (ACT I)

After our return from summer holiday, we are not surprised to find that Bob Filner has resigned. In July already, three long-time supporters of the mayor had called for his resignation, alleging numerous incidents of sexual harassment, including 'inappropriate comments, kissing and groping'. The unidentified victims included an employee on the mayor's staff, a campaign volunteer and a constituent. The mayor had replied that he would defend himself vigorously: a 'fair and independent investigation' would clear him of all charges of sexual harassment. In an emotionally charged speech to the San Diego City Council, the mayor claimed he had become the victim of a 'lynch mob'.

But a few weeks later, on 30 August, after further allegations of sexual harassment (mostly from women among his own staff) and the prospect of legal action taken against him, Mr Filner, defender of the seals at La Jolla Children's Beach, threw in the towel.

THE FALL OF BOB FILNER (ACT II)

The news of Filner's resignation is making headlines all around the country. His position had finally become untenable after a lawsuit was filed against him. In total, 19 women had come forward and publicly claimed that Filner had sexually harassed them, including a retired admiral, a Marilyn Monroe impersonator, a 67-year-old great-grandmother, and a nurse who said Filner demanded a date in exchange for helping a Marine who had suffered a brain injury and PTSD during service in Iraq. It remained for Filner to negotiate the details of his resignation, including a request to the City of San Diego to pay his legal fees. The city council initially refused to do so, voting in fact to sue Filner for any costs incurred by the city due to claims filed against him and the city. However, after three days of mediation, a deal was struck setting up a joint legal defense fund for Filner and the city against claims arising from lawsuits by current or former city employees, as well as providing an additional $98,000 to cover part of Filner's expected legal fees. City Council president Todd Gloria was appointed interim mayor, pending a new election.

ADDING INSULT TO INJURY: 'Ban Filner!'

The Hooters chain of *Playboy*-type family restaurants, best known for their scantily-dressed, shapely and buxom waitresses dressed in hot pants and tight T-shirts, tries to cash in on the media frenzy surrounding the Filner case by publicly announcing a campaign to ban the mayor from its establishments.

WEDNESDAY, 16 October

THE FALL OF BOB FILNER (ACT III)

Today is Bob Filner's day in court. He pleads guilty to charges of felony and misdemeanor and is sentenced to three years of probation, three months of house confinement, and loss of his pension for about six months (from the date of the first allegation to his resignation). He is also barred from ever again standing for elected office and will have to submit to treatment by a mental health professional. He will spend six months in jail if he violates the terms of his probation. This is presumably the end of public life for Mr Filner. He was elected mayor with a 52% majority last November, after having served nearly 20 years in Congress as San Diego's local representative.

The sentence is the result of a plea bargain which saw Mr Filner accept and plead guilty to one count of felony (false imprisonment by violence, fraud, menace and deceit) and two counts of misdemeanor (battery), which could have had him sentenced to three years' jail and $10,000 for the felony and 12 months and $4,000 for each misdemeanor charge. All other charges related to the harassment claims were dropped as part of the deal worked out with the State Attorney-General's office. Curiously, the felony charge of false imprisonment was the result of Mr Filner restraining a woman against her will at a fund-raising event by placing her in what has since become known as the 'Filner headlock'. The other charges related to the former mayor kissing a woman on her lips against her will and touching the buttocks of another one.

On the cover of today's *U-T* is on over-sized photo of the ex-mayor at his public sentencing, with a neat alliterative headline: Filner's final fall. The paper's editorialist speculates about a possible comeback of the once popular ex-mayor, sometime down the track.

FOOD TRUCKS

Ever thought of getting into the gastronomy business? The easy way is to open a pop-up restaurant, or a food truck.

Food trucks are all the rage. There are some 250 of them roaming the San Diego downtown streets and suburban malls, with about 50 considered 'gourmet trucks'. They advertise their position on social media, and their hardcore twitter fans follow them for lunch. Most of these mobile restaurants seem to offer standard American fare: hamburgers, hot dogs, donuts, bagels, sandwiches, tacos, burrito, nachos, sodas, smoothies and shakes, and extra fries. But there is also the Pierogi Truck, Crepes Bonaparte, Mariscos Alex, Mangia Mangia Mobile, New York on Rye, The Green Truck, SoulCal Food, Greengo Grilled Cheese Gastro, and Eat at Recess. As the name suggests, the latter caters to the school crowds; its hot-selling item is a chicken sandwich imaginatively labelled 'Science Project'. And then of course there is: The Mother Trucker Express of New Orleans, Cuisine and Catering, Creole and Cajun Creations.

The problem with food trucks in San Diego City and County is that they are operating in a legal limbo. Rules of operation are ill-defined. Under ex-mayor Bob Filner, a laissez-faire policy was the order of the day. But Interim Mayor Todd Gloria has instructed police and county rangers to enforce the rules, at least the one that is clear and in the books: food trucks are not permitted to do business on private property. Why food trucks are allowed to ply their trade on public streets but not on privately owned land, usually parking lots, is beyond me, but that's the law. Citations have been issued to trucks operating on private parking lots. The problem is that this where the food trucks apparently do most of their business.

But there are other issues. The owners of traditional brick-and-mortar restaurants want a buffer zone between themselves and any food truck. What about rubbish pick-up and toilet facilities, they ask. What about the appropriate proximity (or distance) to schools and bus stops, say concerned parents. And what would be the appropriate operating hours, council rangers would like to know.

I remember from Sydney that any self-respecting 'world-class city' of today seems to have flagged food trucks as one of their claims to global pre-eminence. If only the bureaucrats would take care of the devilishly mundane bureaucratic details.

We decide to give the business a test when we come across the Champions Mariscos Seafood truck on the parking lot between Toys 'R' Us and a Petco warehouse on Morena Boulevard, not far from the airport. This is a private lot, so the seafood champions must be doing their business illegally, although nobody seems to mind. There is a queue of about half a dozen people, and business is brisk. We try a couple of fish tacos, and then we order some more. They are very tasty, with a generous bit of fried fish, and you can help yourself to extra lime, mayo and all sorts of mean looking chili sauces. At a dollar and a quarter a piece this taco is unbeatable. You can also have a dozen oysters on the half-shell for twelve bucks.

248

The truck has quite a few other items on the menu, mostly with imaginative Spanish names. There is *Costa Azul* (shrimp wrapped with cheese and bacon), *Tostada Loka* (Crazy Tostada, which is shrimp ceviche with octopus, clams, scallops and oyster), or *Tostada Viagra* (all seafood, minced and marinated in lime). I decide that my favourite dish is *Aguachile Maleficio* (raw scallops, shrimp and octopus marinated in lime juice, served with onions, avocado, cucumber and chillies).

AN AMERICAN DREAM: A.D. 1925

At tennis during a break, Marv, aged 94, shows us an old photo of a boy in a sailor's uniform. 'That's me,' he says, 'at the age of six, in a sailor's uniform. Mind you, I'm an army man!' he adds slyly.

The photo shows a cute-looking boy in a sailor's suit characteristic of children's fashion in the early 20th century. Marv explains that he had just found the picture among the things squirreled away and left behind by his late wife. He remembers that it was sent by his mother in New York to the *NY Post* newspaper in 1924 or 1925, following an announcement in the press that a replacement for boy-actor Jackie Coogan was being sought. Readers were asked to send in photos of their aspiring young Thespian offspring, and the paper promised to forward them on to the appropriate people in Hollywood. Coogan, who played the title role in Chaplin's *The Kid*, was apparently getting a little too old for the kind of role that had made him famous around the globe, while the studio obviously wanted to continue to cash in on his box-office appeal. 'What if I had gotten a call from Hollywood?' Marv muses.

'The glamour!' I answer. 'Just imagine: the American Dream. The Oscars, the red carpet, the fans, the women, the easy life. You would have been a star.'

'Maybe,' says Marv. 'But I didn't get a call from the studio. I joined the army.'

MONDAY, 28 October

FISHING NEWS No.1: OARFISH ASCENDING, OR 'THE END IS NIGH'

Two giant oarfish have just come to the attention of Californians. Within one week, an 18-foot dead specimen was discovered floating in the waters off Catalina Island, and a 14-foot oarfish was washed up on a beach in Oceanside in North San Diego County five days later. The giant oarfish live in depths of more than 600 feet, and it is exceedingly rare that they make it to the surface.

The fish is a relative of the silver ribbonfish that makes a seasonal appearance at the Sydney Fish Market at a bargain-basement price. Apparently, there is a reasonable supply in Sydney Harbour and estuaries like Broken Bay and Port Hacking. It is a stunning-looking fish, with an elongated sharp mouth, huge eyes and smooth, silvery skin along its very long, snake-like body. Apparently, it's mainly dried and used in Chinese cooking.

Superstition has it that dead oarfish washed up on land are portents of disaster: they warn of impending doom. In Japanese and Taiwanese folklore, they are called earthquake fish; their appearance supposedly foreshadows major earthquakes and volcanic eruptions, with tsunami monster waves to follow.

It's just as well that there was an earthquake emergency drill today at All Hallows Academy. When the siren sounded, the kids had to crawl under their tables and assume the brace, or fetal, position. No panic! Then the all-clear siren sounded and the kids filed out of their classrooms onto the soccer field to be lined up and counted.

Ok, we're ready for the Big One.

FISHING NEWS No.2: TOTOABAS CROSSING THE BORDER

Fish smuggler Jason Jin Shun Xie, 49 years of age, of Sacramento, California, was sentenced in San Diego Federal Court to four months in prison. He was also ordered to pay $3 million (amount to be confirmed by another Federal Court) to the Mexican government as compensation for the loss the country suffered because of dried fish bladders shipped illegally out of the country. Xie pleaded guilty to knowingly trafficking endangered wildlife.

The totoaba, a fish related to the sea bass that can grow up to 6 feet in length, is found only in the Sea of Cortez; they spawn in the Colorado River delta where they can be easily caught and smuggled through the closest US port of entry at Calexico, California. Their swim bladders are filled with gas rather than urine to help control stability and buoyancy. Dried in the sun, totoaba bladders are considered rare delicacies in Chinese soups and highly prized by *connaisseurs* for their alleged performance-enhancing qualities; they fetch between $5,000 and $10,000 a piece.

In Mexico, commercial fishing of totoaba goes back well over a hundred years. It was always a lucrative business; bladders sold for five dollars apiece in the early 1900s. In the 1920s, American fishermen entered the industry, harvesting both the meat for domestic consumption and the bladders for export. By the end of WWII, the US was exporting 400,000 pounds of dried fish bladder to China: a classic case of overfishing from which the Totoaba population never recovered.

Today, the fish are protected under the Endangered Species Act and under an international trade pact. But the demand from China – where prices have reached astronomical heights – remains undiminished, so there is still a lot of poaching going on, including by organized Mexican drug cartels who have discovered a profitable sideline to their traditional business: so-called aquatic cocaine. The illegal trade is now threatening the survival of the species. Scientists in Mexico have been working on a breeding program with the aim of releasing fish to breed again in the wild. The cost of raising a single totoaba to reproduction age is estimated at over $11,000 – and that was the exact amount used to calculate the cost of restitution in the case of fish smuggler Xie. He admitted to trafficking 270 bladders, thus: $270 \times 11,000 = 2,970,000$.

For a while, Mr Xie did quite well out of his illegal export business. He owned a $350,000 mansion in Seattle (which he forfeited to the US government as part of his plea bargain) and his profits were estimated at approximately $3 million.

Now, when he gets out of jail, he'll be back to plus/minus zero.

WEDNESDAY, 30 October

'DEAR ABBY'

The 'Dear Abby' column in Pap Doug's *U-T* is nearly always good for a surprise insight into contemporary American mores and manners, and maybe even for a bit of a chuckle. Today's item is sent in by a 'lady reader' who signs in as a 'Lover of Nature' requesting advice on a matter of religion. She writes that she is a 'practising pagan of long standing' and, before going on a date arranged by a friend, would like to know what to tell the gentleman concerning her faith. The writer takes pain to stress that she looks …well, yes, like the rest of us, at first sight she couldn't be suspected of being a non-Christian. So, what are you supposed to do: tell the gentleman on the first date that you are a practising pagan? How do you break it to him – slowly or being up-front about it? The lady is clearly worried: pagans usually have a bad press, she claims, although they really are 'only nature-loving people with knowledge of home remedies.'

'Dear Abby' wisely counsels a don't-ask-don't-tell strategy. Dear Lover of Nature, she writes, this is not a matter to be broached on a first date, unless if and when the occasion arises. And to satisfy the general readership of her column, she refers to Patheos.com, an online library on the subject of religion that contains a section on paganism.

Very good common-sense advice, I agree. Although, on second thought, if I was 'Dear Abby', I probably would have suggested that the correspondent avoid the somewhat *risqué* term 'pagan' altogether and just tell her date that she is a non-Abrahamic Theist who believes in God but is neither Jew nor Christian nor Muslim. That should offer food for thought and conversation. But then again, is paganism all that bad, really? What about atheism? The late Irish comedian Dave Allen (May His Soul Rest in Peace) used to joke that he was 'a practising atheist, thank God.' What about a practising Devil-Worshipper? I've read somewhere that a parish of satanists in Manhattan have applied to the New York state government for tax exemption status, on the basis that they are a not-for-profit church like any other religious organisation. Now, would you tell a person on a first date that you are a practising satanist?

HALLOWEEN TIME

Pumpkins everywhere. Houses decorated with jack o'lanterns, ghosts and ghouls, witches and vampires, monsters and pirates, skeletons, skulls, tomb stones, spider webs: all made out of scary plastic or chilly synthetic fibres in sweatshops in South East Asia and available at bargain prices at dollar shops across the nation. It's almost like decorating the house for Christmas, a way-over-the-top competition for the neighbours' attention. There are Halloween pop-up stores all over the place where you can buy your scary stuff, if you cannot find it in your local supermarket. A hot and very practical item is a bucket-sized plastic pumpkin with top removed and a carry-handle attached, to put your treats in while trick-or-treating.

Halloween is big business in the US. Nationwide, people are expected to spend some $6.9 billion on candy, costumes and decorations, including $2.6 billion for adult costumes, $1 billion for kids' costumes, and $330 million for pet costumes. Favourite pet costumes are pumpkin, hot dog and devil. Top Ten choices for adult costumes are witch, batman, vampire, zombie, pirate, action hero, superman, Dracula, cat and scary mask (pop version of the famous Munch painting). The equivalent list for kids is essentially the same, except for some girls who apparently prefer to ignore the scary stuff and dress up to kill as princess or fairy. The remarkable similarity in dress code for adults and children is further proof, if needed, of what one learned observer has termed the ongoing infantilisation of contemporary American society.

I had promised Max that we would buy a pumpkin and carve it out to make a Jack O'Lantern, but friends tell us to wait till the last moment because once you carve them, they apparently will start to stink, attract fruit flies and collapse in a day or two. We finally buy a 12-pound pumpkin from Walmart for $3.99 three days before Halloween. I cut off the top, while Max is standing by, eager to help. The first job is to remove the seeds and stringy bits from inside the hollow vegetable. But Max's enthusiasm is quickly gone when he discovers that the icky, gooey, slimy stuff is a little yucky to the touch. I finish the job myself, with Max watching a while before he returns to his iPad. Once the orifices are carved out, Max does the rest, which is putting in a battery-powered LED light, and bingo – it lights up. Jack O'Lantern is ready to be put on the balcony balustrade, facing Draper Avenue and scaring the wits off the costumed customers crossing the street into Sammy's Woodfired Pizzeria below our flat.

Who's got the biggest pumpkin? Gary Miller, of Napa Valley, is the winner of the 40th Annual Safeway World Championship Pumpkin Weigh-Off in the state of California. His monster pumpkin weighs in at 1,985 pounds, and he takes home $12,000, nearly $6 a pound. That a state-wide competition in the second-most populous state of the US presents itself as a world championship goes without saying. Meanwhile, across the country, a Halloween display at the New York Botanical Garden at Bronx Park features a giant pumpkin as its centrepiece. It weighs a record-breaking 2,032 pounds. So, there: New York is still the biggest pumpkin, the California World Championship contest notwithstanding!

(Footnote: One year later in Berlin, I am surprised to learn that pumpkin weigh-offs are not unique to the USA. In a competition held in Ludwigsburg, Germany, a Swiss farmer's plant (or is it a fruit?) weighs in at an impressive 1054 kg, or 2,323 pounds and 10.75 ounces. World record! Eat your heart out, Americans! Let's hear it for the Europeans!)

THURSDAY, 31 October

'PILLAGE THE VILLAGE!'

In the spirit of Halloween, the merchants of the village of La Jolla have joined forces to celebrate and to promote their businesses. The campaign is called 'Pillage the village!' Between 3pm and 6pm the shops are inviting trick-or-treaters to come in and ask for some candy. Along Girard and Fay Avenues, there are hordes of children chaperoned by their moms or nannies roaming the sidewalks, in various stages of costuming. Everybody is carrying a designer shopping bag or plastic pumpkin-bucket to collect the treats on offer. The kids seem very competitive in that special American spirit: 'It's the loot what counts, buddy!'

Some of the adults have dressed up as well, there are ladies with long-flowing black dresses, gothic make-up and gigantic witches' hats, and a few gentlemen showing off as pirates or American Indians with the customary accessoires. One guy dressed in a gorilla suit is riding his motorbike along Prospect Street. It is a fantastic sight, and everybody seems to be having a great time.

Is Halloween an American attempt to provide a carnivalesque experience to its fun-seeking folks? Not really, I conclude. Some things are missing here: alcohol to begin with, but also the free spirit of political satire. There is no ritualised anarchy, no making fun of traditional hierarchies. There are merry crowds, but there is no communal *Schunkeln*, no singing or dancing in the streets as I remember it from my childhood experiences of *Karneval* in Germany. No drunks staggering about, either.

Meanwhile, there is a Halloween Party at All Hallows. The kids don't have to wear their school uniform, they are allowed to dress up. In the afternoon at Barnes, there is tennis practice where the kids can play in their Gothic mode costumes, and that is a lot of fun, of course. Finally, it's trick-or-treating time: Max and Vera, chaperoned by Susan, are off to a street in the foothills of Bird Rock where all the fancy house decorations are on view. They come back with a bucket-full of candy each.

Vera's mother Mary, who is Irish and Catholic, is not a fan of all the Halloween fanfare, and she does not approve of her daughter's school promoting it. Halloween is also All Saints' Day, and the school does not make a great deal out of the Roman Church's liturgical observation of the Lives of Saints, well-known or obscure. It's a shame, says Mary. I agree, though I'm not much of a Catholic. My faith ('the substance of things hoped for on the evidence of things not seen') lapsed many years ago.

SATURDAY, 2 November

Maximilian's birthday is on Halloween Day. As it falls on a Thursday, we celebrate the following Saturday with a party in the park of the La Jolla Recreation Centre. We have booked a jumping castle for the occasion, and there are some 15 kids from his class and from golf who are having a field day jumping up and down on the rubbery structure and sliding down its slide. There is a lot of shouting, running around, playing ball, eating cake and drinking soft drinks. The parents drop off their offspring at the appointed hour, along with boxes of presents, and disappear to do their shopping, or whatever, and return three hours later to pick up the kids. Not everyone is on time. But that's all right, we take it easy, cleaning up and disposing of the rubbish, properly.

In the evening, we drive to Old Town where the Latinos are celebrating their version of Halloween: The Day of the Dead, Día de Muertos. There is a candlelight procession through the dimly lighted, narrow streets, people in skull costumes and ghost make-up peer into living-room windows to marvel at the altars arranged by the residents with memorabilia of death and burial and photos of dear departed. The place is packed with tourists, the bars and restaurants overflowing. We finally manage to buy some tacos at a *cantina* that has set up a few benches in a courtyard, so we sit and eat and watch the tourist parade with quite a few living dead among them in advanced states of inebriation. It is almost midnight when we get home.

SAN DIEGO BEER WEEK, 1-10 November

Following hard on the heels of the *Oktoberfest* beer extravaganza, the San Diego Beer Week is meant to promote the self-proclaimed craft beer capital of the nation. There are 71 boutique-beer companies in San Diego County. Reportedly, there's a special San Diego taste in craft beer – it's supposed to be more hoppy, less sweet, more alcoholic – and its reputation is growing across the country, according to one local self-professed expert: 'We are the Napa Valley of craft beer.' There is 'artisanal' or 'hand-crafted' beer to be imbibed just about everywhere, and there's hardly a single self-respecting pub that does not advertise a list of rotating micro-brews on its posted menus.

Route 78, the Beer Route, cuts across North County for sixty miles from Oceanside to Escondido (west to east); during Beer Week, 24 micro-breweries have opened their doors to visitors, and there is no lack of colourful, imaginative brand names: Prohibition Brewery, Mother Earth Brew, Duckfoot, Toolbox, The Belching Bear, The Nickel Beer Company and – my favourite – Booze Brothers.

The latest trend is pairing beer with food, and the sommeliers of the barley juice are trying very hard to be just as inventive and poetic in their attempts at flowery descriptions as their more experienced colleagues in the wine industry. But they still have a way to go. Take the sommelier at the Marine Room for example where a 'Heirloom Bacon-Wrapped Monkfish with Honey Spice Faro, Ruby Grapefruit and Absinthe Infusion' has just been added to the menu. The appropriately named *sommelière* Miss Lisa Redwine has chosen a Mission Brewery Blonde to accompany this dish, because 'the beer has the richness of ale and stands up to the bacon, without overwhelming the fish.' I find this a little flat.

Or consider The Fishery, my favourite fish place in Pacific Beach. The head waiter suggests a St Archer White Ale to accompany their Spiced Seared Local Yellowtail, a tasty-looking sashimi-type appetiser for customers with very small appetites: thin slices of fish just so seared around the edges crusted with coriander and fennel seed, on a Serrano chili and cilantro emulsification with paper-thin slices of watermelon radish. The white ale, says chef Paul Arias, makes 'total sense with this dish. Yes, it's a light flavour beer, but with a complex profile that contrasts with the spice from the Serrano to create a nice flair.' Ok, nice one, we're getting there.

And what about this pairing at the up-market Hotel La Valencia where chef James Montejano offers a dish of Grilled Octopus to go with a hand-crafted Green Flash Hophead Red? If you think this sounds like a simple proposition, think again. The char-grilled octopus is served on a long, rectangular plate along with oven-roasted tomatoes, *kalamata* olives and *maitake* mushrooms contrasted with a spicy *muhammara* pepper sauce from the Middle East, accentuated with daubs of fig and olive vinaigrette. Says the chef: 'The smoky flavour of the octopus and the saltiness of the olives stand up to the robustness of the beer, and the full-flavored caramel-and-malt-based beer goes well with the spiciness of the *muhammara* and the *umami* of the mushrooms, and brings out a depth of flavour in the dish as a whole.' 'Each component,' the chef proudly proclaims, 'is like a port of call on a cruise around the Mediterranean.' Well, what more can we say?

MONDAY, 3 November

Among the birthday gifts for Max is a voucher for a toy store in Bird Rock. We stop by there in the afternoon so he can

Easy Rider: Getting a Haircut on the Motorbike

choose something to the tune of 20 bucks. We find a curious establishment: half toy store, half barber shop for kids.

Max is fascinated by the special seats that the young customers can sit in while having their hair cut or their curlies done. There is a racing car, a motor bike, a fairy tale coach, a pink pony. Surprisingly, Max does not want a toy, he prefers to have his hair cut. We ask the lady at the cash register whether it's ok to trade in the voucher, and she agrees: sure, why not. Max climbs up on the motor bike, grabs the handle bars, and a young lady with tattered blue jeans, black crop top and blue-pink hair gets to work on him with scissors and comb. He sits on his bike with quiet determination, holding perfectly still, his eyes steadily fixed on the road ahead of him, doing a ton towards Big Sur on Highway 1 north of LA.

THE SEASON FOR TUNNELS

October through December is tunneling season along the border between Mexico and Southern California. Cross-border tunnels are being used to smuggle drugs, and late autumn is the season when the marijuana harvest is at its peak, stockpiles of the plant are high and ready for export. Since 2006, some 75 tunnels have been discovered in the San Diego region. The latest find, on 30 October, was near the Otay Mesa border crossing: one-third of a mile in length, four feet tall and three feet wide, descending to almost 40 feet below ground, equipped with an electric rail system, ventilation and lighting. Its shutdown followed weeks of intensive surveillance and investigation by customs and drug enforcement agencies. Three suspects were arrested and drugs with a street value of $12 million confiscated: 17,000 pounds of marijuana and 327 pounds of cocaine. This is the first time that cocaine has been discovered in connection with a tunnel. The hunt for the people behind the operation goes on.

Obviously, these tunnels are not hand-crafted. They are high-tech industrial operations, designed by professional surveyors and structural engineers, starting inside a warehouse on the Mexican side and connecting to another warehouse on the northern side of the border. The latest discovery is the eighth such large-scale 'super tunnel' that has come to light since 2006; it is believed to be the work of one of the big Mexican drug cartels.

The story brings to mind the hand-dug micro-tunnels used by East German refugees who fled to West Germany in the 1960s and 70s. Interestingly, the Mexican-American tunnels are being used to smuggle drugs, not people.

SATURDAY, 16 November

CONVENTION CITY, SCIENCE CITY

San Diego is Convention City, and this week one of the biggest meetings will assemble some 30,000 research scientists from around the globe for the annual conference of the Society for Neuroscience.

San Diego is well placed to welcome the event. Apart from UCSD and SDSU, which do important work in neuroscience, San Diego is home to a cluster of some of the most prestigious research institutes in the country, such as the Salk Institute for Biological Studies (cutting edge work in fields such as neurobiology, cognitive neuroscience, immunobiology, cell biology and genetics), the Scripps Research Institute (medical applications of biosciences), the Sanford-Burnham Medical Research Institute, the La Jolla Institute for Allergy & Immunology, the California Institute of Regenerative Medicine, and the Brain Corporation. There is also a concentration of some 300 biotech companies operating in San Diego county.

Delegates to the international congress will no doubt be impressed when they hear about recent additions to the research infrastructure at La Jolla. Only a week earlier, the UCSD announced a private donation by philanthropist Denny Sandford of $100 million (the second largest in the university's history). With Sandford's money, the university is going to fund a new unit, the Sanford Stem Cell Clinical Center; it will be used mainly for drug trials. At the same time, the University celebrated the opening of a new enterprise by one of its most distinguished graduates, genome pioneer J. Craig Venter. The J. Craig Venter Institute, opened with a black-tie gala by former vice-president Al Gore, is a private research institute built on environmental principles on land donated by the university: it has a zero-carbon, net-zero energy footprint, a remarkable feat considering that the institute requires huge amounts of electricity to power machinery such as freezers that permanently run at temperatures below zero degree Fahrenheit (equal to minus 18 degree Celsius).

J. Craig Venter, who received both his BSc and his PhD from UCSD, won international recognition for his work on mapping the human genome, and for his ocean exploration genome project that aims at cataloging the genetic diversity in marine microbial communities. He is also well known as a maverick scientist who, when frustrated with the pace of public funding for his work, turned to the corporate world to form joint enterprises. From me personally, he gets the thumps-up for successfully combining scientific research of the highest standard with his own preferred leisure activities. He used his private yacht, the *Sorcerer II*, to collect oceanic microbes, eventually circumnavigating the globe on a two-year voyage that brought back some 60 million marine microbes.

Whether it is basic research digitizing biological specimen and tracking DNA codes or applied studies in clinical trials to develop new therapies and medications, institutes such as Salk, Scripps Research, the Brain Corporation or Venter are in essence private research enterprises that work in close co-operation with universities and specialized companies to achieve their aims, in business as much as in science. Philanthropy is an essential part of their business plan.

AMAZING PHILANTHROPY

Philanthropy is alive and well in the U.S., despite the gloomy *Zeitgeist* that seems to have taken hold in some sectors of American society. But not many rich people are as generous as businessman Denny Sanford who is determined to give away all his money before he dies. (Well, he can't take it with him, can he?) Sanford, born in St. Paul, Minnesota, is a South Dakotan who made his money in credit cards; he has donated huge amounts of cash to universities in his home state and to his alma mater, the University of Minnesota. Like many wealthy Americans, he has a home in La Jolla, where he often chats with scientists in his neighborhood who tip him off about where to invest some of his surplus funds. The gift of $100 million to UCSD is only the latest in a string of grants to local institutions. Previously, he has donated $70 million to the Sanford Burnham Institute and $30 million to the nearby Sanford Consortium for Regenerative Medicine that plays a pivotal role in the 'State of California's Stem Cell Initiative'.

Sanford's source of wealth offers an interesting moral dilemma. He became rich as the founder and CEO of *First Premier Bank*, by providing low limit credit cards to higher-risk clients at comparatively higher rates of interest. That means he made money out of the country's poor (well, perhaps not exactly poor, perhaps more correctly 'the unfortunate-lower-middle-class-fallen-on-hard-times people'). His customers were mostly people who had, for whatever reason, failed to pass a credit history check. But is it not a good thing to offer credit a to person who might otherwise not be able to find one, in a country in which creditworthiness is vitally important?

Sandford emphasises that he's serious about giving away all of his fortune, estimated at $1.3 billion. He is proud to have coined the phrase, 'I aspire to inspire before I expire.'

Sandford will be 78 years old in December, 2013. There are still quite a few greenbacks to be given away. $1.3 billion equals one-thousand and three-hundred million dollars.

THREE COMMENTS ON THE ABOVE

1: Denny Sanford obviously does not mind having his name plaqued on to buildings, just like his competitor in philanthropy, Irwin Jacobs, both following in the tradition of their illustrious predecessor, local philanthropy champion Eleanor Scripps.

2: The current record holders in San Diego philanthropy are Irwin and Joan Jacobs, of Qualcomm fame. The couple donated $120 million to the San Diego Symphony in 2002, $110 million to prop up the engineering faculty of UCSD in 2003, and $75 million to UCSD's Jacobs Medical Centre in 2010.

3: The donation to the SD Symphony came just in time to save the orchestra that had been in deep red for some time. Now it is doing quite well. Under the baton of musical director Jahja Ling, it recently made its debut at Carnegie Hall in NYC (with pianist Lang Lang), and it just returned from a successful tour of China.

MONDAY, 18 November

DRONES IN LOCAL NEWS

USS Chancellorsville returned to her home port of San Diego Naval Base today after an accident involving a malfunctioning unmanned aerial vehicle during exercises in the Point Mugu

Sea Range the previous week. This is a large area of sea and air space near Malibu closed-off to all traffic. The Northrop Grumman-built drone, 13 feet long with a wingspan of six feet, slammed into the portside of the cruiser and blew a big hole in the superstructure. An unspecified number of sailors were injured.

Chance Roth, president of the San Diego Drone User Group, commented that accidents like this are bound to happen in the experimental phase of introducing new technologies. 'At the beginning of the whole airplane revolution planes dropped out of the sky like flies, right?! And we're kind of going through the same things right now,' said Roth, interviewed on local TV as the expert on drones. He flies drones for fun. Regulations insist that he must have visual contact with his craft at all times.

SOUTH OF THE BORDER: DRONES OVER TIJUANA

The mayor of the city south of the border, Jorge Astiazarán, has announced that he is planning to buy drones to help with the surveillance of the city. The vehicles are expected to monitor traffic, detect landslides or illegal rubbish dumps in remote areas and help control wildfires. In an effort to increase the debt-ridden city's efficiency by using advanced technology, the mayor's office is negotiating with 3D Robotics to purchase several Ready-to-Fly 3DR Quad drones. The company is one of several smaller drone companies based in Southern California; its design office is located in San Diego while the manufacturing plant is in Tijuana. The drones weigh only about 3 kilos and can carry about a kilo in video equipment. They cost $599 each, *sans* camera. The company is willing to help with the training of operators.

There are as yet no regulations regarding the use of drones in Mexico. Only one other Mexican city, Puebla, is using them.

There seems to be little public awareness of issues involving privacy and protection of civil liberties, although in Puebla drones have been employed to monitor mass gatherings.

'THE STENCH IS BACK!'

If you walk along Prospect Street in downtown La Jolla, and there is a bit of an onshore breeze blowing, you cannot miss it: the stench is back. After the clean-up of the rocks around La Jolla Cove at the end of May, there was a general sigh of relief: the poop and guano deposits left by the cormorants, seals and pelicans had been eaten up by the bio-active agents applied by the Blue Eagle company in a supposedly environmentally sensitive process, the debris had been washed away into the ocean, and people could breathe freely again without having to hold their noses. But it was not to last.

The birds and pinnipeds are back doing what comes natural, and the local merchants are complaining again that the stench keeps tourists and shoppers away. But this time there is a new twist to the story: it is the sea lions that are predominantly responsible for the stench. They are noisy and stinky, too. They had been away to their island rookeries during the summer, and now they're back in even greater numbers. A marine biologist hired by the city to advise on what to do about the stench explains that the smell is different at different periods, depending on what the sea lions eat. If they feed on schools of greasy fish like sardines or anchovies, the smell is much worse than when their diet consists of local low-oil rockfish (not that the smell is sweet at any time). Also, the adult sea lions climb up higher on the rocks where the tides don't reach to wash away the feces, and the sea lions' urine is apparently pretty rank as well.

So, what to do? The microbial treatment costs about $100,000 a pop, and that's a bit steep for a repeat job every other month or so. Ex-mayor Bob Filner (who had famously promised he'd hoover the rocks himself as a last resort) is no longer available to come to the rescue, so good advice is rarer than rubies. One ingenious suggestion by a local correspondent to *La Jolla Light* is to get the San Diego Fire Department involved: send a couple of fire trucks by once a week and power-wash the rocks clean with the help of a few gallons of concentrated bio-degradable dishwashing detergent, and bingo – job done!

Another imaginative solution would be to remove the fence that was put up by the city council to protect the animals from interference by curious humans. The reasoning is that if people, locals and tourists alike, would be allowed to wander freely on the rocks, seals and birds would quickly abandon the site and go elsewhere. But the cliff face is steep and anything but safe, the rocks are brittle and slippery. What if an unsuspecting Japanese or Chinese holiday-maker were to slip and crash into the water, or worse perhaps, onto the mean-looking, half-submerged cliffs below? What if another curious tourist would be attacked and mauled by an angry sea lion? Well, there is an easy answer to this one, and it is aggressively favoured by some vocal members of the local business community: put up signs to warn people that they are entering the rocks area at their own risk!

MONDAY, 11 November

There was an overnight burglary at the *Symbolic Motor Car Company*, La Jolla's authorised sales and service centre for Rolls-Royce, Bugatti and Bentley. The showroom is conveniently located at La Jolla Boulevard, near the intersection with Pearl Street, a few blocks down from our flat. I take a walk to have a look, expecting a massive crime scene scenario, but there's nothing much to see. The thieves got in by backing up their old pick-up truck through the front door, and they got away with...no, not what you think! Not a pre-loved Bentley Continental GTC Speed, nor a brand-new spiffy Rolls Royce Phantom Series II. They only helped themselves to a mere few accessories, to wit: an unspecified number of Breitling Bentley Wristwatches (Swiss made), worth close to $100,000. They also caused some $50,000 worth of damage to the building.

Currently, the Symbolic MCC is offering a few specials, including a pre-loved 2012 Bugatti Veyron listed at a keen $1,850,000 – a very good deal considering a new model would set you back $3 million. Or you can order a RR Wraith, available in 2014, the newest model of the venerable old coach maker; it is said to be sportier and easier to drive, no longer requiring a chauffeur. Price available on request.

THE SILLY SEASON

As soon as the Halloween decorations are down, the Christmas lights go up. Crude posters appear attached to telephone poles and traffic lights at busy intersections, advertising the services of handymen offering to string up your lights around your trees or along your porch. But we're not merely talking colourful or flashing electric lightbulbs here; there is all sorts of fanciful illuminated scenery: Santa Clauses climbing up on the rooftops and clinging to chimneys, reindeers pulling their sleighs across the gables of suburban homes, nativity scenes artfully arranged on front lawns. Now that winter is approaching, it's getting dark early, around 5pm, and that's when the lights come on.

This is America, and of course there is competition among neighbours trying to out-light each other. The undisputed local champion is a San Marcos resident, Mr Bill Gilfillen, nicknamed 'Mr Christmas', a 75-year-old retired flight engineer who spends three months of the year planning his installation. His house on Knob Hill Road attracts some 10,000 drive-by visitors annually. This year he has put up 100,000 lights to spread the season's cheer. His electricity bill for the month of December – lights are up every day from Thanksgiving to 30 December – will come to roughly $1,200. The centrepiece of his work is a huge plastic foam Santa sitting next to a white Xmas tree in the middle of his front lawn. 'It looks so real that he [Santa, that is] could almost get up and walk away,' says the proud installation artist.

Not content with his engineering work, Mr Gilfillen is also seasoned actor. Every day he dons a velvet Santa suit, hand-crafted jointly by his mother and mother-in-law, and sits on a chair in front of his house, asking children to join him and to tell him about their wish lists while the excited moms snap pictures on their smartphones. The line of kids waiting their turn can be a block long. Last year Mr Gilfillen had exactly 2,732 young visitors sitting on his lap. He keeps track of them by counting the candy canes that he hands out.

MORE ON YOGA AND RELIGION

At Encinitas, an elderly man has been seen parading in front of local schools' entrances with a placard saying: 'PROTECT YOUR CHILDREN! OPT OUT OF YOGA! Luke 17:2.' If you check the biblical passage in question, and I thank columnist Logan Jenkins of the *U-T* for doing so, you will read: 'It would be better for them to be thrown into the sea with a millstone tied around their neck than to cause one of these little ones to stumble.' Oh, dear! This is heavy stuff: yoga is turning little children into sinners, the lonely protester is saying. Adult teachers or parents responsible should be taken a dozen nautical miles out to sea and thrown overboard! I wonder, though: are millstones easy to come by this day and age? Probably not. Would a cement block do instead?

Predictably, a local court ruling that allowed yoga to be taught to San Diego elementary school children has provoked a sharp response from concerned Christians. An appeal has been lodged by the National Center for Law & Policy, and the case may well end up before the Supreme Court. That could take a few years, though. The Soledad Cross story comes to mind.

In the meantime, some parents at Encinitas are upset about the elderly man who is exercising his constitutional right to free speech. Apparently, he is the grandfather of one of the 50 or so children whose guardians have decided against yoga classes. But other parents complain that granddad is 'fanning the flames of controversy' in front of the innocent little ones. They don't like to see controversy at the schools' gates. Why should children be exposed to politics and conflict and opposing viewpoints at such tender age? About ten percent of parents' responses to his placard are 'wicked and nasty', according to granddad.

CHARITY SEASON

The weeks leading up to Christmas is the season for fundraising and charity drives, and the local charity benefit circuit is in full swing. There is one event after another, and it seems there's not a single not-for-profit organization that does not hold a fundraising gala, nor a club that celebrates itself and its members by organizing an auction sale or festive lunch or black-tie dinner in aid of this or that good cause. There is a mind-boggling choice to spend your hard-earned dollars to do good, give something back, help others in need.

Charity begins at school. All Hallows Academy is holding a cake sale, and kids are asked to bring in cash to buy cupcakes (at one dollar a piece) to help fundraising for the school. In the American spirit of competitiveness, the class who will raise most money will get an honourable mention, over the school's intercom and in its newsletter. In the Catholic tradition of missionary charitableness, children and parents are also asked to collect food for the hungry. The kids are asked to bring in donations, not cash this time but canned foodstuffs and durable goods, to be distributed among the needy people of the Greater San Diego Community. Do we have any surplus items in our pantry? Not really, so it's off to Vons to stock up on some pasta, canned tomatoes, cereal, etc. We buy everything in twos, with half the stuff going into special bags to be taken to school as charity supplies.

Charity continues at the supermarket. At the entrance to Vons, we are astonished to find plastic boxes set up with signs asking for seasonal donations. Now, here's an interesting idea to stimulate the economy by generating more turnover and simultaneously reducing distribution problems while you are doing your daily good deed at the same time: buy the stuff you'd like to donate to the poor and hungry and leave it in the store, right behind the cash register, and the good people of Vons will take the boxes where needed.

Charity at Walmart: the collection boxes at Vons recall a recent Thanksgiving story concerning a Walmart in Ohio that went one step further in its charity drive. The store had set up plastic containers in its entrance, with signs saying: 'Please donate food items here so Associates in Need can enjoy Thanksgiving Dinner.' In other words: you are being asked to buy stuff in the store and then leave it there for its poor employees. Pure genius, and *honi soit qui mal y pense*. Nevertheless, the novel charity drive created a great deal of attention and a fair bit of criticism all across the nation. Couldn't the Walmart managers pay their workers, or associates as they call them, a decent wage so that they would not need to ask for charity? But this is unfair, surely. After all, Thanksgiving is the season of good cheer and good will, and Walmart is certainly supportive of sharing and doing its part to spread the festive spirit, without forgetting of course that its principal commitment must be to its shareholders who expect to see a decent return on their investment.

MONDAY, 16 December

NO DRONE TESTING IN SOUTHERN CALIFORNIA

San Diego, the hub of the country's military drone industry, lost out today in its bid to have Southern California chosen as one of the six regions in the continental USA where flight testing will be conducted with the aim of opening the country's airspace for use by unmanned aircraft. This is not about the military use of drones, but commercial and private applications. The plan proposed by a coalition of political, business and military leaders had comprised almost all of the southern half of California, excepting the LA metropolitan area, along with the airspace over the Pacific off San Diego. Instead, the Federal Aviation Administration selected areas in less densely populated parts of the country: Alaska, Nevada, North Dakota and Texas. The main concern of the project is to evaluate safety issues to prevent possible collisions between civilian drones and manned aircraft, and to develop a regulatory system for drones akin to that in place for conventional air traffic.

Local officials and business people seem to be genuinely upset about what is perceived as a snub to San Diego: How could the government NOT select US? What about our manufacturing strength? The two largest drone producers in the country based right here! And what about our sunny skies? Meanwhile, concerned Californians worried about safety and the possible invasion of privacy breathe a gentle sigh of relief. With recent revelations regarding security agencies like the NSA collecting 'bulk data' of its citizens by monitoring cell phone communication, not to mention listening in to the phone conversations of allied foreign leaders in Europe, and with advertisers or internet companies tracking their consumers online, people are increasingly suspicious of Big Brother-activities by Big Government or Big Business.

Spokesmen for the drone manufacturers in San Diego have remained silent on the right-to-privacy issue. However, they continue touting the civilian use of their new models, particularly Northrop Grumman's latest, the 'Bat' and the 'R-Bat'. This is the drone equivalent of the Stealth Bomber, an unmanned plane that can fly deep into enemy territory without being detected by advanced radar and surface-to-air missiles. But, says the company, they can also be used in agriculture (plant surveillance, crop dusting), looking for oil leaks along the Alaskan pipeline, or border surveillance. The applications ?are limitless, according to a spokesperson who also announced a significant expansion of the company's facilities in San Diego.

XMAS IN RIO

We decide to take advantage of our close proximity to Latin America (well, relatively speaking, compared to Sydney) to spend the holiday in Rio de Janeiro, Brazil. We stay in a hotel in *Cinelandia*, opposite the fancy *Teatro Municipal*, but we can't get any tickets to the Christmas Ballet Extravanganza, everything sold out, so instead we book a tour through the lovely old building itself with its golden cupolas and the beautiful tiled mosaics in the cool *Cafe do Teatro* in the theatre's basement. It's hot in Rio at this time of the year, just like the Down Under Sydney Summer. The beaches are crowded, and so are the tourist sites where we faithfully join the long queues to take the cog train up to *Christo Redentor* on Corcovador and the cable car to the top of Sugar Loaf Mountain. Next stops: Copacabana and Ipanema. I've done it all before, but for Max and Susan it's all new, and I don't mind doing it again.

Max is having great fun playing soccer with a couple of Brazilian boys on Ipanema beach, while Susan and I watch the action from a pop-up bar on the promenade, slurping our *caipirinhas*. Max is indefatigable, he runs and runs and heads and kicks the ball and sweats profusely in the oppressive, tropical heat. We wonder what is going through his mind right now: playing soccer with the Brazilian boys who everybody expects to be world champions in six months' time. Later, we eat at a *churrascaria*, and Max becomes the favourite of the waiters as he wolfs down incredible portions of lamb and beef and pork.

On my previous visit to Rio, one of the highlights for me was a tandem flight on a paraglider down the mountain at Niteroi, just south of the city, 25 minutes of exhilarating flying in the brilliant blue sky over the jungle and the high-rise buildings and the ocean, the cityscape with its avenues and parks and *favelas* laid out like a map underneath your feet, and finally landing on a grassy strip next to the beach. A few years ago, it only cost US $80, and I wouldn't mind doing it again today at whatever price they'd be charging. I try to convince Susan to have a go, but she is not game enough, and Max is too young. Too bad: I resist the temptation to go it alone. I love Rio. We need to come back another time.

LAST WORD ON THE STENCH?

The businesspeople on Prospect Street whose properties overlook La Jolla Cove have decided it is time to do

Australia vs Brazil: Max Playing Soccer with the Boys from Ipanema

something decisive about the infamous stench drifting up from the sea lion colony on the rocks below. They are angry with the San Diego city councillors for not doing their job. On 2 January, at the Valencia Hotel, a new not-for-profit group, Citizens for Odor Nuisance Abatement (*ONA*), was founded.

Mr George Hauer, the proprietor of 'George's at the Cove' restaurant and president of the exclusive club that consists of some twenty-odd members, announced that those present (by invitation only) paid one dollar each to join. It is not anticipated that members of the public will be asked to come on board. The aim of ONA is to force the city of San Diego to clean up excrements from rocks in La Jolla Cove and to take down the fence that limits public access. It is claimed that the fence was erected without public notice or consultation, without an environmental impact study, and that fencing off the public led to the build-up of sea lion excrement and cormorant guano, causing noxious odours.

Now, an innovative solution to make the stench disappear has been proposed by a former animal trainer at SeaWorld: he offers to housetrain the sea lions to defecate somewhere else, and he proposes to do this for a fee of $30,000. There are no details about how this is going to work, but – on reflection – it seems the obvious way to go. Perhaps a floating pontoon (the SLL, for Sea Lion Loo) could be anchored some distance away in the bay, and then the sea lions would be trained to use this as a toilet (or restroom, as the American vernacular has it). When the sea lions need to answer nature's call, they would just swim over, jump up on the platform (which presumably would have some appropriately-sized holes cut into it), do their business (with the wave action serving as a natural WC), they would get a reward by means of an automated sardine dispenser (ASD) and then swim back to shore to happily loll about on the rocks of La Jolla Cove, where they would be marvelled at by the tourists who could now enjoy a stench-free lunch at the desirable tables near the open windows of George's and La Valencia, overlooking the peaceful waters of the blue Pacific Ocean.

The Friends of the Children's Pool, who advocate getting rid of the harbour seals on the old Mia Casa beach, are following developments with interest. They approve of the objective of *ONA* but think its focus is too narrow. The aim should be, says Ken Hunrich, president of the Friends of the Children's Pool non-profit club, 'to clean up the entire coast...through better wildlife management, and not just at the Cove.'

Meanwhile, the attorneys are waiting in the wings.

TENNIS PHILOSOPHY: MARV ON LIFE

On late-night TV, I watch a pop concert live from Buffalo, New York. It is a benefit for FarmAid with an anti-fracking theme. As in California, people in New York State are deeply divided over fracking, with many small family farmers thinking that exploiting the oil shale beneath their land will mean the end of their precarious economic situation. The New York Farm Bureau also supports fracking. Others support a moratorium and more environmental studies to make sure that fracking is safe.

The artists at the concert, among them Willie Nelson, John Mellencamp, Neil Young and Pete Seeger, take a united stand against hydraulic fracturing. Pete Seeger, at the age of 94 a frail performer but lively and engaging as ever, had devised a new stanza to the old popular stand-by, Woody Guthrie's 'This land is my land'. I could not quite catch all the words, but the chorus went something like this: 'New York is my state / New York is your state / from the Hudson Valley / to the Catskill mountains / ... / New York was meant to be frack-free.'

The next day at tennis, while we're having a drink of water between a change of ends, I ask Marv what he thinks of the folk singer, his contemporary? 'Pete Seeger?' he asks back. 'Never heard of him.' I just manage to hide my surprise and explain that Seeger is the same age as Marv, a prominent popular artist and political activist with a nationwide and international following for more than half a century. Marv just shrugs his shoulders.

I realise, once again, there is more than one America.

Later, Marv tells an anecdote from the Korean War. Some buddies of his would walk every night out of their camp through a snowed-in minefield to a cabin with some prostitutes, 'and they would stick it in to these whores.' 'It's not survival that's man's basic instinct in life,' says Marv, 'that's all garbage. The basic instinct is fornication.' 'Yeah,' Brian says. 'Interesting, isn't it?' We all laugh.

IMMIGRATION REFORM: THE CALIFORNIA MODEL

While the ideological debate on immigration reform (Obama's agenda) or immigration restriction (Republican opposition) is heating up in Congress, there are a myriad of day-to-day occasions where immigrants, illegal or otherwise, are affected by rules and regulations specifically designed for them. In California, pragmatism reigns. Here's a sample, in response to standard assumed opinions, concerning drivers, lawyers and low-wage guest workers.

1. 'You cannot survive in California without a driver's licence!' – 'Many people do.'

The California government has announced that illegal immigrants will be allowed to apply for a driver's licence. Applicants must prove their residency, pass a vision test and complete a written driving exam and road test – just like I did, in fact. The new law is to come into effect on 1 January 2015, and it is expected that thousands of illegal immigrants will apply for a licence. Driving without one is a risky business in California. If you get caught, your car might get impounded, you certainly will get a fine, you may lose your job. But you cannot survive in California without a car.

To the Republican opponents of Governor Brown, the new regulation is another example of big government doing the wrong thing. To handle the expected surge of applications, 822 additional employees will be added to the state's payroll. The licence will cost $30, but the real cost of supplying a document to an undocumented immigrant is likely to be much higher. The opposition is calling for a surcharge of $100 to be paid by applicants: user pays. While the new licences will look just like regular ones, there will be one exception: the top right corner will say 'Federal Limits Apply'. That means the licence cannot be used to board an airplane or enter a federal building. The trauma of 9/11 sits deep.

2. 'You cannot be a lawyer in California if you are an illegal resident!' – 'Yes, you can.'

The California Supreme Court has cleared the way for illegal immigrants to qualify for admission to the state bar. Following legislation introduced by San Diego State Assemblywoman Lorena Gonzales and passed with bipartisan support by the Governor and the State Legislature, Mr Sergio Garcia of Chico, CA, can now practise law in California. Lawyers for the U.S. Department of Justice opposed Mr Garcia's application on the ground that Mr Garcia is a 'deportable legal alien', but the California Supreme Court ruled that 'no federal statute precludes a state from issuing a law licence to undocumented immigrants.'

The unauthorised immigrant who is now a proud attorney-at-law had come to the US with his parents as a one-year old, attended California schools, studied law, got a degree and passed the bar exam at first attempt. However, he was subsequently barred from taking up his licence by a review committee on the basis that federal law prohibits unauthorised immigrants from becoming lawyers. Mr Garcia has applied for legal status, but his case has not been heard because of a backlog and might not be decided for years.

Ironically, Mr Garcia cannot be employed to work for a law firm because of a federal ban on hiring people who are in the country illegally. But he can, of course, open a legal practice and work on his own. It's a free country, after all.

California is the first state in the union that has paved the way for non-legal residents to become lawyers. Following her win in court, Assemblywoman Gonzales announced that she would seek similar rulings in other cases, such as doctors or pharmacists. Lorena Gonzales is herself a lawyer and a child of immigrants. The good people of San Diego who are represented by her in Sacramento are justifiably proud of her.

3. 'The boat is full!' – 'It's the economy, dummy!'

In the *U-T*, local businessperson Andrew Puzder adds his voice to the immigration debate. He is worried that government inactivity will do nothing to increase America's economic competitiveness and this should be 'an overriding concern for those who serve us in office.' According to Puzder, the 'immigration system is broken,' it hurts 'businesses, like ours, that create jobs and economic growth.' Puzder exhorts the pollies in Washington to 'stop fear mongering and political posturing' and 'find a rational compromise.'

What does Puzder advocate? 1. Stronger border security. 2. More visas for high-skilled workers. 3. Electronic programs to help employers verify the immigration status of job applicants. 4. Temporary visa programs for farm labourers and other low-skilled workers. 5. Path to legal status for undocumented immigrants. 6. Bipartisan commitment to immigration reform.

Andrew Puzder is CEO of CKE Restaurants which owns the Carl's Jr. and Hardee's chains of fast-food franchises. They also own Red Burrito and Green Burrito. It is a global enterprise with headquarters in Carpinteria, just south of Santa Barbara, that currently operates 3,318 outlets in 42 states and around the world. New projects aim at bringing an additional 100 units to Brazil, expanding the existing presence in Russia, and first-time moves into Denmark, Guatemala and Puerto Rico.

Traditionally, business interests have supported moves to ease immigration restrictions to make sure a sufficient supply of cheap labour is available. In the 1970s, agri-business groups around Delano in Central California tried to run their own guest worker scheme by importing agricultural workers from Egypt and Yemen in response to the strike by the mostly Hispanic United Farm Workers Union. Today, things have become more complicated. Powerful conservatives want the government to deport all undocumented aliens. They propose building a wall to keep Latinos out of the country. Yemen has become a country where US drones kill alleged terrorists.

MONDAY, 20 January

LAST WORD ON DRONES?

An unmanned aircraft operated by the U.S. Customs and Border protection agency was deliberately destroyed after a mechanical failure and drowned in the Pacific Ocean 20 nautical miles off Point Loma. The vehicle broke apart on impact with the water. The navy sent a ship to retrieve the debris in an attempt to investigate the causes of the accident. Meanwhile, all drones under the control of Customs and Border Protection, a division of the Department of Homeland Security, have been grounded across the nation out of 'an abundance of caution'.

The drone that went down in the Pacific was identified as a *Maritime Variant Predator B* aircraft, built by General Atomics in San Diego, worth $12 million.

Protest groups along the US-Mexican border opposed to drone use, from California to Texas, have used the incident to speak out again. They cite safety concerns and loss of privacy caused by constant surveillance of the border area. 'Drones are dangerous and set a bad precedent for protecting our civil liberties,' says Pedro Ricos, director of the American Friends Service Committee in San Diego. He adds that drones are expensive, too; the money could be put to better use, for 'meeting community needs such as hospitals, better schools, improving city infrastructure.' There is the old, big, pacifist dream again: butter instead of cannons, swords into ploughshares.

THURSDAY – SUNDAY, 23–26 January

FARMERS OPEN AT TORREY PINES

It's our last weekend in La Jolla, and the focus is again on golf. This time we are happy to watch. At the Farmers Open at Torrey Pines, seven-times winner Tiger Woods misses the cut and makes an early exit. All the attention is on local hero Phil Mickelson. The crowds following him are immense, and it's very difficult to get close to the action, not the least because stands have been put up all over the place, including around some of the greens. They are reserved for VIP ticket holders. Food is average and drinks are expensive. Luckily, I've learned to ask for a 'military special' (from a soldier standing next to me in line at a kiosk): the Grey Goose Vodka Lady gives me a triple shot in a tall glass with a spritzer of lime and cranberry juice, and, thus fortified, we can follow another group of golfers from tee box to green.

Alas, Mickelson withdraws before the last round due to a back injury. The crowds jostle to catch a glimpse of him as he makes his way to the carpark, waving and signing autographs, including one on Max's white base cap. We feel sorry for the local champion, but it is not important anymore. We enjoy walking around the south course in the sunshine for a last time. We say goodbye to Jenny and watch the sun slowly sink into the ocean while the colourful hang gliders are flying back and forth along the cliffs.

A lot of sport is happening during our last week in California. We watch the Australian Open on TV: the blistering temperatures during the early days at Melbourne Park have given way to more temperate weather, Federer has made a marvelous comeback to reach the semi-finals, with quite a few people speculating he might win another Grand Slam on this occasion, only to see him lose in the final against his old nemesis, Nadal, who finishes him off cleanly in straight sets. Then there's Li Na's convincing win in the women's final followed by her hilarious victory speech where she thanked her agent for making her rich. She also acknowledged her husband, a 'lucky guy to have found me', for fixing her drinks and lugging her rackets around.

On Monday after school, Max and the other tennis kids meet the US Davis Cup team at Barnes Kids' Day. They exchange a few rallies with the pros, get their caps signed and complimentary T-shirts as gifts. I am not familiar with the names of the players who practise at Barnes' in preparation for the match against Great Britain. It seems the US do not have any top-ranked tennis players at the moment. A new generation is trying to make its mark.

Meanwhile, at La Jolla Tennis Club, the older generation (Marv and Irv) are doubtful about the venue chosen for the Davis Cup tie. A specially prepared temporary stadium with a clay court is being built inside Petco stadium in downtown SD. It will cost a huge amount of money. And why clay – to stop British hotshot and Wimbledon grass specialist Andy Murray? Nonsense! Why not use the posh La Jolla Beach and Tennis Club with its excellent facilities where big tennis events have been staged before? The seniors shake their heads. They are not amused.

On Wednesday, Susan and I play our last mixed-double sets against Marv, Irv, Brian, Hettie, Karen and Val. We shake hands, say goodbye and wish each other well. It was a privilege playing with you guys, I say. Thank you very much. We had a lovely time. We most certainly had.

I would have loved to watch the Davis Cup, but we won't be here anymore. By the end of the tournament, we're already in Berlin and read about San Diego's glorious weather in the paper.

27 JANUARY 2014: IN MEMORIAM PETE SEEGER

Pete Seeger has died, aged 94, in a hospital in Manhattan. He was a wonderful man, a proud American and a great artist. Reading his obituary in the *U-T*, I feel sad, but I am glad that I could see him perform, if only on TV, at what seems to have been his last concert, the anti-fracking gig at the FarmAid benefit. On stage, surrounded by his peers, he appeared almost larger-than-life, a seemingly solitary survivor of the great cultural upheaval that began in the late fifties. More than half a century later, he was treated with great respect, even reverence by his younger colleagues like Neil Young.

And I remember Marv's indifferent comment: 'Never heard of him.'

Pete Seeger was a man of principle who never wavered in his commitment to fight for a better, more civil and just society. To be sure, he was a sort-of-communist in his early years, one of the few activists who did not flinch when they were hauled before the infamous committee of Senator Joseph McCarthy to rat on their mates and to answer charges of being anti-American. The *U-T* obituary has an interesting local detail about the most difficult phase of Seeger's career. After he was cited for contempt and sentenced to prison,

Seeger was asked by the San Diego City Council to sign a statement that he was not a communist and an enemy of the United States, otherwise a scheduled concert at San Diego State University would not go ahead. He refused, and the concert was cancelled. A quarter of a century later, to their infinite credit, the councillors reversed themselves. They issued a unanimous apology and invited Seeger back.

In recent years, Pete Seeger had lent his voice to support the environmental movement. Among other activities, he had sailed his sloop, the *Clearwater*, along the Hudson River to draw attention to efforts to clean up the polluted waterway.

FRIDAY, 31 January

We have packed our bags and cleared out the things we won't be able to take with us. Max reluctantly agrees to leave his surfboard in Maggie's garage: no surf beaches in Berlin. We tell him Kenny will look after it until we come back, though I doubt whether Kenny will use the surfboard much; he has become greatly obsessed with golf recently. The giant soft toy turtle goes to Kenny's little sister. We drive around to our friends to say goodbye.

For the last time, I drive the now familiar route up north to LA on I-5, past San Onofre and San Juan Capistrano. Again, we take the Route 73 tollway, the fast detour that skirts Irvine, before joining the I-5 for the final stretch past Long Beach to Torrance. We'll stay with Xiaofang, Bill and Brianna for one more night. We've arranged to sell the car to a Chinese couple who have recently arrived in California, so we drive across the whole LA metropolitan area to their place near Pasadena where they invite us to dinner. We show them the car, and they do a test drive back to Torrance. We sign a contract for sale, exchange car and registration papers for $2,000 in cash, and watch the murky-green Mercury Grand

Marquis V8 disappear around the corner. The next morning, while Bill is already at work delivering the mail for the US Postal Service and day-dreaming about a second career as a personal fitness coach to the Hollywood Rich and Famous, Xiaofang and Brianna take us to LAX and drop us off at the overseas terminal. They promise to visit us in Berlin.

EPILOGUE

When we disembark at Tegel airport, there is half an inch of snow on the ground, but it is gone two days later and from then on, clear skies rule.

We live in the *Rheingau* quarter of *Wilmersdorf*, a quiet, leafy and solidly bourgeois district of the Old West Berlin, far away from the now trendy, hip and chic areas of the re-unified New Berlin like *Prenzlauer Berg* or *Friedrichshain*, and even further away from the precarious suburbs of the Old East Berlin like *Marzahn* or *Hellersdorf*. Life around *Rüdesheimer Platz*, the centre of our neighbourhood, has changed very little since I first spent some time here in the late 1970s. There are the familiar flower shops (on just about every corner), little specialty stores and restaurants and cafés; new arrivals are the bio-baker and bio-butcher in addition to a smallish bio-supermarket. Every Tuesday and Friday, the lively street market along *Eberbacher Strasse* brings throngs of shoppers in search of fresh fruit and veggies and the various seasonal specialties of the *Havelland* region around Berlin. There's white asparagus in late spring, cherries and plenty of berries in summer, chanterelles and porcini mushrooms in autumn. A fishmonger plies his trade next to a Polish sausage maker, there are Greek and Turkish delis to stock up on dips and olives, and you can always eat a *Currywurst* – epitome of Berlin culinary art – unless you feel like Chinese noodles for a change. The *Pastis* opposite the subway entrance is a new place that becomes my favourite eatery, a tiny French brasserie that serves fresh Atlantic oysters to be washed down with a glass of *Entre-Deux-Mers*. From May to October, the daily *Weinfest* on Rüdesheimer Platz (with visiting vintners from the Rhine selling their wines) makes this the liveliest, fun-filled place in all of Berlin.

We enroll Maximilian in *Carl Orff Grundschule*, a normal state primary school with a curricular emphasis on music education. There is a special class for non-native students (quite a few of the pupils have migrant backgrounds: Turkish, Russian, Albanian, Syrian), but after two months the teacher informs us that Max can move to the regular German class. His progress is quite astonishing; clearly, he had picked up much more of a passive knowledge of the language than I had been aware of.

We quickly settle in. It's not laid-back La Jolla, but life here is easy, too, and we're in a buzzing metropolis. We don't have a car, and we don't need one. In 30 minutes, by bus and subway, we are at the Brandenburg Gate, or one of the three opera companies, dozens of theatres, countless cinemas, concert halls, museums and art galleries. Public transport will also take you to most of the city's numerous forests and parks and lakes and rivers and canals. Berlin has more bridges than Venice.

We waste no time to begin to explore Berlin. We buy a yearly ticket that covers all the city's main museums, and we spend nearly every Sunday afternoon exploring the treasures of the *Stiftung Preussischer Kulturbesitz*. Max joins a football club, the *FC Grunewald*, that trains on a pitch just across the corner from our house and, as part of his team, soon plays in the little league all over Berlin. Soccer is, of course, the big thing in Germany during this summer. Like everyone in his class, Max collects and trades the photo cards of the German national team, *die Nationalmannschaft*, and he has soon committed to memory every player, their clubs, number of goals scored and number of international matches played. By the time the world cup in Brazil comes around, he knows as much about soccer as every other kid on the block. But there's more to life than football. His mother finds a Chinese piano teacher for him, with a lesson every Sunday morning, there is also a Chinese school on Saturday mornings, and soon Max's life is as busy as it was in La Jolla.

And then there is golf. When we left California, we thought we'd give golf a rest. In Germany, golf is considered a marginal sport, with a reputation for snobbishness and something that elderly people do. There are only two golf courses in Berlin, and about half a dozen in a radius of about a hundred kilometers in the surrounding countryside of Brandenburg (compared to some 200 courses in Sydney alone).

The club closest to us is at *Wannsee*, in the South of Berlin just inside the city borders. It was used by the American military before the wall came down; perhaps Rudy Duran played here. It's a members-only club, one of the oldest in Germany, with great facilities. There is a beautiful club house with a sizeable veranda looking out over the practice greens and the wide, undulating fairway leading up to the 18th hole. It is all very lush and green, and there are some lovely old trees. Amazingly, one can get there by public transport in just under three-quarters of an hour: from Max's school by bus to the city rail station at *Grunewald*, from there by train to *Wannsee* station, and then another bus towards *Glienicker Brücke* (where the spies used to come in from the cold). The bus stops at *Schäferberg* across the road from the back entry to the club, just next to the driving range and locker rooms.

We find out, more or less by coincidence, that the club has an active youth department. They organise a selection process every year where they invite kids who are interested in golf and perhaps have some experience to show what they can do in front of the coaches and pros, and the kids with talent and potential are invited to join the club's *Jugendförderprogramm*. The aim is to train young players to eventually play in the top German League, the *Bundesliga*. It's an ambitious, long-term project, modeled on similar programs run by the different national sports organizations in Germany to ensure that their young players can compete successfully at a high level, ideally even in international competitions, or at the Olympics. Or perhaps become pros, and play for the European team for the Ryder's Cup.

We register Max for the selection, and he is one of four kids (out of some 40) offered a place in the program. A couple of weeks later he receives an official invitation and becomes one of the youngest members of the *Golf- und Landclub Berlin-Wannsee*. The annual fee is only 180 euros; it includes a locker where Max can keep all his gear, twice weekly coaching, unlimited free play on the club's two courses, one nine-hole and one championship course (on the short course you don't even need to book a tee time). Range balls on the two-level driving range are also free. In winter, there is fitness training in the gym.

Thus, Max starts playing golf again. He has grown out of his old clubs, so we buy him a new set and a buggy. He joins the other kids for training and quickly makes new friends. There is a weekly tournament, the Youth Challenge, and at the end of the year, it turns out that Max has won the series. He is the club's youth champion. His trophy is a miniature version of the youth department's mascot, a Disney-like duck swinging a golf club sculpted in fibreglass, and a welcome change to the usual dust catchers.

Dragon Mom's dream is back on the agenda.

Player of the Year: Max with Duck Trophy at Wannsee Golf Club, Berlin

ACKNOWLEDGEMENTS

This book is based on journal entries made during our stay in San Diego from February 2013 to January 2014. Some of the names have been changed for reasons of privacy.

I gratefully acknowledge, as noted in the text, the *San Diego Union-Tribune* as the main source for local information. A special mention goes to Gary Warth and Roxana Popescu, both at *U-T*, for stimulating articles on yoga as religion and on Indian matriarch Ida Brown, respectively.

I also acknowledge the free local weekly *La Jolla Light* with its extensive real-estate section and up-to-date info on celebrity gossip and village affairs.

On Media and Boston Marathon Bombing: the great cartoon by caricaturist Bob Gorrell is at <gorrellart.com>.

On 'Papa' Doug Manchester: I gratefully acknowledge Dorian Hargrove, 'Got a permit for that, Manchester?', *San Diego Reader*, 42/18 (May 2013), 2-3, 46, and Rob Davis, 'San Diego's Cheerleader in Chief', *Voice of San Diego*, 20 January 2012.

The helicopter photo of San Onofre Nuclear Power Station is by Andrea Swayne.

I acknowledge Phil Constantin (*Times of San Diego*) for the image of seals on Children's Pool Beach in 2001, and *LA Times* (latimesblogs.com) for the aerial image of the beach a decade later.

The picture of the La Jolla Reading Room (1898) is in <lajollabluebook.com.

Thank you to Steven Morrison of SMDESIGNS and Joel Naoum of Critical Mass Consulting.

Thank you also to Tom Thompson of ETT Imprint, and to Wolfgang Ihl, Jon von Kowallis, Haiqing Yu and Tracy Liu.

With thanks to Rudy Duran, Todd Smith at Colina Park, Jenny Liu at Torrey Pines, and Miriam Hiller and her team at Wannsee; to Maggie and family; Vera and family; Chuck and Tim; Louise and family; to Marv, Irv, Brian and Val, Hettie, Karen at LJTC; Bernd and Axel at Schlaraffia; John and Todd at UCSD; Wally and Kay; Ken and Jeffrey; the Principal, staff and parents at All Hallows Academy; the Principal, staff and parents at Carl Orff Grundschule.

A special 'thank you' to Bill, Xiaofang and Brianna at Torrance, and of course to Dragon Mom Susan and Little Dragon Max

www.ingramcontent.com/pod-product-compliance
Lightning Source LLC
Chambersburg PA
CBHW021218090426
42740CB00006B/270